SEVERA
STORIES
high

The Language of Story
Penelope Marsterson

GW01390018

INTRODUCTION

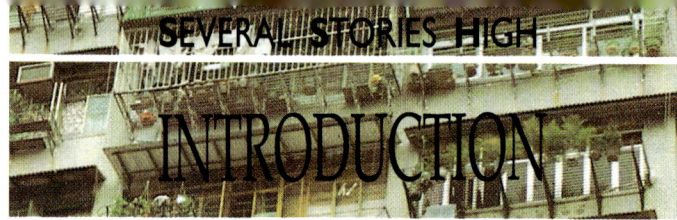

Initiatives is about language – what it is, what it does and where it comes from.

This Resourcebook is arranged in units, each of which looks in detail at one aspect of language. Tapes and photocopy repromasters run alongside each unit, and together they present a range of options to choose from, which may include:

- discussion in large or small groups
- role playing
- drafting your own response in writing
- presenting findings to the group as a whole
- experimenting with new forms of writing
- making radio programmes
- interviewing people in the community
- research and analysis
- looking at paintings
- responding to poetry and prose
- thinking about accent and dialect
- questioning your own assumptions about language and people.

Some of the activities you will be invited to tackle may be quite difficult. Don't be put off by your first response; use that response and build on it – share it with other members of the group, talk about it with your teacher, discuss it at home. Your ideas and feelings are crucial in coming to an understanding of how language works.

Whatever you're investigating, **share** your ideas, **comment** on each other's opinions, **follow up** new ideas that occur to you – above all, use your own **initiative!**

CONTENTS

THE
IMPORTANCE OF STORY

EVERYDAY STORIES

Stories form an important part of our everyday lives – most conversations are built around stories of one kind or another. They surround us as entertainment, as a means of developing relationships, as a way of explaining things as we find them, as a means of selling goods and services, to avoid trouble, or as a way of making sense of our experiences and maintaining our individuality.

The following section concentrates on the way stories can begin and end, and how a writer or speaker develops, changes or manipulates a story in order to say something. Stories don't have to end in a certain way for instance, but can be adapted for a different outcome. This is very clear when you can see how one story will use the plot of another, and our enjoyment and understanding depends on our knowledge of the first story.

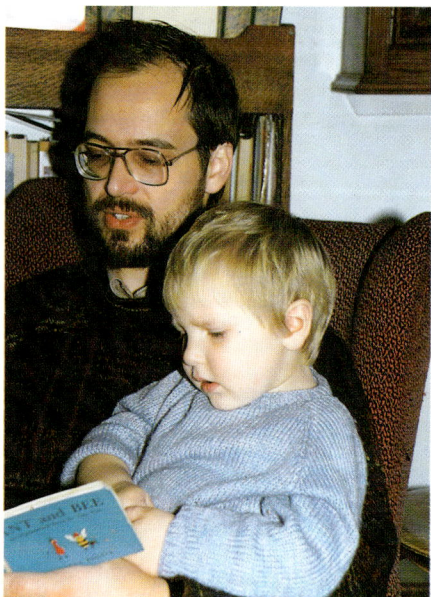

On the tape you can hear students talking about story. How far do their comments reflect yours?

Story *n*. **1.** a historical narrative or anecdote; historical writing or records; history as a branch of knowledge, or as opposed to fiction; a recital of events that have or are alleged to have happened; a series of events that are or might be narrated.

2. (*with possessive*) a person's account of the events of his/her life or some portion of it; the series of events in the life of a person, or in the past existence of a thing, country or institution considered as narrated or a subject for narration.

3. a narrative of real, or more usually, fictitious events, designed for the entertainment of the hearer or reader; a series of traditional or imaginary events forming the matter of such a narrative; a tale (specifically a nursery or folk tale).

4. traditional, poetic or romantic legend or history.

5. an incident related in order to illustrate some remark made, an anecdote.

6. an allegation, a particular person's representation of the facts in a case; a mere tale, a baseless report.

7. a narrative or descriptive article in a newspaper or other media, the subject or material for this.

A Variety of Meanings

● In groups, each choose one of the definitions given above and tell, retell or devise a 'story' to illustrate that particular meaning of the word.
eg a newspaper 'story';
    a 'story' which is only one person's understanding of events;
    a 'story' which is a piece of history.

● Story can mean both fact and fiction, more often a mixture of both. Put all the stories you have prepared on a large poster, titled, 'The meaning of a story'. Make sure that they are clear and readable so you can draw connections and make comparisons. Using drama, work on the scenes. You may need a presenter to link the separate items which explore the various meanings of story.

Personal Checklist

● With the help of *Repromaster 1*, if you find it useful, note down as many stories as you can recollect that you have read, overheard or come across in the last week.

● Using the books to hand in the classroom, try to identify types of stories.

● List favourite stories of your own at different ages – do you still read them? Share these with the group and compare notes.

● Which *three* TV programmes in the last week have stayed in your mind?

● How fascinating do you find stories in instalments?

● How much of TV and Radio output uses the format of a serial?

● How many current pop songs tell a story?

You will find it helpful to jot down any ideas or findings that emerge from discussions in the form of a response log.

So Many People – So Many Stories

● Study the illustration above showing scenes in a motorway restaurant.

What life stories could you construct from the fragments of conversation you can hear?

● In groups, dramatise the scene depicted above, allowing the audience to focus on each different conversation in turn, whilst the remaining groups chat quietly. You will have to decide what the rest of the conversation is in each case.

● Invent your own 'case histories' for each of the groups and individuals in the motorway restaurant at the same time. Why are they here? Where were they yesterday? Where will they be tomorrow? Try putting the characters into other situations eg at home or at work. How do you use the character clues in the original exchange?

● Write the story of each group, explaining what has brought them together on this occasion. If you need to, you can change the basic dialogue for each to develop another story.

Stories We Tell – Ideas for Discussion

● How basic is the urge to tell a story?
● How basic is the urge to hear a story?
● How basic is the urge to live out a story?
● Why are people willing to watch the same film, or read the same book a second time, when they already know what happens in it?
● Why do we often find ourselves drawn to someone who arrives and says, "You really won't believe this, but . . ."
● Why does the classroom often fall silent when people realise that someone is telling a joke they haven't heard before?
● If a film starts by revealing the end of the story, what is it that keeps us watching? Why is it that we often enjoy a repeat showing of a programme?

EVERYDAY STORIES

Writers build stories from all kinds of experiences. In this extract, Joseph Conrad explains how Nostromo *came to be written.*

The Inception of *Nostromo*

. . . the first hint for *Nostromo* came to me in the shape of a vagrant anecdote completely destitute of valuable details.

As a matter of fact in 1875 or '6, when very young, in the West Indies, or rather in the Gulf of Mexico, for my contacts with land were short, few, and fleeting, I heard the story of some man who was supposed to have stolen single-handed a whole lighter-full of silver, somewhere on the Tierra Firme seaboard during the troubles of a revolution.

On the face of it this was something of a feat. But I heard no details, and having no particular interest in crime *qua* crime, I was not likely to keep that one in my mind. And I forgot it till twenty-six or seven years afterwards I came upon the very thing in a shabby volume picked up outside a second-hand bookshop. It was the life story of an American seaman written by himself with the assistance of a journalist. In the course of his wanderings that American sailor worked for some months on board of a schooner, the master and owner of which was the thief of whom I had heard in my very young days. I have no doubt of that because there could hardly have been two exploits of that peculiar kind in the same part of the world and both connected with a South American revolution.

Yet I did not see anything at first in the mere story. A rascal steals a large parcel of a valuable commodity – so people say. It's either true or untrue; and in any case it has no value in itself. To invent a circumstantial account of the robbery did not appeal to me, because my talents not running that way I did not think that the game was worth the candle. It was only when it dawned upon me that the purloiner of the treasure need not necessarily be a confirmed rogue, that he could be even a man of character, an actor and possibly a victim in the changing scenes of a revolution, it was only then that I had the first vision of a twilight country which was to become the province of Sulaco, with its high shadowy Sierra and its misty Campo for mute witnesses of events flowing from the passions of men short-sighted in good and evil.

Such are in very truth the obscure origins of *Nostromo* – the book. From that moment, I suppose, it had to be. Yet even then I hesitated, as if warned by the instinct of self-preservation from venturing on a distant and toilsome journey into a land full of intrigues and revolutions. But it had to be done.

Joseph Conrad, Preface to *Nostromo* (1904)

The next two extracts also show different ways in which authors start their stories.

Pigs is Pigs

In the end we all know that stories are a game, a pretence, an imagined set of people working through an imagined set of events that a writer has selected to make certain points. But it is selectivity that allows fiction to be exciting and relevant, which allows it to float free from everyday circumstances and work in a heightened and self-aware way.

We are all able to write stories. What we need to learn and improve is the ability to select and fashion the imagined consequences of those stories so that we can entertain our readers and perhaps convey our perceptions to them as well. Like anybody else, it is a process I am still working through and expect I always shall be.

David Harmer, *Pigs is Pigs*

The Paths of Common Life:
Jane Austen's *Emma*

. . . the author of novels was, in former times, expected to tread pretty much in the limits between the concentric circles of probability and possibility; and as he was not permitted to transgress the latter, his narrative, to make amends, almost always went beyond the bounds of the former. Now, although it may be urged that the vicissitudes of human life have occasionally led an individual through as many scenes of singular fortune as are represented in the most extravagant of these fictions, still the causes and personages acting on these changes have varied with the progress of the adventurer's fortune, and do not present that combined plot (the object of every skilful novelist), in which all the more interesting individuals of the dramatis personae have their appropriate share in the action and in bringing about the catastrophe. Here, even more than in its various and violent changes of fortune, rests the improbability of the novel.

Walter Scott, Review of *Emma* (1815)

Stories – Your Own Ideas

● In small groups consider the following questions:

1. How far do you think stories are built from the imagination and how far from 'real life'? Which kind of stories do you prefer?

2. How far is it a combination of the two? Is it possible to separate the two?

3. Do you think it is important that a story should be 'true'?

4. Can you think of a story which could be described both as 'true' and 'not true'?

The tape features writers and storytellers explaining the significance of story in their own work. Is there a common thread in what they say, or does story mean different things to different people?

REASONS FOR TELLING STORIES

Pages 6–9 have considered how much stories are a part of daily life, and have touched on how writers develop ideas for stories. The 'How?' and 'What?' of stories, if you like. That does not answer the question 'Why?'

● How many reasons can you list, either individually or in groups, for telling stories in every sense of the word?

One Good Reason

● In groups compare the following anecdotes.

A) "We had a special lecture in assembly this morning about the danger of wearing earrings because one girl had her earlobe torn off in a gym lesson," a boy says one evening.

"We've heard that story too," his sister replies, "I don't think that kid ever existed!"

B) "My mum was going to book us a holiday on the cheap rate for half term because we hadn't got away in the summer. I said we ought to go somewhere where we could guarantee warm weather in October, so we'd decided on Tunisia, but then my boyfriend told me that everyone who's been there has had the most awful diarrhoea. If they don't get it there, they have it when they come back!"

● One person is enthusiastic about something they hope to do/they have bought/someone they have met. The other person has some dreadful experience to tell which puts the first person right off it! How far does the enthusiast alter his/her view?

● Improvise a scene in which someone uses the words: "That story changed my life!" Compare the various scenes to see how many different situations have been thought of.

● "I wouldn't if I were you!" Devise and write a scenario for another group to act out which begins with this line.

The Second Good Reason

A) A doctor once travelled to an African country to research a public health scheme. As soon as he got out of the plane he was excited by a low background throbbing – the sound of tribal drums. He became less enthusiastic when night came and his sleep was disturbed. He complained to the hotel management the next morning but was simply told, "The drumming must never stop."

The next day he travelled out into the bush to inspect levels of sanitation in the native villages. There he saw the drummers, keeping on with their interminable drums. It went on, everywhere he travelled and everywhere he tried to sleep. In the bush, the savannah, always there was drumming. When he had been told 'The drumming must never stop' for the hundredth time, he lost all patience.

"Why? Why? Why must it never stop! I can't sleep. It's driving me crazy. Why must it never stop?"

The chief explained, "Because if the drummers stop then the bass guitar begins!"

B) A photographer had reached the peak of his fame and could take the time to set up really perfect photographs. He wanted to take the best photograph that had ever been taken of a field of wheat. He searched a long time and found the ideal field, and sat in the wheat all hours of the day and night to find the perfect moment for the lighting. At last he arrived for the final shot, and sat down among the wheat stalks. The combine harvester came along and cut off his legs.

C) Get stoned – drink cement.
Picasso was framed.

Options

● Conduct a spot survey on the favourite comedians of the class. Is there an overall favourite? Comedians complain that television means they have to produce new material every week. Are there any comedians whose work you find repetitive? Why do they continue to be popular? Can you identify particular styles of comedy? What percentage of the week's programming on any channel would you guess was devoted to comedy? Check your guess against a copy of the *Radio* or *TV Times*.

● In different groups, decide on a particular kind of joke ('knock, knock' jokes, graffiti jokes, elephant jokes) and collect them together for a poster. Research Joke Books. Within your groups find out if there are differences in sense of humour.

● In pairs, take it in turns to try and make your partner laugh. It is up to the straight-faced person to hold out as long as they can.

● Construct a drama based on a funny incident – is it different, funnier or less funny when acted out?

The Third Good Reason

● Can you recognise yourself in any of the following?

"I really have done my homework but I left it on the bus."

"I put my homework in my history book and it looks just the same as my chemistry book so I've brought the wrong one."

"Our cat has gone missing and on the way home I thought I saw it in a garden and I put my bag down to go to it and then a dog started chasing it and I ran after it and when I got back my bag had gone."

"We had a power cut last night so I wasn't able to do my homework as we'd only got one candle and my mum needed it in the kitchen."

● Produce the most far-fetched excuse you can for not doing homework. (It should be believable.) Improvise a scene around it. If you can tape it, listen again to the way language is used.

● Take the parts of the accuser and the accused. The accuser thinks up something to blame their partner for, and it is up to the other person to think of convincing excuses to keep out of trouble. How easy is it to think up excuses? Do you find yourself using real-life experiences?

REASONS FOR TELLING STORIES

The Fourth Good Reason

● Which are the most expensive programmes we see on television?

● Read the following two examples. Is there a connecting factor in the two stories?

A) The family lawyer tells the lucky heir that he has inherited millions, but as his great uncle was a strange man, he has to fulfil one condition to qualify for the inheritance. He has to spend the first ten thousand pounds in exactly twenty-four hours.

He goes to the Stock Exchange, finds the company least likely to succeed and buys all the shares he can. Once the message is passed round the dealers they suspect 'insider trading' and begin to buy shares in this useless company. The value rises on the market and the unlucky man can sell at a profit!

He rushes to a car showroom to buy the most expensive model – and finds he is their thousandth customer and entitled to a free car! In despair he goes into a pub and orders a pint of their most expensive lager. He is amazed at how expensive it is – he orders drinks on the house all round – and qualifies for the inheritance!

B) The waiter in the restaurant is very tired waiting only for the last customers to go, but a very romantic young couple are lingering over their meal. At last the man asks for the bill, and the woman says could she have just one more cup of coffee?

Behind the kitchen door, the waiter isn't going to bother with the coffee machine and grinding coffee beans. He makes a series of noises imitating a coffee machine and as the couple pay, the woman gives the waiter a grateful smile and says, "Lovely coffee! Could we have another?"

● Having read the two examples decide:
1. Which are the most popular 'story' adverts among the class?
2. Can you recall an advert's story, but not the product it is selling?
3. Do some companies keep a theme or character running through the stories in their commercials?

● Try devising a story to sell a product. The whole story must be told in exactly 30 seconds of screen time. *Repromaster 2* allows for the use of storyboard, and could be used for a written presentation of this.

The Fifth Reason – But Maybe Not a Good One

● Have you ever been told something by someone which you found out later was not true? Something about their own life, or about somebody else, or about a particular place you both know?
How did you feel when you found it wasn't true?
Had you been led to admire or to despise someone on false pretences?
Can you work out why people tell 'stories' of this kind?

'Rumour' or 'gossip' is a common theme in girls' magazine stories.

● Devise your own story which illustrates this title, using any of the suggestions in the discussion section above but replacing yourself with a fictitious character.

The Sixth Good Reason

● Read the following two folk tales to see what they have in common.

A) After the great flood, man became very hungry as there was nothing left growing on the earth and so he went into the forest to hunt. Previously the animals and birds had been his companions but when they realised they were in danger they withdrew. The birds had been warned of man's approach and so he was left alone and afraid to go back into the forest. Instead, he devised a canoe to float on the water, and caught himself fish to eat.

However, the great sun-spirit Arawidi, used this creek as his favourite fishing place after his day's work was done and he became concerned lest man take all the fish. He realised that man was afraid to go into the forest and decided to give him a companion so that he could hunt again.

Taking the form of a man, Arawidi visited the man in the evening where the day's catch was laid out before the cooking fires. He picked up a fish and altered the shape of its body, shorter and heavier, and pulled out legs from the fish's body, and made the tail longer and thinner. Finally he reshaped the fish face into a dog face. All the time he held the fish/dog by the nose so that part of the dog remained cold and always has done. And the dog has remained to guard man's house and keep him company and always has done.

From the West Indies

B) Once two girls living in the Land of the Long White Cloud heard the old people talking of the fire-that-never-goes-out which gave unending life. Without explaining where they were going, they set off on the terrible journey to reach the entrance to the underworld. They took a basket of sweet fruits of the earth to give to the spirits who lives in the underworld. Many times on the way they were hindered by the very trees and bushes, mountains and hills, which tried to keep them back from their terrible quest. In the end the courage of the girls overcame all obstacles and they arrived at the sea where a huge tree grows from a cliff. The spirits of the dead pause to lament in the branches of the tree before going beneath its roots to the underworld.

The girls entered between the tree roots and followed a long dark passage. They found three spirits sitting round a fire of three sticks, the fire which never goes out. Whilst one girl offered them fruits the other snatched a burning stick and they ran back. The spirits ran after them and caught at the girl holding the burning branch just as she broke through to the world above. Her sister tried to pull her out, but the spirits had her tight. She had to lose hold of the flaming stick to escape which meant unending life, but instead of dropping it back, she threw it far into the sky above and wrenched herself free of the grasp below. The spirits sank back, unable to enter the light of the world of the living and the sky god caught the flaming stick and set it in place where it could light up the night sky when the sun was away. It was not good for mortal men to have unending life but everywhere the courage of the girls was thanked when people saw the moon shining in the dark sky.

From the Pacific Islands, Maoriland

Options

● Working in a group, discuss and write down your thoughts about these six good reasons for telling stories. You may well come up with others.
Use this as a script for a Presenter, who will link six improvisations, each of which shows one of the reasons for 'Telling a Story'. The individual scenes could take any form – monologue, dialogue, short play.

● Try drafting out a story based on any of the following statements.
1. I wish I had listened to what I was told about it/him/her.
2. I had been so upset and it turned out to be only a rumour.
3. Real life is funnier than made-up stories.
4. So now you know why dogs turn round before they sleep/the stars shine/the sea is blue.
5. I had to think quickly if I was to stay out of trouble.

HOW STORIES CHANGE

A story can work in different ways. If you cast your mind back to the fairy tales and stories which you enjoyed as a child, you can see how many different ways the same story can be presented.

The Audience

● Look at the following examples and decide what audience they are aimed at.

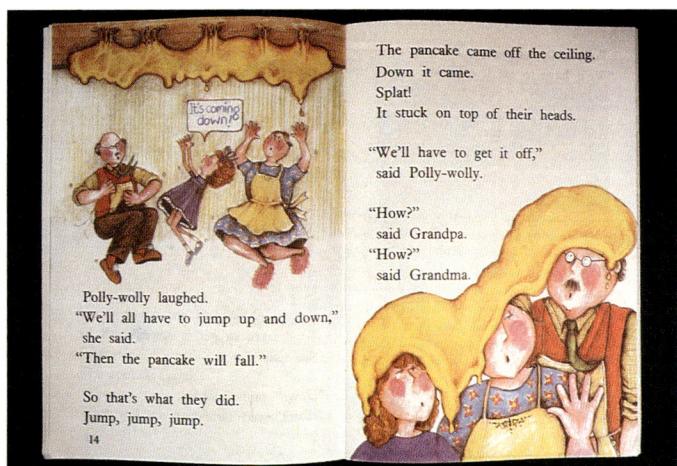

The pancake came off the ceiling.
Down it came.
Splat!
It stuck on top of their heads.

"We'll have to get it off,"
said Polly-wolly.

"How?"
said Grandpa.
"How?"
said Grandma.

Polly-wolly laughed.
"We'll all have to jump up and down,"
she said.
"Then the pancake will fall."

So that's what they did.
Jump, jump, jump.
14

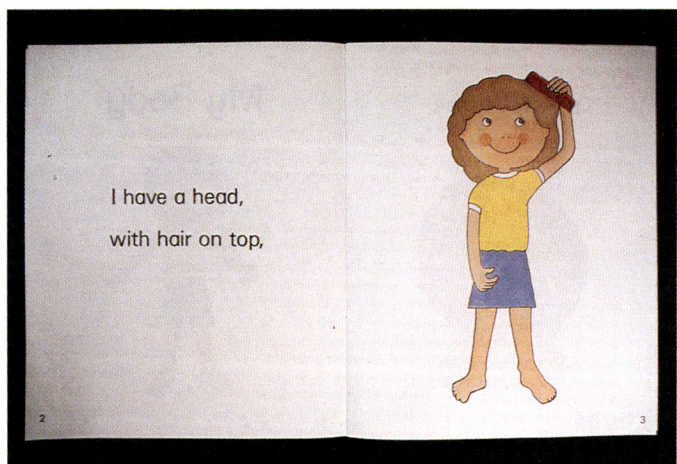

I have a head,
with hair on top,

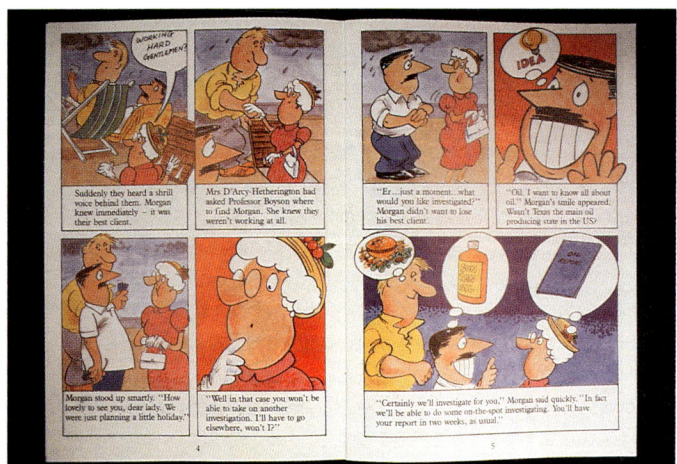

● Decide on a story you know well – a fairy tale, a commercial, an episode of a serial, something you have read recently in school. Individually or in pairs, try to present that story in a different way. You can choose from any of the following, or think of your own.
Picture strip with captions/without captions/with speech bubbles
Straightforward narrative
Play format – dialogue with directions
Verse storytelling/rapping.

Many modern writers are fascinated by the way that stories can be worked or changed, and prefer not to tie themselves and their readers down to one version of the events. They make it clear to their readers that a story, like life, can have many possible openings and many possible outcomes.

The following extract is from the book by Italo Calvino with the title **If on a winter's night a traveller.**

In the first chapter he says: "A situation that takes place at the opening of a novel always refers you to something else that has happened or is about to happen and it is this something else that makes it risky to identify with, risky for you the reader and for him the author."

● Bear these ideas in mind as you study the following extract. What is it that 'has happened'? What is it that 'is about to happen'?

You may find the story quite difficult to follow. Repromaster 3 *is based on this story and helps with the difficulties of the text.*

If on a winter's night a traveller
Extract A

The novel begins in a railway station, a locomotive huffs. . .

. . . In the door of the station there is a passing whiff of station café odour. There is someone looking through the befogged glass, he opens the glass door of the bar, everything is misty, inside, too, as if seen by nearsighted eyes, or eyes irritated by coal dust . . .

. . . It is a rainy evening; the man enters the bar; he unbuttons his damp overcoat; a cloud of steam enfolds him; a whistle dies away along tracks that are glistening with rain, as far as the eye can see . . .

I am the man who comes and goes between the bar and the telephone booth. Or, rather: that man is called "I" and you know nothing else about him, just as this station is called only "station" and beyond it there exists nothing except the unanswered signal of a telephone ringing in a dark room of a distant city. I hang up the receiver, I await the rattling flush, down through the metallic throat, I push the glass door again, head towards the cups piled up to dry in a cloud of steam . . .

Something must have gone wrong for me: some misinformation, a delay, a missed connection; perhaps on arriving I should have found a contact, probably linked with this suitcase that seems to worry me so much, though whether because I am afraid of losing it or because I can't wait to be rid of it is not clear. What seems certain is that it isn't just ordinary baggage, something I can check or pretend to forget in the waiting room. There's no use my looking at my watch; if anyone had come and waited for me he would have gone away again long ago, there's no point in my furiously racking my brain to turn back clocks and calendars in the hope of reaching again the moment before something that should not have happened did happen. If I was to meet someone in this station, someone who perhaps had nothing to do with this station but was simply to get off one train and leave on another train, as I was to have done, and one of the two was to pass something to the other – for example, if I was supposed to give the other this wheeled suitcase which instead has been left on my hands and is scorching them – then the only thing to do is to try to re-establish the lost contact.

I have already crossed the café a couple of times and have looked out of the front door onto the invisible square, and each time the wall of darkness has driven back inside this sort of illuminated limbo suspended between the two darknesses, the bundle of tracks and the foggy city . . .

. . . it is not wise for me to move away from here where they might still come looking for me, or for me to be seen by other people with this burdensome suitcase . . .

A man whom I do not know was to meet me as soon as I got off the train, if everything hadn't gone wrong. A man with a suitcase on wheels, exactly like mine, empty. The two suitcases would bump into each other as if accidentally in the bustle of travellers on the platform, between one train and another. An event that can happen by chance, but there would have been a password that that man would have said to me, a comment on the headline of the newspaper sticking out of my pocket, on the results of the horse races. "Ah, Zeno of Elea came in first!" And at the same time we would disentangle our suitcases, shifting the metal poles, perhaps also exchanging some remarks about horses, forecasts, odds; and we would then go off toward different trains, each pushing his suitcase in his own direction. No one would have noticed, but I would have been left with the other man's suitcase and he would have taken away mine.

A perfect plan, so perfect that a trivial complication sufficed to spoil it. Now I am here not knowing what to do next, the last traveller waiting in this station where no

more trains arrive or leave before tomorrow morning. It is the hour when the little provincial city crawls into its shell, again. At the station bar the only people left are locals who all know one another, people who have no connection with the station but come this far through the dark square perhaps because there is no other place open in the neighbourhood . . .

. . . I, in fact, find myself here without a here or an elsewhere, recognised as an outsider by the nonoutsiders at least as clearly as I recognise the nonoutsiders and envy them. Yes, envy. I am looking from the outside at the life of an ordinary evening in an ordinary little city, and I realise I am cut off from ordinary evenings for God knows how long, and I think of thousands of cities like this, of hundreds of thousands of lighted places where at this hour people allow the evening's darkness to descend and have none of the thoughts in their head that I have in mine; maybe they have other thoughts that aren't at all enviable, but at this moment I would be willing to trade with any one of them. For example with one of these young men who are making the rounds of local shopkeepers collecting signatures on a petition to City Hall, concerning the tax on neon signs, and who are now reading it to the barman . . .

. . . "What about you, Armida? Have you signed yet?" they ask a woman I can see only from behind, a belt hanging from a long overcoat trimmed with fur, the collar turned up, a thread of smoke rising from the fingers gripping the stem of a glass. "Who says I want to put a neon sign over my shop?" she answers. "If the City is planning to save money on street lights, they certainly aren't going to light the streets with my money! Anyway, everybody knows where Armida's Leather Goods is. And when I've pulled down the metal blind, the street will just stay dark, and that's that."

"That's a good reason for you to sign," they say to her. The address her familiarly, as *tu*; they all call one another *tu*; their speech is half in dialect; these are people used to seeing one another daily year after year; everything they say is the continuation of things already said. They tease one another, even crudely: "Admit it, you like the street dark so nobody can see who comes to your place! Who visits you in the back of the shop after you've locked up?" . . .

. . . I too, though I have other things to think about, there I let myself go, I speak to her, I strike up a conversation that I should break off as quickly as I can, in order to go away, disappear . . .

"What stories do they tell?" I ask. "I don't know a thing. I know that you have a shop, without a neon sign. But I don't even know where it is."

She explains to me. It is a leather-goods shop, selling suitcases and travel articles. It isn't in the station square

HOW STORIES CHANGE

but on a side street, near the grade crossing of the freight station.

"But why are you so interested?"

"I wish I had arrived here earlier. I would walk along the dark street, I would see your shop all lighted up, I would go inside, I would say to you: If you like, I'll help you pull down the shutter."

She tells me she has already pulled down the shutter, but she has to go back to the shop to take inventory, and she will be staying there till late . . .

She looks around, as if making fun of me; I point my chin at her; she raises the corners of her mouth as if to smile, then stops: because she has changed her mind, or because this is the only way she smiles. "I don't know if that's a compliment, but I'll take it as one. And then what?"

"Then I am here, I am the I of the present, with this suitcase."

This is the first time I mention the suitcase, even though I never stop thinking about it.

And she says, "This is the evening of square suitcases on wheels."

I remain calm, impassive. I ask, "What do you mean?"

"I sold one today, a suitcase like that."

"Who bought it?"

"A stranger. Like you. He was on his way to the station, he was leaving. With an empty suitcase, just bought. Exactly like yours."

"What's odd about that? Don't you sell suitcases?"

"I have a lot of this model in stock at the shop, nobody here buys them. People don't like them, or they're no use. Or people don't know them. But they must be convenient."

"Not for me. For example, just when I'm thinking that this evening could be a beautiful evening for me, I remember I have to drag this suitcase after me, and I can't think about anything else."

"Then why don't you leave it somewhere?"

"Like a suitcase shop," I say.

"Why not? Another suitcase, more or less."

She stands up from the stool, adjusts the collar of her overcoat in the mirror, the belt.

"If I come by later on and rap on the shutter, will you hear me?"

"Try."

She doesn't say good-bye to anyone. She is already outside in the square . . .

"Chief Gorin is arriving later than all the predictions tonight," someone says, because at that moment the chief enters the bar.

He enters. "Good evening, one and all!" He comes over to me, lowers his eyes to the suitcase, the newspaper, mutters through clenched teeth, "Zeno of Elea," then goes to the cigarette machine.

Have they thrown me to the police? Is he a policeman who is working for our organisation? I go over to the machine as if I were also buying cigarettes.

He says, "They've killed Jan. Clear out."

"The suitcase?" I ask.

"Take it away again. We want nothing to do with it now. Catch the eleven o'clock express."

"But it doesn't stop here . . ."

"It will. Go to track six. Opposite the freight station. You have three minutes."

"But . . ."

"Move, or I'll have to arrest you."

The organisation is powerful. It can command the police, the railroad. I trail my suitcase along the passages between the tracks until I reach six. I walk along the platform. The freight section is at the end, with the grade crossing that opens into the fog and the darkness. The chief is at the door of the station bar, keeping an eye on me. The express arrives at top speed. It slows down, stops, erases me from the chief's sight, pulls out again.

Italo Calvino, *If on a winter's night a traveller*

Sharing Ideas

● In groups agree one answer for each of the following questions.

When you have completed all ten, swap your answers with those of another group and see whether you agree with their interpretation. Why do you agree or disagree with them?

1. Why at first did you think the man with the wheeled suitcase was so nervous?

2. Who do you think it was who bought the wheeled suitcase from Armida's leather goods shop?

3. What do you think is in the suitcase he is going to exchange?

4. Which of the suitcases are empty?

5. Who do you think are his bosses?

6. Why is the man surprised by the identity of the person who finally comes in and gives the code words to him?

7. How do you know that Jan was the person he was to exchange suitcases with?

8. How could it have been Armida who betrayed them? Do you think this is likely?

9. In what way has his organisation been able to 'command the police, the railroad'?

10. What do you think will happen next?

Activities Using Beginnings

● Work in pairs on a scene where two agents meet. Leave it for the audience to decide what might happen next.

● In a group, present a scene in a public place where there are several people gathered. Gradually it becomes clear that one of these people is an outsider. Drop a few hints about what his purpose might be, but leave the audience guessing.

● Improvise a scene based on the exchange of two identical objects, like suitcases. Suggest why these people might have arranged for this exchange.

HOW STORIES CHANGE

Throughout these first sections there are suggestions as to how an idea or issue might be improvised, or presented in a dramatic way, in a way that is suitable for writing. These alternatives in themselves are examples of the way that stories can be organised.

When working on the drama suggestions above, a group produced the following:

A) "Flight 207 is preparing to leave at terminal 4. Will all passengers on this flight please make their way to the area immediately. Thank you." The speakers switched off with a loud click.

"Listen Kuba, I've got to go – the plane's about to leave. I'll see you in Cairo." Grant put down the phone and headed towards the plane. Once he was acquainted with the person sitting next to him, who was going to see her son in Egypt, he prepared for the long flight to Egypt. The plane soared on across the night sky like an eagle and when it landed he made his way quickly to the checkout point . . .
Jonathon, Nick, Soumen

One of the group simply stood and read out the carefully written narrative, whilst the others went through the motions. This was altered and improved, as a dramatic way of telling a story until all that was left was this:

B) *Scene – a busy airport.*
ANNOUNCER: Flight 207 is preparing to leave at terminal 4. Will all passengers on this flight please make their way to the area immediately. Thank you.
GRANT (*speaking into airport phone*): Listen Kuba, I've got to go – the plane's about to leave. I'll see you in Cairo.
Scene – on the plane.
VOICE ON INTERCOM: Good afternoon ladies and gentlemen, this is your pilot speaking. We shall shortly be landing at Cairo airport, local time, 4.30pm temperature 20 degrees. We hope you have enjoyed your flight. Please be sure to take all baggage with you.
Scene – at the taxi rank.
DRIVER: Where to, sir?

Spot the Difference

● In pairs decide:
1. What is included in A that is omitted in B?
2. What is included in B that is omitted in A?
3. What kind of audience have the writer of A imagined they are addressing?
4. How many voices are required to put A across to an audience?
5. How will B need to be presented – what extra people will be required to show the audience what the location is and what is happening there?
6. How do the words of the Announcer or the Voice on the intercom instantly tell the audience where the action is taking place?
7. What general guidelines could you now draw up on the difference between telling a story and acting a story?

Options

Choose from one of the ideas below and write the story suggested.
● An agent's contact fails to turn up. What has gone wrong? Who are they working for? What are they trying to achieve?
● A traveller is delayed at an unfamiliar station and gets into conversation with a lady who has a reputation locally . . .
● Two suitcases are accidentally exchanged on a busy railway platform and the owners catch different trains, unaware of what has happened.
● A chance meeting that changed your life.

If on a winter's night a traveller
Extract B

You have read Italo Calvino's idea that it is 'risky' to identify with a narrative, a story and the whole of his book deliberately torments the reader.

The next extract comes from the chapter immediately after the assignation of the secret agents in the railway station, but as you will see, does not continue the story of the traveller on the winter's night at all but addresses the reader directly.

You have now read about thirty pages and you're becoming caught up in the story. At a certain point you remark: "This sentence sounds somehow familiar. In fact, this whole passage reads like something I've read before." Of course: there are themes that recur, the text is interwoven with these reprises, which serve to express the fluctuation of time. You are the sort of reader who is sensitive to such refinements; you are quick to catch the author's intentions and nothing escapes you. But, at the same time, you also feel a certain dismay; just when you were beginning to grow truly interested . . .

Wait a minute! Look at the page number. Damn! From page 32 you've gone back to page 17! What you thought was a stylistic subtlety on the author's part is simply a printers' mistake: they have inserted the same pages twice. The mistake occurred as they were binding the volume: a book is made up of sixteen-page signatures; each signature is a large sheet on which sixteen pages are printed, and which is then folded over eight times; when all the signatures are bound together, it can happen that two identical signatures end up in the same copy; it's the sort of accident that occurs every now and then. You leaf anxiously through the next pages to find page 33, assuming it exists; a repeated signature would be a minor inconvenience, the irreparable damage comes when the proper signature has vanished, landing in another copy where perhaps that one will be doubled and this one will be missing. In any event, you want to pick up the thread of your reading, nothing else matters to you, you had reached a point where you can't skip even one page.

Here is page 31 again, page 32 . . . and then what comes next? Page 17 all over again, a third time! What kind of book did they sell you, anyway? . . .

The next day, as soon as you have a free moment, you run to the bookshop, you enter, holding the book already opened, pointing your finger at a page, as if that alone were enough to make clear the general disarray. "You know what you sold me? . . . Look here . . . Just when it was getting interesting . . ."

The bookseller maintains his composure. "Ah, you, too? I've had several complaints already. And only this morning I received a form letter from the publisher. You see? 'In the distribution of the latest works on our list a part of the edition of the volume *If on a winter's night a traveller* by Italo Calvino has proved defective and must be withdrawn from circulation. Through an error of the bindery, the printed signatures of that book became mixed with those of another new publication, the Polish novel *Outside the town of Malbork* by Tazio Bazakbal. With profound apologies for the unfortunate incident, the publisher will replace the spoiled copies at the earliest possible moment, et cetera.' Now I ask you, must a poor bookseller take the blame for the negligence of others? We've been going crazy all day. We've checked the Calvinos copy by copy. There are a number of sound volumes, happily, and we can immediately replace your defective *Traveller* with a brand-new one in mint condition."

Hold on a minute. Concentrate. Take all the information that has poured down on you at once and put it in order. A Polish novel. Then the book you began reading with such involvement wasn't the book you thought but was a Polish novel instead. That is the book you are now so anxious to procure. Don't let them fool you. Explain clearly the situation. "No, actually I don't really give a damn about that Calvino any more. I started the Polish one and it's the Polish one I want to go on with. Do you have this Bazakbal book?"

"If that's what you prefer. Just a moment ago, another customer, a young lady, came in with the same problem, and she also wanted to exchange her book for the Polish. There, you see that pile of Bazakbal on the counter, right

under your nose? Help yourself."

"But will this copy be defective?"

"Listen. At this point I'm not swearing to anything. If the most respected publishing firms make such a muddle, you can't trust anything any more. I'll tell you exactly what I told the young lady. If there is any further cause for complaint, you will be reimbursed. I can't do more than that."

The young lady. He has pointed out a young lady to you. She is there between two rows of bookshelves in the shop, looking among the Penguin Modern Classics, running a lovely and determined finger over the pale aubergine-coloured spines. Huge, swift eyes, complexion of good tone and good pigment, a richly waved haze of hair . . .

She smiles. She has dimples. She is even more attractive to you.

She says: "Ah, indeed, I was so anxious to read a good book. Right at the beginning, this one, no, but then it began to appeal to me . . . Such a rage when I saw it broke off. And it wasn't that author. It did seem right away a bit different from his other books. And it was really Bazakbal. He's good, though, this Bazakbal. I've never read anything of his."

"Me either," you can say, reassured, reassuring.

Italo Calvino, *If on a winter's night a traveller*

Understanding the Situation

● In pairs decide why the reader's copy of *If on a winter's night a traveller* does not continue the story but just starts again at the beginning when it gets to page 33?
Which other book has been bound inside the wrong cover?
Which book does the bookseller say the reader has actually been reading?

But the author has another surprise in store when you move onto the next chapter, hoping to find out what happened to the agent when he caught the eleven o'clock express specially made to stop for him. It is another opening chapter for quite a different novel called **Outside the town of Malbork.**

ENDINGS

"And then I woke up and it was all a dream."

"And so they married and lived happily ever after."

How Do Stories End?

● These type of endings often occur in fairy tales or stories you read when you were young. What other types of story endings can you think of?

● Note down the ways you hate stories to end.

1. Do you hate a sad ending?

2. Do you like to know what happened to every single character?

3. Do you like to see characters getting what they deserve, be it good or bad?

4. Do you prefer an ending which is more 'lifelike' or inconclusive?

● In a group compare your notes and see how many different endings you have described.

● In pairs:

1. Collect last lines from books you know or can find in school or at home.

2. Mount them all on a poster. What do they suggest about the stories they conclude?

3. If you do not know the story, can you guess what sort of a story it was?

All good writers realise the importance of a strong ending to their story and try to think their way through to the ending before actually writing the story. Others, however, feel that a conclusive ending does not represent their experience of life – that stories never actually stop but just pause for a while.

X. maintains that a good novelist, before he begins to write his book, ought to know how it is going to finish. As for me, who let mine flow where it will, I consider that life never presents us with anything which may not be looked upon as a fresh starting point, no less than as a termination. "Might be continued" – these are the words with which I should like to finish my *Coiners*.
Andre Gide, *Les Faux Monnayeurs* (1925). *Part III, chapter xiii, transl. Dorothy Bussy* (1952).

● In groups devise a short scene which has two possible endings, one of them conclusive/decisive, one of them more open ended/'might be continued'. Present both scenes one after the other.

● Alternatively this could be written as a story which has two possible endings.

Ideas for Alternative Endings

One structure which allows for this is to include in the story a situation which is decided by tossing a coin, and then to provide the two different outcomes depending on each side of the coin coming down.

● You could use any of these last lines or re-use any of the 'famous last lines' collected on the poster project above in order to try out this idea for 'alternative endings'.

I married him.

It was his contact.

She/he had failed him/her.

And that was the beginning of . . .

So the country began to open up.

At last I could look him/her in the face.

It was a triumph.

What was to come next, no one knew.

So they moved forward together.

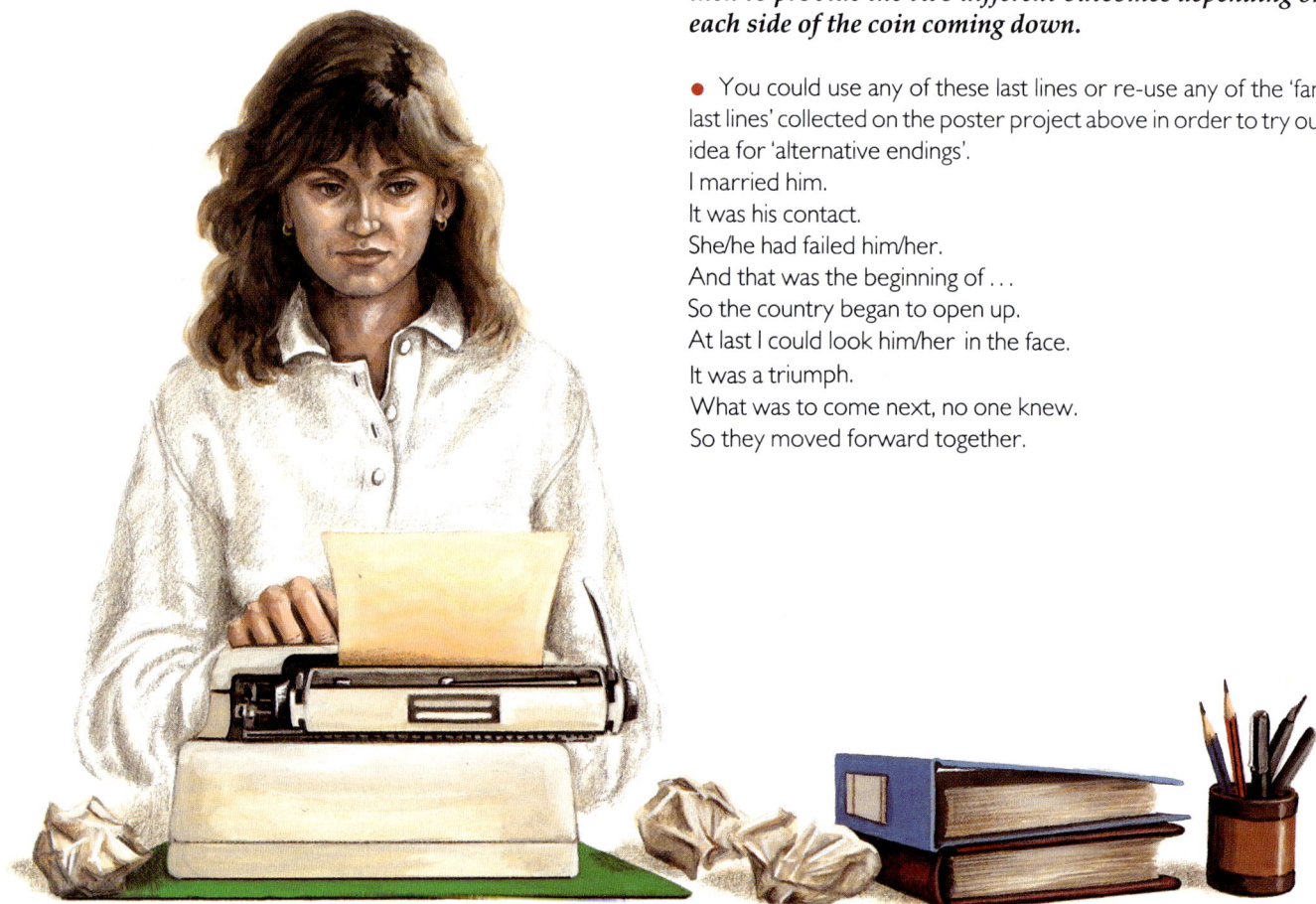

Pages 14–19 of this unit showed how the modern writer Italo Calvino deliberately exploited the reader's expectations of the beginning of a novel. In the next examples, well known writers do much the same with the expectations of how a story should end.

Vanity Fair

In the novel **Vanity Fair** *by WM Thackeray, a very long book, the writer gives a summary of the future lives of many of the characters – but consider the final short paragraph.*

The Baronet lives entirely at Queen's Crawley, with Lady Jane and her daughter; whilst Rebecca, Lady Crawley, chiefly hangs about Bath and Cheltenham, where a very strong party of excellent people consider her to be a most injured woman. She has her enemies. Who has not? Her life is her answer to them. She busies herself in works of piety. She goes to church, and never without a footman. Her name is in all the Charity Lists. The Destitute Orange-girl, the Neglected Washerwoman, the distressed Muffin-man, find in her a fast and generous friend. She is always having stalls at Fancy Fairs for the benefit of these hapless beings. Emmy, her children, and the Colonel, coming to London some time back, found themselves suddenly before her at one of these fairs. She cast down her eyes demurely and smiled as they started away from her; Emmy skurrying off on the arm of George (now grown a dashing young gentleman), and the Colonel seizing up his little Janey, of whom he is fonder than of anything in the world – fonder even than of his 'History of the Punjab'.

'Fonder than he is of me,' Emmy thinks, with a sigh. But he never said a word to Amelia that was not kind and gentle; or thought of a want of hers that he did not try to gratify.

'Ah! *Vanitas Vanitatum!* Which of us is happy in this world? Which of us has his desire? or, having it, is satisfied? – Come children, let us shut up the box and the puppets, for our play is played out.
WM Thackeray, *Vanity Fair*

● How do you think this ending changes the reader's attitude to the story they have just been involved in?

The French Lieutenant's Woman

The French Lieutenant's Woman by John Fowles is well known for the author's provision of two alternative endings, one a conventional happy one, but the other possibly a more satisfactory outcome for the book's heroine.

And now, having brought this fiction to a thoroughly traditional ending, I had better explain that although all I have described in the last two chapters happened, it did not happen quite in the way you may have been led to believe.

I said earlier that we are all poets, though not many of us write poetry; and as so are we all novelists, that is, we have a habit of writing fictional futures for ourselves, although perhaps today we incline more to put ourselves into a film. We screen in our minds hypotheses about how we might behave, about what might happen to us; and these novelistic or cinematic hypotheses often have very much more effect on how we actually do behave, when the real future becomes the present, than we generally allow.

Charles was no exception; and the last few pages you have read are not what happened, but what he spent the hours between London and Exeter imagining might happen. To be sure he did not think in quite the detailed and coherent narrative manner I have employed; nor would I swear that he followed Mrs Poulteney's postmortal career in quite such interesting detail. But he certainly wished her to the Devil, so it comes to almost the same thing.

Above all he felt himself coming to the end of a story; and to an end he did not like. If you noticed in those last two chapters an abruptness, a lack of consonance, a betrayal of Charles's deeper potentiality and a small matter of his being given a life-span of very nearly a century and a quarter; if you entertained a suspicion, not uncommon in literature, that the writer's breath has given out and he has rather arbitrarily ended the race while he feels he's still winning, then do not blame me; because all these feelings, or reflections of them, were very present in Charles's own mind. The book of his existence, so it seemed to him, was about to come to a distinctly shabby close.
John Fowles, *The French Lieutenant's Woman*

Playing With Endings

A child at infant school wanted the part of Joseph in the Christmas nativity play, but was annoyed to be told he was to be the innkeeper. At the performance, with all the parents watching, Mary and Joseph came wearily to the inn and asked if there was room for the night. The innkeeper replied, "Yes, plenty. Come right in and make yourselves comfortable!"

● Choose a story which most people know well (Cinderella, Hansel and Gretel, Snow White etc.). Rewrite the ending so that there is a distinct surprise, a contradiction of what the audience are expecting. This can be presented as written narrative, an improvisation or a radio play.
● Choose a text, novel or play, that you have recently read and provide a different ending for it. The characters should behave consistently with the way they are portrayed in the text.
● Take a serial, series or soap opera you know and write a final episode for it. Round off the stories of most (if you can't manage all) of the characters.
You will find more ways of ending and beginning, of beginning at the end or of ending at the beginning, on pages 30–37.

TITLE SEQUENCES AND TRAILERS

The beginning could be said to be the most important part of a story. It offers a wealth of possibilities and it is this openness which television producers exploit in title sequences and trailers. They want a large audience for their programme, so they carefully construct the information which goes out in advance of the programme. Do you ever find a programme is not as good as you were lead to expect by the trailer, or the title sequence?

Title Sequences

● What kind of programme would follow each of these title sequences:

A) The camera follows puzzling shapes, then as it pans upwards we see reflections in the rain soaked streets. Mournful jazz music is heard and then in the distance a solitary figure is seen, in a raincoat and a trilby hat, leaning against a bus stop.

B) A rapid sequence of images follows one another – tossing waves, a boat, a diver dropping over the edge, a nineteenth century print of a whaler, a clip from 'Moby Dick' the famous whale film, back to the tossing waves . . .

C) A pattern of stars explodes across the screen and then reshapes into galaxies which are sent spinning in ever expanding circles. A new collection of lights emerges which focuses into the naked light bulbs around a stage or screen star's make-up mirror.

● Having decided what kind of programme is to follow, use *Repromaster 4* on 'Storyboard' to devise your own title sequence. The example below shows you how it might be done.

● Watch the title sequences of three similar or three different kinds of programmes. Write an account of each of them, with an introduction and a conclusion which draws attention to the differences and similarities you have noticed between them. How important do you think the title sequence is in establishing in the viewer's mind what it is they are about to see?

	Vision	Sound	Script
1.	Very long shot lots of blue water white caps on the waves distant seagulls.	Britannia rules the waves Seagulls screaming.	VOICE OVER: When Britain was great she ruled the waves but . . .
2.	Gradually coming closer a tiny speck can be seen.	Britannia rules fades away into sound of water.	. . . nobody seems to have told Cuthbert's dad.
3.	It is a battered old fishing boat with a crusty old Geordie on board.	A jews harp plays very quietly the tune *Dance to yer daddy*.	DAD: Howway yer great dope, oor Cuddie!
4.	Cuthbert, a handsome youth appears on deck.	Vocal line of tune becomes audible *You shall have a fishie when the boat comes in.*	CUTHBERT: Why've ye hoyed me oot?
5.	Picture fades to give way to series title – 'All the nice girls love a sailor'.	Words of song give way to Northumbrian rant based on this tune.	

There are two ways in which producers give a taste of their story – in advance, with a trailer, or in the case of a series episode, with a version of 'the story so far'.

● Using *Repromaster 4* on 'Storyboard', observe and record the narrative of trailers, the way they hint at the story to come. What is the connection between the pictures on the screen and the commentary provided by the 'voice over'? Compare the results of your research and try to work out a list of the ingredients for a successful trailer.

● Devise your own trailer for a future programme – drama, discussion, game show, or any other. Write a summary of what would be said by the voice over.

● Create a group of characters for a mini series (you could use suitable pictures from newspapers and magazines). Under each portrait, write the narrative spoken at the same time, explaining the part this person has played in the story so far.

● Make a comparison of the difference between television and radio treatment of introductions.

● Tape your own introductions for two different radio programmes, using suitable music and writing the script for the presenter/announcer.

STORIES WHICH BREED

Stories are important to advertisers on television as they hope the audience will remember the story and so remember that particular product.

● Consider the following two advertisements and see what they have in common.

A) A passionate love scene is taking place on wild Yorkshire moorland between a fierce dark handsome man and a lovely girl. They are obviously Cathy and Heathcliff from the great love story *Wuthering Heights*. Their favourite wild rocky place, Penistone Crag, towers above them. Suddenly the lovers are distracted, they are in danger! The rocks begin to fall, one or two at first and then a hail of rocks. They look at each other and say:

'He's shaking the set!' and then turn accusingly to the viewer and chant together, 'Should have rented from . . .'

B) A very insignificant wild west character is being chased by the posse who catch him in their lasso. The screen image changes to the typical lovers' scene in a misty evening garden, advertising a collection of romantic hits on record. Suddenly whooping breaks out in the distance as the posse gallop by the startled lovers, demolishing the garden hedges as they do so.

Again the screen image heralds a new commercial, for detergent as the typical housewife is just reaching for a packet from the supermarket shelves. To her amazement, behind the packet of washing powder is the face of the underfed cowboy, grinning apologetically. Again the pursuers come galloping through the supermarket after their victim.

Finally a 'wanted' poster appears, with our friend's weasely face on it, but he doesn't seem at all perturbed considering the big smile he gives and the kind of lager he is said to drink.

Commercials – Your View

Some writers have suggested that we relate to stories, works of art and fiction in a particular way: rather than interpreting what we hear or read by relating it to our understanding of the 'real world', they suggest, we understand stories by relating them to other stories we know, or other works of the same type, or genre.

1 How do these two examples illustrate this point of view?
2. What other kinds, or genres, of television commercials do you have to be familiar with to enjoy the story described in example B?
3. What other examples of this kind of commercial have you seen?

● Make a list of several commercials many people have seen recently. Choose one which could be easily imitated or sent up and present it in any dramatic form you choose.
● Devise your own commercial for any product which uses the idea of another.

FRIDAY MATTERS

ODD MAN OUT

Martyn Harris

THE DAILY TELEGRAPH, FRIDAY, NOVEMBER 18, 1988

I WENT along to the Advertising Effectiveness Awards this week — partly because it seemed a contradiction in terms.

Admen are forever giving each other awards for creativity and innovation. They are always boasting about how original, sophisticated and witty British adverts are, and how many admen become Hollywood directors. But I've noticed they keep rather quiet about how effective advertisements are in shifting the cans of beans off supermarket shelves.

In my more puritanical youth I liked to take the Marxist line on advertising as "the rattle of the stick in the swill bucket". Like most people I still refuse to believe that advertising really works, or at least, that it works on me. I'm proud that I can't remember if the TV dinner party with the sexy Englishwoman and her French fancyman is selling After Eights or liquers. And is it Chum, Winalot or Pal that top breeders recommend? I'm pleased to say I haven't a clue.

I enjoy the TV mini-dramas for Red Mountain coffee, but carry on buying Safeway's own brand. I am impressed by the profligacy of the Peugeot car racing through the burning canefields, but still drive a

Why tell me to buy British Gas? I can't buy it anywhere else

Volkswagen. I love the man who bellows about Allied Carpets on the cheap, late-night slots, but can't believe his sweaty entreaties have ever sold so much as a doormat.

Corporate adverts perplex me too. After years of expensive propaganda I am ready to concede that BP, ICI and Hanson Trust are indeed very big companies which make lots of useful things all over the world. But so what?

Some are so obscure that I'm not sure what they are selling in the first place. There is one which features spooky little pipe-cleaner men with no feet, marching about in a Waiting for Godot landscape. After watching it about 20 times I finally grasped it was for the Royal Bank of Scotland, but why do they want their bank associated with miserable little pin men? And what are they actually selling? Mortgages? Insurance policies? Pensions? Where do I buy these things? There's definitely no branch in the Holloway Road.

I don't understand either what those public monopoly advertisements are for, those pacy TV spectaculars for gas and electricity, which chew through the budget of a feature film in 60 seconds. What am I supposed to do if I like an electricity advert? Turn on all the cooker rings to celebrate? And why tell me to buy gas from British Gas? I can't buy it anywhere else. Surely one of the main points of a public monopoly is that it doesn't have to waste customers' money on advertising.

The commercials they are proudest of, though, are the psycho dramas, like Pirelli, Red Mountain and Apple Computer, which, through great

The Hofmeister bear dodges yobbishness but stays street-smart

compression, tell quite complex stories.

These only work, according to Hamish, because Britain has a uniquely sophisticated TV audience, nurtured on high-quality dramas and series — mostly from the BBC. It is also a very coherent audience which sees the same programmes and the same advertisements — and talks about them the next day. A spoof ad like Carling Black Label, imitating Levis and Old Spice, works only when there is a common television culture, which, of course, we won't have much longer.

One Man's Opinion

- Study the newspaper article and then discuss your reactions to it with your group.
- Consider the relevance of the final paragraph to the idea of 'Stories that breed'. Why do admen believe that such commercials only work in Britain?
- For each of the following statements, decide whether you agree or disagree with Martyn Harris:

1. "I still refuse to believe that advertising really works."
2. "I enjoy the TV mini dramas … but carry on buying Safeway's own brand."
3. "I am ready to concede that … are indeed very big companies … but so what?"
4. "Some are so obscure that I'm not sure what they are selling in the first place."
5. "I don't understand what those public monopoly advertisements are for."

- Explain your attitudes to the issues outlined in the article, providing your own evidence from commercials you have seen to explain your ideas.

The implications of some of the ideas covered in this unit are explored in more detail on Repromaster 5. *This will give you a chance to look at genre, bookcovers, sequels, comedy, photostory, advertising.*

STORIES WHICH BREED

A 'story' is a phrase often used to describe a joke. Many comedy sketches depend on the audience recognising the setting and the characters before the action or dialogue begins. When the dialogue does begin, it exploits our expectations.

A down and out approaches a prosperous looking businessman and asks in a wheedling tone for (the money for) a cup of tea.

What would you expect to be the next line or piece of action?

TRAMP ''Have you got 20p for a cup of tea, guv?''
MAN   ''No! Certainly not!''
TRAMP ''Well, here you are then.''
The tramp then gives the man 20p.

Cartoons can also use our knowledge of particular stories, or advertising can use the conventions of the photo-story in the teenage romance magazines, like the one on this page.

Repromaster 6 *contains further work on the way stories can be used commercially in advertising.*

Absurd Comedy

• Read the photo-story *The Bank Manager in the Bri-Nylon Suit*. Most of you will have seen a photo-story magazine and will know the kind of pictures and dialogue to expect.

1. Which of the photos are posed in a typically exaggerated way?

2. Which of the pictures are not really appropriate to the situation?

3. Whereabouts do you find people speaking inappropriately or out of character?

4. Find examples where the writer is clearly making fun of the bad writing to be found in such stories.

5. How realistic do you find the presentation of Mum and Russell?

6. Find examples of references to the fact that this is not reality but just a stereotyped photo-story.

7. In their advertising banks have to overcome the fact that most people find banking boring. How successfully has this been done here?

8. If you had never seen a photo-story, would this advertisement be successful in obtaining your attention?

• Use the existing photos from a photo-story magazine.
Cut up the separate frames from different stories and combine them to produce a totally new story, which could be quite ridiculous.
Cut out or blank out the writing in the speech bubbles and replace it with new text which could be inappropriate to the character or the situation.
Display the stories which you have manipulated into new stories, alongside examples of the published version, and see which are most effective.

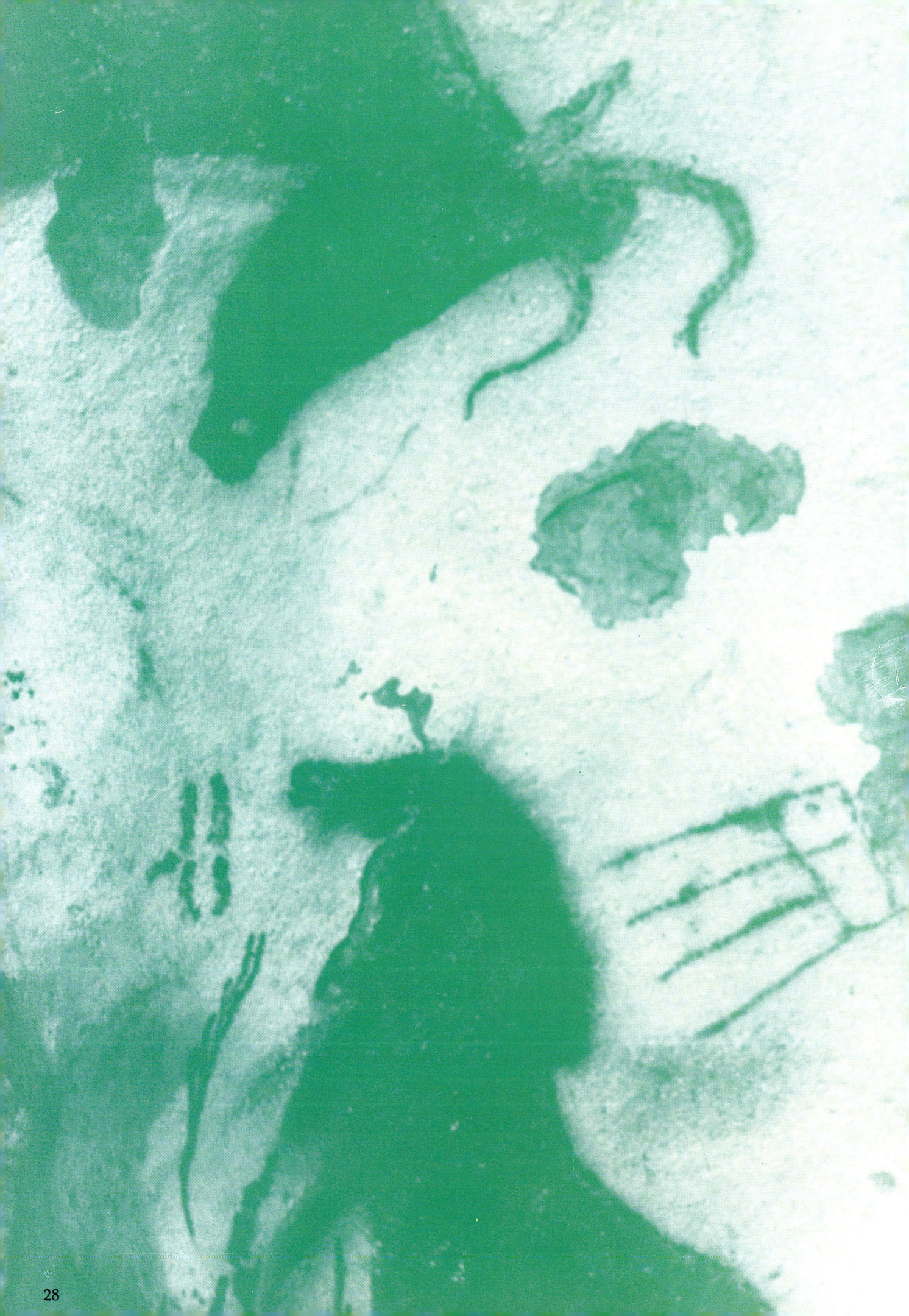

STRUCTURE IN NARRATIVE

PLANNING AHEAD

Have you ever heard the phrase 'meanwhile, back at the ranch . . . ?' What is it used to suggest? A well-told story is one which has an interesting shape to it. If you simply say 'and then' your listeners will become bored. You must try to get their interest by making them wonder what might happen, or give them lots of different people to follow.

Before you start this unit listen to the tape, where students discuss the nature of storytelling and the shape of narrative.

Groupwork Research and Analysis

● If at all possible, use a tape recorder to record people of different ages telling a story they know well. Concentrate on younger people and try to represent different stages of development eg a three year old, an eight year old and a teenager.

● Ask them to tell you a story they have heard at home or at school, or tell you what happened in a recent episode of a soap opera or serial they may have watched on television.

● In order to compare the different retellings it may be necessary to transcribe them from the tape onto paper. More information about how to tackle this can be found on *Repromaster 8.*

● Note down the obvious differences between the ways the stories are told.
1. Where do problems occur for the narrators?
2. Do they all tell the story in the 'correct' time sequence?
3. Can they organise a story which involves two different groups of people in different places?
4. How important are names?
5. How is dialogue introduced?

Obviously, when approaching a written story, it is important to plan ahead so that when the story begins to open out, your readers will be able to enjoy following all parts of the story. Firstly, however, you need a gripping opening. You will find examples of this on **Repromaster 9** *which will explore the idea in detail.*

A Story Which Will Develop

● Read through the following typescript with the notes the author then made as she began to work on her idea.

> *too informal?*
>
> The house was far older than ~~you~~
> realised until you stepped inside. Then
> the low floors, lower than the pavement
> *is this the right word?*
> outside, and the crumbly beams marching
> *do I need to make this more obvious?*
> across the low ceiling let you know how
> many generations had lived there before.
> She hated it at first, after the stately
> rooms of the house the family had left
> in the North, feeling as though they had
> left a part of themselves there, torn
> out, leaving a wound which continued to
> bleed from time to time, and ache
> *make it clearer who this is?*
> quietly all the time. *is this too far "over the top"?*
> She had the nicest room, with two
> windows catching the morning sun, as she
> had made most fuss about moving. Mummy
> *too childish?*
> had asked, "Well, shall we stay here and
> Daddy will go on visiting us at
> weekends?"
> *find a better phrase*
> "No, that's not fair on him." But she
> went on and on, about the stricter
> discipline at the new school and the
> friends she wasn't making. Perhaps it
> was the unhappiness which awoke the
> sleeping spirits from the house's long
> past. Supernatural manifestations are
> often associated with disturbed
> teenagers: *this gives the game away - too obvious!*
> The story could be worked out from the
> deeds, where a widow had given up her
> right to continue in the house, in
> favour of another person, whose name can
> be seen in the local graveyard.
> *the other plot - what happened in the past - must be introduced in a better way than this*

● What other alterations might you have made?
● Present a scene where a family come home together after their first day at school/work to a house they have just moved into. Decide on each character and their reactions to the move.
● Rewrite the story above focusing on the tragic event in the past. Why was the lady a widow? What had happened to her husband?
● Rewrite the story opening from the viewpoint of the parents in the family.

On **Repromaster 10** *you will find a story which can be cut up so that the different strands in the story can be interwoven.*

Begin At The Beginning?

● Consider the following examples:

Assignment – Write a story which takes this as its opening paragraph:
"The notice said: There is no public ferry service at the river. No petrol, no accommodation and no communications. Do not travel when the road is in a wet condition. If you proceed beyond this point you are travelling at your own risk."
NEA Examining Board

Ian ignored the notice. He wanted to know what was over on that side of the river. Nobody had ever crossed it, but Ian had to know. He had dragged a small dinghy with him for crossing the river. He had to bring the dinghy on foot because it was a stormy night and the rain had washed away the road. Ian was cold and wet, but that was not going to stop him. He had decided that tonight was the night. He dragged the dinghy down to the river bank and he got into it. He set off across the river. The river was flowing and he found it difficult to control the boat. Several times the boat got turned over. It took about an hour for him to cross. When he reached the bank he crawled up exhausted and just lay there. He fell asleep.

When he woke up he was in a bed and a doctor was standing over him.

He said to the doctor "Why am I here?" The doctor answered "A tree branch broke and . . ."
Neil

I read the sign. It didn't calculate in my brain. I just kept on driving, the river getting nearer and nearer. I finally stopped the car. The engine made an enormous sound, it was getting old. I was getting old too.

The misty air surrounded me, the sky grey. It all looked familiar, the mucky, cold river looked even more dull than ever before. I suddenly felt cold, remembering the night before. Those cruel words, those violent fists, all the screaming and shouting never seemed to stop.

One day I shall laugh at this, maybe even tell someone. But right now it's fresh in my mind. Daniel was always the one to begin the arguments, I was the one to end them. It had been a long and tiring day. The night was drawing . . .
Jane

Group Decisions

● In both cases the character in the story ignores the warning. In groups discuss the following questions:
1. Why this is a good way of involving the reader's interest?
2. What makes you want to know what happened?
3. Are you surprised at what happens to Neil's hero?
4. Look more closely at Jane's opening – do you in fact find out what happens to her heroine when she crosses the river?
5. Which direction in time is Jane's story moving in when it reaches the fourth paragraph?
6. What is it that you want to know about now, the future or the past?

You can contrast the two uses to which the opening paragraph has been put – Neil has used it to start his story, but it looks very much as if it is going to be the end of Jane's story.

So you may in fact not begin at the beginning of the story, but at the end and the reader will be involved in finding out, not what IS going to happen but what HAS happened in the past to arrive at this present . . .

BEGIN AT THE END

The example in the previous section shows how the same opening paragraph can be used to make a story which begins at the beginning of its time sequence, or one which begins at the end.

You might think at first it is odd to reveal the ending so early but many writers have chosen to start at the end of the story they are going to tell.

Openings

● Read the following brief examples.

A) "Last night I dreamt I went to Manderley again. It seemed to me I stood by the iron gate leading to the drive, and for a while I could not enter, for the way was barred to me."
Daphne du Maurier, *Rebecca*
In fact, Manderley has been destroyed by fire before the story begins.

B) "When Tusker Smalley died of a massive coronary at approximately 9.30 am on the last Monday in April, 1972, his wife Lucy was out, having her white hair blue-rinsed and set."
Paul Scott, *Staying On*
This death is in fact the last event dealt with in the book.

C) MRS JOHNSTONE (*singing*):
   Tell me it's not true
   Say it's just a story.
The narrator steps forward
NARRATOR (*speaking*):
   So did y'hear the story of the Johnstone Twins?
   As like each other as two new pins,
   Of one womb born, on the self same day
   How one was kept and one given away?

   An' did you never hear how the Johnstones died,
   Never knowing that they shared one name,
   Till the day they died, when a mother cried
   My own dear sons lie slain.
The lights come up to show a re-enactment of the final moments of the play – the deaths of Mickey and Edward. The scene fades.
Willy Russell, *Blood Brothers*

● In groups:
1. Work out the questions which a reader or audience might want to ask after reading these openings.
2. Why does someone dream about somewhere in particular?
3. Why is the idea of dying alone so distressing?
4. What possibilities are there that two people might never know they were related?
5. How are your reactions to a story different when you already know the outcome of the story?

● Present a scene which is a typical ending, either a happy ending or a sad ending, a family reunion, a marriage, a death, a separation of some kind. Then develop this to show how it was in fact the beginning and let the audience know how that ending was arrived at. You may need some kind of presenter or narrator to do this.

● Devise a scene containing the words, "You may think that this is the end . . ."

Dramatic irony is the term given to a situation where the reader or audience is 'in the know', when the characters, ignorant of what is in store for them, work their way to the pre-determined conclusion. This takes a story a long way from its simple beginnings and gives the reader a very complex involvement with the characters and events.

Write a story which begins . . .
1. By the time you read this I shall already be dead.
2. Now I was definitely going to find out what it was that drove the tenants away from the Goole house.
3. Tell me, Grandpa, why it was that you never married again.
4. If you want to know why I gave up playing the violin, well, it's a long story!
5. If the environmentalists are determined to clear out the ruined section of the Madely Canal, they're in for a very nasty surprise.
6. My mother had me christened James, but you will never hear my father call me by that name.
7. Going through my father's papers after his death I found his marriage certificate – but it wasn't my mother's name with his upon it.

Grave Fascination

The end of anybody's story must be the writing on their gravestone even if it only tells us their date of birth and death. If you spend time reading gravestones you will soon find the ends of many fascinating stories as very often more than one person is listed on the stone.
You can compare the ages of husband and wife.
You can work out how many children a couple have.
You can see how many times a man married (women were more likely to die than men in the past).
You can see what their children thought about the parents.
You can find out how few people lived to maturity.
You can see where people died and what they died of.

● Visit your local graveyard and copy out some of the inscriptions – simply lettering them out on tombstone-shaped pieces of paper and then mounting them on green card makes a display – then invent a life story, or even a family saga, to fit the inscription you find most interesting.
● Here are several examples of gravestone inscriptions which have been collected for their interest. Use them to answer some of the research ideas above.

Further exploration of these ideas based on epitaphs can be found on Repromaster 11.

Tombstone Stories

First

- In pairs, invent several epitaphs for tombstones, which all relate to different members or generations of the same family. (You may find the examples from the Hertfordshire church on *Repromaster 11* useful.)
- Write each one on separate pieces of paper.
- Turn the language into something you think sounds old.

Then

- Pass your examples on to another pair and receive someone else's epitaphs.
- Use these to work out some episode from the story of the family concerned, perhaps as a presentation of family history for local radio.

Then

- Tape, or otherwise share, all the different news items with the rest of the class, comparing them with the original epitaphs.
- Did the pair who received your epitaphs interpret them as you had intended?

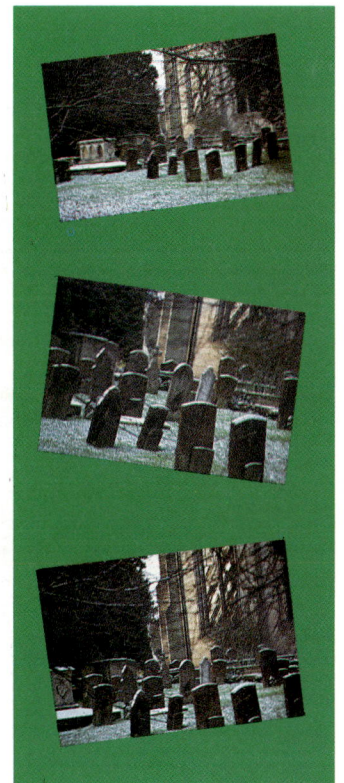

THE IMPORTANCE OF THE PAST

Often when we are puzzled by someone's behaviour or attitudes the answer can be found to lie in the past. A disagreement long ago may explain a silence or hatred between people now, a deprived childhood may explain present extravagance, an unhappy relationship with a parent may explain a similar unhappy relationship with a child.

All these examples could form stories in themselves and people continue to be fascinated by the influence of the past.

Writers often provide background information from the past to build up their characters, and this can be introduced in two ways.
1. There may be a sort of 'pre-title sequence' which describes an episode taking place long before the main events of the story.
2. The past is suddenly recalled in the middle of the present, in someone's mind, or through a conversation or the discovery of a document. This is called a 'Flashback'.

● To which category do each of the following examples belong?

The Mayor of Casterbridge

This is the title of a novel written in 1886. The following extract comes from the opening of the book when the future

mayor is a young man who, in a moment of drunkenness does something he is to regret for the rest of his life. It is kept a secret and when the episode described here becomes public he loses his position in society.

"For my part, I don't see why men who have got wives and don't want 'em, shouldn't get rid of 'em as these gipsy fellows do their old horses," said the man in the tent. "Why shouldn't they put 'em up and sell 'em by auction to men who are in need of such articles? Hey? Why, begad, I'd sell mine this minute if anybody would buy her!"

"There's them that would do that," some of the guests replied, looking at the woman, who was by no means ill-favoured.

The fuddled young husband stared for a few seconds at this unexpected praise of his wife, half in doubt of the wisdom of his own attitude towards the possessor of such qualities. But he speedily lapsed into his former conviction, and said harshly –

"Well, then, now is your chance; I am open to an offer for this gem o' creation."

She turned to her husband and murmured, "Michael, you have talked this nonsense in public places before. A joke is a joke, but you may make it once too often, mind!"

"I know I've said it before; I meant it. All I want is a buyer."

But a quarter of an hour later the man, who had gone on lacing his furmity more and more heavily, though he was either so strong-minded or such an intrepid toper that he still appeared fairly sober, recurred to the old strain, as in a musical fantasy the instrument fetches up the original theme. "Here – I am waiting to know about this offer of mine. The woman is no good to me. Who'll have her?"

The company had by this time decidedly degenerated, and the renewed inquiry was received with a laugh of appreciation. The woman whispered; she was imploring and anxious: "Come, come, it is getting dark, and this nonsense won't do. If you don't come along, I shall go without you. Come!"

She waited and waited; yet he did not move. In ten minutes the man broke in upon the desultory conversation of the furmity drinkers with, "I asked this question, and nobody answered to 't. Will any Jack Rag or Tom Straw among ye buy my goods?"

The woman's manner changed, and her face assumed the grim shape and colour of which mention has been made.

"Mike, Mike," said she, "this is getting serious. O! – too serious!"

"Will anybody buy her?" said the man.

"I wish somebody would," she said firmly. "Her present owner is not at all to her liking!"

"Nor you to mine," said he. "So we are agreed about that. Gentlemen, you hear? It's an agreement to part. She shall take the girl if she wants to, and go her ways. I'll take my tools, and go my ways. 'Tis simple as Scripture history.

Now then, stand up, Susan, and show yourself."

"Don't, my chiel," whispered a buxom staylace dealer in voluminous petticoats, who sat near the woman; "yer good man don't know what he's saying."

The woman, however, did stand up. "Now, who's auctioneer?" cried the hay-trusser.

"I be," promptly answered a short man, with a nose resembling a copper knob, a damp voice, and eyes like button-holes. "Who'll make an offer for this lady?"

The woman looked on the ground, as if she maintained her position by a supreme effort of will.

"Five shillings," said some one, at which there was a laugh.

"No insults," said the husband. "Who'll say a guinea?"

Nobody answered; and the female dealer in staylaces interposed.

"Behave yerself moral, good man, for Heaven's love! Ah, what a cruelty is the poor soul married to! Bed and board is dear at some figures, 'pon my 'vation 'tis!"

"Set it higher, auctioneer," said the trusser.

"Two guineas!" said the auctioneer; and no one replied.

"If they don't take her for that, in ten seconds they'll have to give more," said the husband. "Very well. Now, auctioneer, add another."

"Three guineas – going for three guineas!" said the rheumy man.

"No bid?" said the husband. "Good Lord, why she's cost me fifty times the money, if a penny. Go on."

"Four guineas!" cried the auctioneer.

"I'll tell ye what – I won't sell her for less than five" said the husband, bringing down his fist so that the basins danced. "I'll sell her for five guineas to any man that will pay me the money, and treat her well; and he shall have her for ever, and never hear aught o' me. But she shan't go for less. Now then – five guineas – and she's yours. Susan, you agree?"

She bowed her head with absolute indifference.

"Five guineas," said the auctioneer, "or she'll be withdrawn. Do anybody give it? The last time. Yes or no?"

"Yes," said a loud voice from the doorway.

All eyes were turned. Standing in the triangular opening which formed the door of the tent was a sailor, who, unobserved by the rest, had arrived there within the last two or three minutes. A dead silence followed his affirmation.

"You say you do?" asked the husband, staring at him.

"I say so," replied the sailor.

"Saying is one thing, and paying is another. Where's the money?"

The sailor hesitated a moment, looked anew at the woman, came in, unfolded five crisp pieces of paper, and threw them down upon the table-cloth. They were Bank-of-England notes for five pounds. Upon the face of this he chinked down the shillings severally – one, two, three, four, five.

"Now," said the woman, breaking the silence, so that her low dry voice sounded quite loud, "before you go any further, Michael, listen to me. If you touch that money, I and this girl go with the man. Mind, it is a joke no longer."

"A joke? Of course it is not a joke!" shouted her husband, his resentment rising at her suggestion. "I take the money: the sailor takes you. That's plain enough. It has been done elsewhere – and why not here?"

"'Tis quite on the understanding that the young woman is willing," said the sailor blandly. "I wouldn't hurt her feelings for the world."

"Faith, nor I," said her husband. "But she is willing, provided she can have the child. She said so only the other day when I talked o't!"

"That you swear?" said the sailor to her.

"I do," said she, after glancing at her husband's face and seeing no repentance there.

"Very well, she shall have the child, and the bargain's complete," said the trusser. He took the sailor's notes and deliberately folded them, and put them with the shillings in a high remote pocket, with an air of finality.

The sailor looked at the woman and smiled. "Come along!" he said kindly. "The little one too – the more the merrier!" She paused for an instant, with a close glance at him. Then dropping her eyes again, and saying nothing, she took up the child and followed him as he made towards the door. On reaching it, she turned, and pulling off her wedding-ring, flung it across the booth in the hay-trusser's face.

"Mike," she said, "I've lived with thee a couple of years, and had nothing but temper! Now I'm no more to 'ee; I'll try my luck elsewhere. 'Twill be better for me and Elizabeth-Jane, both. So good-bye!"

Seizing the sailor's arm with her right hand, and mounting the little girl on her left, she went out of the tent sobbing bitterly.

A stolid look of concern filled the husband's face, as if, after all, he had not quite anticipated this ending; and some of the guests laughed.

"Is she gone?" he said.

"Faith, ay; she's gone clane enough," said some rustics near the door.

"Well, the woman will be better off," said another of a more deliberative turn. "For seafaring natures be very good shelter for shorn lambs, and the man do seem to have plenty of money, which is what she's not been used to lately, by all showings."

"Mark me – I'll not go after her!" said the trusser, returning doggedly to his seat. "Let her go! If she's up to such vagaries she must suffer for 'em. She'd no business to take the maid – 'tis my maid; and if it were the doing again she shouldn't have her!"

Thomas Hardy, *The Mayor of Casterbridge*

THE IMPORTANCE OF THE PAST

Staying On

In the following extract although a death from heart attack is not a laughing matter, the writer sees much that is quietly comic in the lives of this retired couple, who have decided to stay in India as they can afford to have a servant, Ibrahim.

● How does this opening begin to build up Tusker's obstinate character?
How does it show the attitude of Ibrahim to his employers and the English generally?

Tusker Smalley's death can be fixed as having occurred at approximately 9.30 am rather than say twenty minutes later when the dog stopped whining and began to howl, causing Mrs Bhoolabhoy to shriek, because the dog, Bloxsaw (the Indian pronunciation of its real name, Blackshaw), was generally recognised as too stupid to be aware of the moment its master's soul departed; and Dr Mitra, Tusker's physician, pronounced the coronary as having been so massive as to have caused death at the moment of his fall.

About twenty minutes before his fall, that is at about 9.10 am, Tusker had dragged Bloxsaw into the garage, locked him in, then told Ibrahim that he was dismissed and could clear out right away. He had paid him off. That was at 9.15.

Ibrahim knew it was 9.15. Having taken his money he glanced at his watch to work out how much longer Lucy-Mem would be at the hairdresser and so how long it would be before the business of negotiating his reinstatement could begin. If it ever did. The paying off had been an ominous variation on the theme of getting the push.

For another few minutes Ibrahim hung around, out of sight, anticipating a yelled complaint that the breakfast egg was off, but the only sound was the racket made by the dog using the garage door as a punch-bag . . .

. . . the Smalleys usually ate in the main hotel dining-room or had Ibrahim bring trays over.

Tusker Sahib occasionally had crazes for going to the market and bringing back fresh food which he made a hash of, burning the potatoes, over-spicing the stew. Ibrahim was prepared to make tea, toast, cook eggs, squeeze fruit juice, pour from the packets of cornflakes, oversee the stocking of the refrigerator with butter and milk, and in winter have a go at making the morning porridge which kept his master's and mistress's old bones warm. If either was ill he could and did turn his hand to anything in the line of nursing and commissariat. Years younger than both he felt for them what an indulgent, often exasperated but affectionate parent might feel for demanding and unreasonable children whom it was more sensible to appease than cross.

He had spoiled them both three months before when Tusker Sahib had been taken seriously ill for the first time in his seventy-odd years, and Dr Mitra had ordered him to bed, either in hospital or at home, preferably the hospital. 'Bugger hospital,' Tusker had shouted. 'Come to that, bugger bed. Ibrahim'll look after me, so will Lucy if she can get her arse off the chair.'

One of the pleasures of working for Tusker Sahib was the further insight it gave him into the fascinating flexibility and poetry of the English language . . .

For days after Tusker's confinement to bed he had gone round muttering, 'Bugger bed, and get your arse off the chair.' For days, too, he and Lucy-Mem separately or together shopped for the ingredients of the good nourishing-broth which would keep Tusker's strength up without overheating his blood. Separately or together they had slaved over the rarely used electric oven at The Lodge that was either not hot enough or too hot, somehow not in either their separate or combined competence, a regular djinn of a stove, one moment exhaling smoke and flames and at the next as cold as Akbar's tomb; while in the bedroom or on the verandah Tusker Sahib lay either incomprehensibly docile – like a man (Ibrahim thought) who knew he'd left it too late to go to Mecca or, at other times, pronouncing anathema, against the broth, his wife, Ibrahim, Dr Mitra, and the Shiraz whose tall shadow darkened The Lodge's garden in the mornings until the sun got high enough for the five-storeys to emit heat rather than cast shadow, and cut The Lodge off from the cool breeze that sometimes came at midday in the warm weather. Chiefly, though, Tusker pronounced anathema against Mrs Bhoolabhoy whose chief *mali* was supposed to tend The Lodge's garden as well as the kitchen-garden and the ragged flower pots in the hotel's own compound.
Paul Scott, *Staying On*

After The First Death

Miro is the youngest of a group of Middle Eastern terrorists who have hijacked a bus transporting young children to an American summer camp.

● How is his attitude to children affected by his own childhood?

As he placed the tape on the last window, he felt a tug at his pants. He looked down. A small blond boy was looking up at him, smiling. The boy did not seem frightened of the mask. He had two missing teeth in the front of his mouth, and the gap in his teeth gave him a clown look. Miro continued to apply the tape and the boy kept tugging at his pant leg. Miro ignored him and hurried to finish the job.

The children were meaningless to Miro. They all looked the same to him: small human beings, without identity, strangers who did not arouse his interest or curiosity. He could make no connection with them. He had never played with children when he was growing up. His only companion had been his brother, Aniel. Aniel had been two years older than he. Neither of them had been children, really. They had scrounged for a living in the refugee camps, although it had been Aniel who had done most of the scrounging, an expert, drifting out into the steaming mornings among the thousands who came and went in the camps and returning later with scraps of food or sometimes clothing – an old jacket, shirts or socks – he had either begged or stolen. Once, Aniel had brought him a small wooden object. Orange. In the shape of an animal.

''What is it?'' Miro had asked.

''A toy,'' Aniel had replied.

The word held no meaning for Miro. He recognised the shape of the toy as an elephant. For some reason, the small object held his attention. He would pretend that the elephant was walking across the desert and that he was riding on it and bad men chased them. And then he awoke one morning and the elephant was gone. He and Aniel searched for it in vain. When Miro had fallen asleep in the abandoned shelter, the elephant had been standing near his face, on the dirt floor. Someone stole it in the night, Aniel had explained to Miro. One of the people with whom they shared the shelter for a while, perhaps.

Miro had accepted the explanation without complaint. Stealing was a way of life. But a dim knowledge took shape within him, just as the wooden object had taken on an animal shape. And the shape of the knowledge was this: Do not seek to own anything, do not try to make anything belong to you, do not look for pleasure in anything. It will be taken from you sooner or later just as you must take from other people.

The boy tugged again at Miro as he finished with the taping. Miro brushed his hand away and went towards the back of the bus. He walked softly, not wanting to stir the children. He did not want to become involved with them. He wanted to get involved with no one, the girl included. All he wanted to do was follow orders and complete this particular operation.

Robert Cormier, *After the First Death*

THE IMPORTANCE OF THE PAST

Changing Stories

● Make a chart to show what event in the past influenced the present behaviour or fortunes of each group of characters, and how this information is conveyed, like this:

Characters	Past Event	Present Effect	Means of conveying information
Michael Henchard Mayor of Casterbridge		Loss of position	
	Tusker's earlier illness	Death from heart attack	
		Lack of understanding for children	Flashback

● Improvise a scene based on the extracts from *Staying On* or *After the First Death*, which would replace that particular flashback as a pre-story episode.

● Improvise a scene based on the extract from *The Mayor of Casterbridge*, which uses this episode in a flashback. Present this as a radio play, and show how Susan might come back many years later, recognise her husband as the now famous mayor, and recall what he had done to her in their youth.

Courtroom Drama

A court scene is often enlivened with a stunning revelation from the past, in the form of new evidence, or an outburst by someone else in the court.

● Present a 'courtroom drama' based on one of the extracts above, eg:

1. Miro is brought to trial for his cruel treatment of the children.
2. Michael Henchard is brought to trial for selling his wife.
3. Ibrahim is accused of causing Tusker's death.

● Alternatively you could devise your own court case which brings something from the past to light.

● Improvise a scene which contains the line: "I never thought my past would catch up with me."

Writing the Important Line

● From the three extracts, work out which is the sentence where the reader's attention is switched from the present to past events – the important line which introduces the flashback.

● Try putting together a story which includes one of the following sentences:

1. Suddenly it all came rushing back, that summer on the island.

2. He might think no one knows, but I'm going to ruin his future now.

3. After the funeral, Hari came home and began to open his mother's desk, knowing it contained many of her old letters.

4. My aunt arrived unexpectedly in the middle of the row. We went into the front room.

5. "I think you're old enough now to know," she said.

● In a group work out an explanation for someone who has never seen a flashback in a film and therefore doesn't know what it is. Describe how it would be introduced and how you would know that this event was not part of the main time sequence of the story. Give examples from films you remember or make up an example of your own.

Restructuring Stories

● Choose from any of the outlines below, or invent your own.

1. An immigrant father opposes his son's plans to return and work in their home country. Why?

2. The mother of a schoolgirl seems very unhappy at her daughter's new choice of boyfriend, and does not want her daughter to visit the boy's family. Why?

3. A teenager tries to get her grandmother to become more involved in family life, as she is becoming a recluse. Why?

4. A man refuses to allow his family access to a certain drawer in his desk. Why?

5. A businessman, although successful, is obsessed with the idea of taking over a particular company. Why?

Write out an extract from the story using the part which took place in the past.
First: as a prologue, or pre-title sequence.
Secondly: as a flashback.
Compare the two versions and decide which makes the better story in this case.

PLOT AND SUBPLOT

Longer stories will maintain their reader's interest by relying on the interaction of more than one group of characters in more than one location. We want to find out what each group has to do with the others and how they will finally converge.

Sometimes the key may be found in the activities of one individual who belongs to both groups.

Suspense can be created if the writer deliberately leaves one group of people to make us concentrate on what has been happening to somebody else in another place – 'meanwhile, back at the ranch'.

This is a very common way of shaping stories to be told dramatically, on the stage or on television.

Different Strands

● Listen to the tape, where you'll hear TV director Ric Mellis talking about narrative structures in soap operas. How often have you noticed the same theme running through a soap opera episode?

● Then using the grid provided on *Repromaster 12*, watch a drama or serial episode on television and note down each different strand of the story which is taking place in each location.

● Decide which you think is the *main story* (the plot) and which is the *subplot* (the less important story).

● In pairs compare the results each of you have found and then work out a list of the effects which complex narratives have.

● Consider: the effect of the variety of location; the different status of the various groups of characters; largely male or largely female groups; the tensions and benefits of the interaction of one story with another.

A Radio Presentation

● In groups consider your ideas about radio drama or serials, and how the change of scene is conveyed to the listener.

● Choose two different locations and groups of characters which will both belong in the same story. There could be a family link between them, or they live in the same town, work in the same school or office.

● Draft out the script for two or three scenes, which could be part of a serial so you don't have to present a complete story.

● Decide how you will show that the time or the place has changed between scenes (sound effects? music?).

● Tape the sequence and then play it to another group.

The ideas of plot and subplot, showing how the different elements of a narrative converge and work towards a combination at the conclusion, are explored in more detail on **Repromasters 13–15**. *However, you will also be familiar with the kind of complete story in which everybody starts off together, but then they split into different groups each of which becomes involved in its own plot. Here you can say that the plots diverge.*

Dr Greenslade Theorises

In this extract from the first chapter of **The Three Hostages** *by John Buchan, the narrator's interest in thrillers (called 'shockers' in this old fashioned story) is derided by a friend, who explains how they are written.*

It was a cold night and very pleasant by the fireside, where some scented logs from an old pear-tree were burning. The doctor picked up a detective novel I had been reading, and glanced at the title page.

"I can read most things," he said, "but it beats me how you waste time over such stuff. These shockers are too easy, Dick. You could invent better ones for yourself."

"Not I. I call that a dashed ingenious yarn. I can't think how the fellow does it."

"Quite simple. The author writes the story inductively, and the reader follows it deductively. Do you see what I mean?"

"Not a bit," I replied.

"Look here. I want to write a shocker, so I begin by fixing on one or two facts which have no sort of obvious connection."

"For example?"

"Well, imagine anything you like. Let us take three things a long way apart –" He paused for a second to consider – "say, an old blind woman spinning in the Western Highlands, a barn in a Norwegian *saeter*, and a little curiosity shop in North London kept by a Jew with a dyed beard. Not much connection – simple enough if you have any imagination, and you weave all three into the yarn. The reader, who knows nothing about the three at the start, is puzzled and intrigued, and, if the story is well arranged, finally satisfied. He is pleased with the ingenuity of the solution, for he doesn't realise that the author fixed upon the solution first, and then invented a problem to suit it."

"I see," I said. "You've gone and taken the gilt off my favourite light reading. I won't be able any more to marvel at the writer's cleverness."

John Buchan, *The Three Hostages*

Discussion Ideas

1. Which kind of narrative is Dr Greenslade describing – a convergent or a divergent one?
2. What does he mean when he says that the reader follows the plot 'deductively' whereas the author has written the story 'inductively'?
3. What are the three things 'a long way apart' which the doctor suggests a story might be constructed from?
4. How would you guess the actual story of *The Three Hostages* itself develops from this point?
5. What locations and characters do you think might crop up in the main plot?

Options

● Devise an improvisation which contains:

1. These three characters:	An Asian postmaster
	A school student
	An electrician
2. These three lines:	'Let me out of here!'
	'And so that was how we lost.'
	'Fancy a coffee?'
3. These three elements:	Environmentalists keeping a footpath open
	A lonely old lady
	A leather jacket.

● Use the plot you have produced in the activity above for either a radio script, an actual sound tape, a written story, a play with props and costume.

● Think of 'three things a long way apart', which might be combined into a narrative. If you prefer, use three characters, or lines of dialogue.

● In groups redistribute the 'three things a long way apart' you have chosen individually so that everyone has a different set of three things to work on, and produce a story.

● The finished stories can be presented or displayed so that the rest of the class has to guess what the origin of all 'three things' were for each narrative.

MULTIPLE AUTHORSHIP

Writing a longer story with several plots is a much larger undertaking and in the previous section it has been suggested that a group of friends could divide the writing up between them.

Group Writing

In this assignment, each member of the group, or even of the class, contributes a section to the story, with one following after the other.

● If the members of your group wish to write their own sections simultaneously, follow the advice given on *Repromaster 13* about planning a story in advance.

When all the parts have been written, the group should hold an editing conference, and make sure that:
1. Each section fits smoothly with the ones before and after.
2. The characters are consistent.
3. There is no needless repetition.

● Alternatively, the members of your group can develop the story from the point it has reached, as it is written.
1. One person starts the story and writes the opening 'chapter'.
2. This is then taken and developed by the next person, who follows the clues to the characters, the setting and the plot.
3. The two sections are then read by a third person who contributes the third 'chapter'.
4. Do not plan the story out in advance, but simply take it up as it comes to you and develop it as seems most appropriate for the kind of story being written.
Warning: This activity must be interspersed with others, as only one person can work on it at a time. But you can be writing more than one story, so that everyone has something to work on. Each story will then be passed round to another member of the group rather like the game of 'Consequences'.

Suggestions

Here are some opening sections of stories written by fifth year pupils. If you wish to use these for your assignment first you must identify what kind of story might be following, as each one is written in a particular style familiar to modern readers.
Then base your own next section on this style. Follow clues to the characters, the setting and the plot.
When you have finished your section, pass it on to the next person to write the third, and so on.

A) Chanceford flipped the alert switch back into its usual 'all green' position and began making his way back to the bridge. That was about the twelfth time the alarm on the containment system had malfunctioned in about as many days, so he was not concerned about any danger. He would simply get it repaired when he reached Cee-port 6.

Chanceford was the deputy operations manager on Spartan 4, an astro-cargo-carrier on its way to Cee-port 6, a huge research laboratory on Earth.

He personally did not know what the ship was carrying, but he did know that it was very unstable, because it had to be kept under 112°C for it to be safe to transport. The cargo was contained in a huge refrigerator the size of a house, which in turn was contained in an even bigger lead-lined containment system that was usually used to transport fuel rods to the dumping site. The Captain had told Chanceford that the container had been remodified to carry the 'Top Secret' cargo that was in the over-sized chest freezer in there, and that it could warn of its escape. The Captain was the only one who knew what the cargo was . . .
S. Mullally

B) It was thirty seven years to the day that Vladin Mernik had been arrested. Like so many of the arrests that happened in those days before reform, there was no reason given for his arrest, except that he had been 'unfaithful to the State'.

Vladin Mernik had owned a small bookshop on the outskirts of Korishen, a large town to the east of Moscow.

He had run the bookshop for his father, and when he died, he was left it.

Because of Government policies very few new books entered the country, so Vladin did little business. To increase profits Vladin started selling books by leading Russian writers even though they were not favoured by the State.

He had been selling many books in the first few months and was doing well. But one morning as he arrived to open his shop he noticed a police car outside and that the door was open.

Not knowing what was going on he ran into the shop. Inside were four policemen standing among his torn and ruined books.

One looked at him and said, "Vladin Mernik, you are under arrest for being unfaithful to the State . . ."
Andrew Barling

C) It was the coldest winter in the Alps for living memory; ice would form on the warmest of days, and the bitter north wind bit deep into the thick layers of winter clothing, but because of this, the snow was very deep and perfect for skiing.

In our group there were three of us – myself, Dave and Derek. We all worked in the City and at the thought of all that snow in the Alps, we packed and went. We had a taster of what was going to come even before we left England as on the night before we left the first snow of the year fell, but nothing was to prepare us for the arrival at Berne airport. A blizzard more accustomed to K2 met us, and a normally perfect landing was interfered with by the skidding of the plane on the frozen runway, but eventually we arrived at the resort, hungry and four hours late . . .
Chris Saunders

ADVENTURE GAME BOOKS

In this assignment alternative outcomes are provided for each section of the plot and a different person needs to write the section dealing with each possibility.

When all the sections are bound together in a folder, the pages can be numbered and the story enjoyed as an adventure game book. Here is how one class was started off:

Unknown to your friends you are a secret agent and one summer morning you are sitting peacefully at the table eating toast and marmalade when you hear on the news the announcement of another kidnapping. The daughter of a South American diplomat has disappeared and is thought to have been taken back to her native Peru. Then you see that the newspaper is getting stuck in the marmalade so you wipe it clean, and in doing so you notice that there is a notice in the personal column:

"Fred, come home please, all is forgiven, Mum." This is the code for you to report to your chief, so in twenty minutes' time you are on the London train.

"Ah, Fred," said your boss as you came in (you aren't really called Fred), "do sit down. We have a little assignment on behalf of a Bond Street jeweller. He's worried that a packet of emeralds he is expecting from Peru won't get further than Heathrow. Could you pop down there and keep an eye on the arrivals from South America? The man who is supposed to be coming over with the jewels will be wearing a jersey with llamas knitted into the pattern, but we'd be interested to know if he has any other little friends waiting around the airport."

"If I decide to do this job my own way – I have the usual freedoms?" you asked.

The chief replied, "Sure enough. You're experienced enough to know when the best way to get from A to C is not through B."

As you walked out into the street you just happened to notice a woman move away from the corner of the block. As she put her hand up to the strap of her shoulder bag you saw a huge green emerald glinting on her finger. Do you:

1. Follow this woman? Turn to page
2. Go to Heathrow airport? Turn to page
3. Go to the library to read up about Peru and emeralds? Turn to page
4. Get the next flight to South America? Turn to page

As you can see, each of the four alternatives now need writing up. Each one of these can end in several alternatives but at some stage the adventure will have to end.

How to Start an Adventure Game Book

It is possible to plan the structure of an adventure game book in advance, in which case it will look something like this:

The plan shown divides the story up into very small units but has the advantage that you can see how the story doubles back on itself.

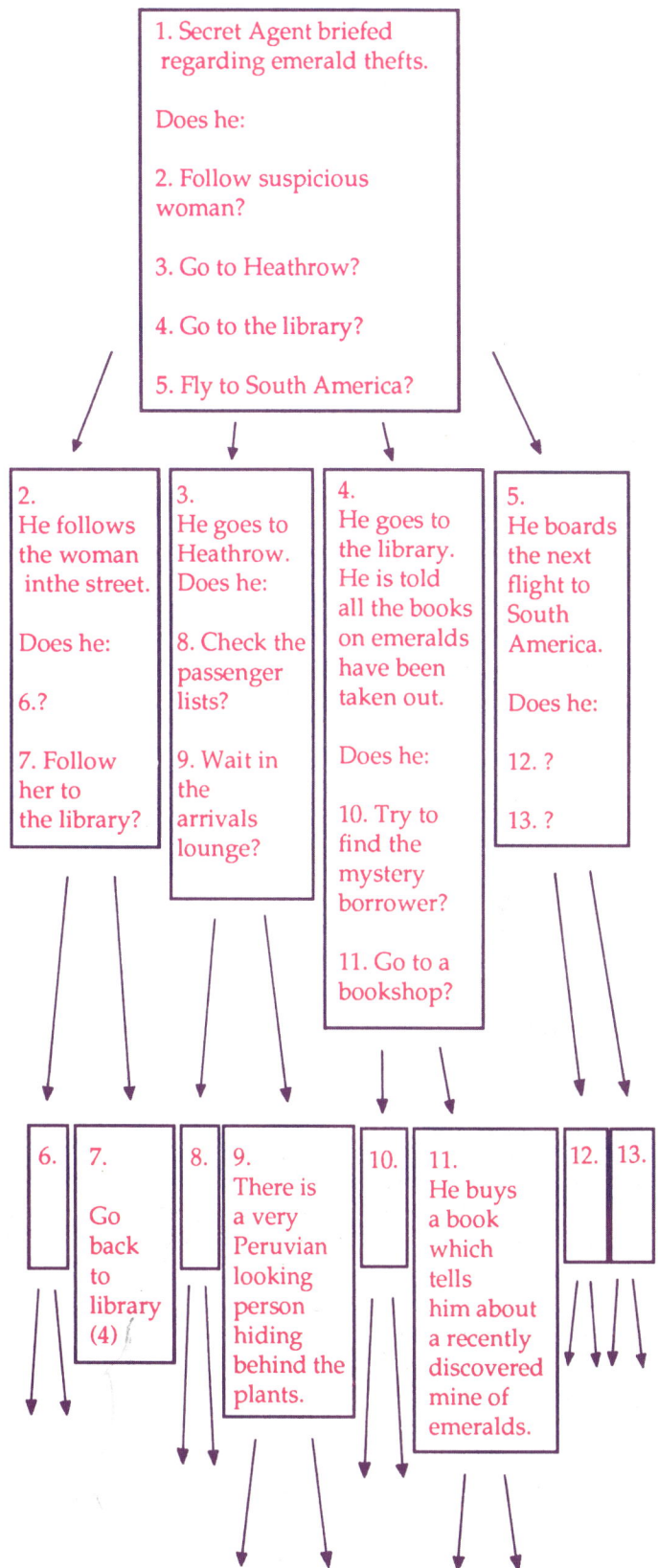

1. Secret Agent briefed regarding emerald thefts.

Does he:

2. Follow suspicious woman?

3. Go to Heathrow?

4. Go to the library?

5. Fly to South America?

---

2. He follows the woman in the street. Does he: 6.? 7. Follow her to the library?

3. He goes to Heathrow. Does he: 8. Check the passenger lists? 9. Wait in the arrivals lounge?

4. He goes to the library. He is told all the books on emeralds have been taken out. Does he: 10. Try to find the mystery borrower? 11. Go to a bookshop?

5. He boards the next flight to South America. Does he: 12. ? 13. ?

6.

7. Go back to library (4)

8.

9. There is a very Peruvian looking person hiding behind the plants.

10.

11. He buys a book which tells him about a recently discovered mine of emeralds.

12. 13.

ADVENTURE GAME BOOKS

1. You are on the edge of a desolate moor. Ahead of you is a circular wall with towers and a gatehouse. Inside the wall is a group of standing stones. You can go left around the wall (2) right around the wall (3) or up to the gate-house (4).

2. You continue around the wall and nothing new comes into sight except more of the wall and a small group of trees. Do you wish to go into the copse (5) continue around the wall (6) or back to the gatehouse (7)?

3. Around the wall you meet a small number of people sitting round a fire talking. You can go up to them (8) or go back to the gatehouse.

4. There are two entrances, a massive gate which is ajar and could be opened (9) or a small door set deep into the wall (10).

5. In the copse you find a minute phial of potion and a stone slab set into the ground. You can leave the wood with the potion (11) or try the stone slab to see if it will move (12).

6. Suddenly a large Orc leaps in front of you – it appears you will have to escape (13) or try to persuade it not to harm you (14).

7. Turn to 4.

8. They appear friendly and offer you a drink from the bottle they are passing round. Will you accept (15) or risk their anger by refusing (16)?

9. The door creaks open ominously and a bat flies out at you. You duck to avoid it and slip, falling through a trap set in the floor. You land in an underground passage which leads left (17) and right (18) – it's your choice.

10. Through the door is a small room with a niche in the wall which contains a gold key. You pick it up and since there is no other exit you return through the door you came in by (4).

Your Own Adventure Game Book

In groups of four:
- Read through the outline of the Adventure Game Book shown above.
- Plan out the structure of the story in a flow chart (as on page 43). Continue the plan to reach a conclusion.
- Write out your story in detail. Divide the work out sensibly between the group.

Remember the following points.
- number each unit of the story.
- each unit takes up one page (this avoids confusion when doing an adventure game book yourself).
- check that each number is used only once.
- to make it more complex you can occasionally double back.
- it could be possible to decide the main outline of the story and then allocate different units to members of the group.

– write each unit on one side of the paper so that they can all be spread out on a table in the correct pattern.

– when you are perfectly sure of the pattern you can then arrange the separate sheets on top of each other as the pages in a book. They are already numbered for you (as the example below shows), if you have followed this correctly!

Don't Forget!

The importance of a good beginning.
The importance of the past.
To use a plot and a subplot.
To decide on the basic storyline together first.

SOAP OPERA

Most viewers appreciate the way that the narrative of soap opera is developed depending upon popularity ratings for certain characters and the availability of certain stars.

Once characters and situation have been created, a group of writers will meet every so often to discuss the plot of the next series of episodes.

A violent death always does something for the audience ratings – and then there is the mystery of who did it.

...What about conflict with parents?.. Say, not staying on at college..

How much longer can we use Steve? He's announced his intention of leaving in the press.

What about some current issue? Could there be some child abuse in the Close?

Isn't it time we did something about A? He's been unemployed for ages now..

B is proving a big hit with the teenage audience. We need something they can identify with more closely

A Script Conference

● In groups of six decide on the roles to be taken by each member of the group for this soap opera script conference, eg writer, casting director, director, producer, designer, representative of technical team. (Many of these roles can be doubled.) *Repromaster 15* explores in detail the role played by each of these characters.

Work out:
future story lines;
different options open to various characters;
different solutions to particular situations.

It may be useful to use flow charts in order to reach your decisions.

This is an outline of the serial you are dealing with:

A family run the local garage on an access road to a major motorway.
The local council are opposing plans to develop a service station on the motorway.
A wealthy developer will make a lot of money if the service station goes ahead on the motorway.
The daughter of the owner of the local filling station has been secretly meeting the son of the developer.
The children at the local school are studying the effects of development in their area.
The planning officer is shortly to inspect the area prior to the planning committee meeting.
Other characters use the local filling station and its shop regularly.

SOAP OPERA

Character Briefing

● In your groups decide on two or three characters you might find in this soap opera.

Divide the group into production team and actors.

Each actor has an interview in which they are prepared for the character they will be playing. The actor must come full of questions whose answers will help them in playing their part really well. The production team must also have a clear idea about how they want to see their ideas developed.

Conduct a Survey

● Rather than writing your own soap opera you might learn a lot about people's understanding of how narrative works and what they enjoy by conducting your own survey into responses to soap opera. Working as a group devise a series of questions to put to people by thinking about the kind of things you want to find out.

● Conducting a survey is a way of seeing whether popular opinions are in fact borne out by what a majority of people say.

For instance:

It is often said that the general public are so ignorant they believe the characters in their favourite soaps are real.

What can you find out from those whom you question?

● Another commonly repeated worry is that children are affected by the soap operas they watch early in the afternoons.

How well do the children you question understand the way these stories are put together?

Will the audience really swallow plots which go over the top?

● Imagine you are going to launch a new soap opera, which you want to overtake an existing successful one.

Decide on the audience you hope to attract. (Age? Occupation? Viewing habits?)

Decide whether you are going to use radio or television.

Set about finding out what that audience would like from a new soap opera eg issues discussed, types of characters, location.

Each member of the group could interview several people and then the responses could be pooled.

● Write an episode from a soap opera. You could base it on research you have done in the other questions, or on one of the role plays.

Firstly summarise the narrative content, what actually happens in the story in this episode.

You could choose an important episode, when a character is 'written out', or a new one introduced.

Then write the script for some of the scenes.

You could take the summary of a forthcoming episode from the *Radio* or *TV Times* and use that as the basis for scriptwriting.

Constructing a Convergent Narrative

It is always interesting to read a story which brings together several different threads at the end, and this is another format which can be divided out among a group so that something much longer can result.

A famous convergent plot occurs in **Murder on the Orient Express** *where it is discovered that most of the people on the train at the time of the murder had a hand in the killing, as they all bore a grudge or a vendetta against the victim, for a whole variety of reasons.*

In large groups or as a whole class, choose one of the following places or events where people are gathered together:

an airport departure lounge;

a smash and grab raid;

a doctor's waiting room;

a funeral;

a sponsored event for fundraising;

or any other of your own.

1. Decide on characters and group them together in twos or threes.

2. Improvise a scene where all the characters are together at the place or event.

3. Then present individual scenes for each small group of characters which explain why they might be together at the same time (these scenes will be working backwards in time from the first one).

4. Working as a group, decide on the place or event which brings all the characters together – a disaster, a murder, a newspaper announcement of some kind, a will.

5. Decide on the different characters to be involved and agree together in what way they are all connected to the final event.

6. Each, separately, write the individual stories.

7. When the separate stories have been shared, the final event where they all converge can be written. It could come at the end, or at the beginning as it does in the example above.

VIEWPOINT IN NARRATIVE

Enraged husband carries out revenge attack

DIFFERENT VIEWPOINTS

So far the focus has been on the content of story, and on providing suitable structures and techniques for organising narrative into a lively and intriguing shape. Yet the identity of the storyteller themself is crucial. For example, when you hear a piece of information or gossip you want to know where it has come from, to assess its reliability.

In this section the focus is on the importance of viewpoint, the narrator's stance, or angle, from which they see the events. In many cases there appears to be an almost different account of the events when they are seen from different viewpoints. It is vitally important that we all learn to see life from the other person's viewpoint in order to understand each other, but you might be in for a surprise when you start to see things through the eyes of others!

● Read these short stories. They will take longer to think about than to read.

The Architect
Extract A

He contracted to do the rebuilding.

Over the scarred surface of the land were laid courses of rubble, clay and earth. Hills were fashioned, grass was sown. A diverted river snaked smoothly across the plain. Vegetation was provided, and animals to keep it in check. Finally, as a memorial, a tree was planted. This, he personally supervised.

And on the seventh day, he rested.

Bob Taylor, *Tale Enders*

Graffitti in University Toilet
Extract B

God is not dead but alive and well and working on a much less ambitious project.

Brainstorming on Viewpoint

● In your groups consider:
1. What subject items A and B above have in common.
2. Which role is the subject of both A and B carrying out?
3. How well has the subject coped with it in B?
4. What kind of job does he seem to have in A?
5. What kind of person would make the statement in B? What relationship would they have with the person they were describing?
6. Pick out any words in A which gave you a clue to the fact that this was no ordinary architect's job.
7. Which sentence in A suggested that the story was taking place after some other event?
8. What did you assume that event to be?
9. What parallel with the situation in A suggests that this story originally took place before any other event at all?

Both these items derive their originality by taking a look at something familiar from a fresh angle.

The Valley of Death

Here is another of Bob Taylor's stories where the clue comes right at the end when you know whose viewpoint you are seeing through.

He had scurried through the trenches of the Somme; been a witness of that senseless carnage. As one of the remaining survivors of that dying generation, he was in much demand as a speaker. Though now frail and old, he never refused an invitation.

His talk had been received with rapt attention. It was as if the audience had been searching in his account for some key to the mystery of their own behaviour.

"Why, in your opinion," asked a questioner, "is there this instinct for self-destruction?"

He cleared his throat and considered. There was a peculiar tension in the silence which awaited his answer.

"From my experience, and from all that I have observed –" he began, but a sudden pain knifed through his chest. He faltered.

"Yes?" pursued the questioner.

"I believe it is because – because –" The rat choked on his words, then shuddered and lay still.

The audience of lemmings blinked, unanswered.
Bob Taylor, *Tale Enders*

DIFFERENT VIEWPOINTS

After the First Death

This book tells of a hijack drama when a small group of Middle Eastern terrorists capture a bus of children travelling to an American Summer camp. What is unusual about the book is that the reader follows the story through a series of different viewpoints. Two of the most important viewpoints are those of Miro, the youngest terrorist, and Kate, the girl who was driving the bus. She condemns the violent action of the terrorists, but the reader is lead to understand how they are motivated, by seeing the situation from Miro's viewpoint as well.

● Compare the first two extracts which describe the attitude of each of them to the black ski-masks which the terrorists wear to disguise themselves.

If what we are doing is heroic, to deliver our people and restore our homeland, why must we hide who we are? He once asked Artkin. And Artkin had told him that there were many laws in the world, good laws and bad laws, right laws and wrong laws. According to the wrong laws, their mission, their work, was condemned. But these laws had been made by their enemies. So they had to disguise themselves to remain free under the wrong laws.

Miro held the mask in his hand now. It was black with red stitching around the eyes, nostrils, and mouth. The moment when he first put it on in an operation was always exhilarating; it was the gesture that divided his life. Without the mask, he was Miro Shantas, the boy without even a real name to identify him to the world. With the mask, he was Miro Shantas, freedom fighter. He often wondered which person he really was . . .

"I know what you are," she said. She did not recognise her voice: it was strident, off key, too loud in her ears, the voice of a stranger. "You're holding us hostage and you've made demands. You're going to hold us here until the demands are met. You're—" She faltered, unable to say the word. Hijackers. Her mind was crowded with newspaper headlines and television newscasts of hijackings all over the world, gunfire and explosions, innocent persons killed, even children.

"This is no concern of yours," Artkin said, his voice cold, the words snapping like whips. "The children are your concern. Nothing else. See to the children."

She drew back as if he had struck her.

Turning to Miro, Artkin said: "It is time for the masks."

She saw them take the masks out of their jackets. They pulled them over their heads. They had suddenly become grotesque, monstrous, figures escaped from her worst nightmares. And she saw her own doom in the masks.

Now that you are more familiar with this writer's technique, read the next extract where, in an interval of waiting, Kate and Miro start talking to each other.

This is why Miro did not like waiting. It gave him too much time to think, to ponder, to wonder about things he should leave to Artkin. He wondered now about the girl, squinting his eyes to see her at the front of the bus. He had tried to engage her in conversation, attempting to follow Artkin's orders, but she had been uncommunicative. Miro pondered what she was thinking. Did she suspect that she would die before this incident was over? . . .

When Kate heard the sound of helicopter, she had been sitting despondently in the driver's seat, clutching the wheel uselessly, unable to face the children any longer and unwilling to look at the boy Miro. She knew she was doomed. She had known it the moment she saw them put on the masks. The knowledge had sickened her, causing her stomach to lurch with nausea. They had allowed her to see them unmasked. She could recognise them anywhere, identify them, point them out in police lineups, the way it happened on television cop shows. The children perhaps didn't represent a threat to the hijackers; the testimony of five- and six-year-olds probably wouldn't hold up in court. But Kate knew they couldn't afford to let her go. Or let her live . . .

Kate had retired to the back seat and sat there, pondering the time ahead and what she must do. One of the things was winning Miro over. Or at least getting him to talk, to let down his defences. She had seen that look in his eye and had to take advantage of what that look meant. He had to look upon her as a human being. More than that: as a desirable young woman, and not a victim. She knew the perfect terrible truth of the situation: she had to make it hard for him to kill her. Thus, when he looked her way on his return as he checked the children, she forced a smile to her lips. A weak substitute of a smile maybe, but it had done the trick. After a few moments, Miro came and sat beside her on the back seat. He removed his mask and placed it on the seat beside him.

And now they were talking about some kind of war, something she hadn't expected when she'd started this conversation. But, she thought: At least, we're talking, we're communicating.

"The war is going on all the time," Miro continued. It was a topic he loved, a topic they had discussed much in the school. "Our duty is to let the people know the war exists, that the world is involved in it, that no one is free from war until our homeland is free." He wished Artkin was here to listen to him, to see how well he had learned his lessons.

"Where's your homeland?" Kate asked.

"My homeland is far from here. Across the ocean."

Kate detected a wistfulness in his voice. "What's its name?"

Miro hesitated. He had not said the word of his homeland for so long – like his own name – that he wondered how it would sound on his tongue. And he hesitated also because he did not know how much he should tell this girl. He wanted to win her confidence, but he must not betray himself or the others. If he did not say his name aloud to Artkin, how could he tell this girl the name of his homeland? "You do not know the place," Miro said. "But it is a place of beauty."

"Tell me about it." Kate said.

"I have never been there. I have never seen my homeland."

"You've never seen it?" Kate asked, incredulous. "How do you know your homeland is so beautiful then and worth all – all this?"

"I have heard the old men talking in the camps and they have said how beautiful it is. They say that if you take off your shoes, you can feel the richness of the land on the skin of your feet. The orange trees are fruitful and the flight of the turtle dove and the lark is balm to the eyes and spirit." He was quoting the old men now, and his voice was like music. "The river there is gentle and the sun is a blessing on the earth and turns the flesh golden. The sky is the blue of shells washed by fresh rains."

Kate thought: This strange, pathetic boy.

And then remembered that he carried a gun and one child had already died . . .

Kate sensed that she was losing him, that she had said something to turn him off. He had been so open one moment and then his face had closed her out, his eyes dropping away. Maybe it hurt him to talk about his parents and his dead brother. Maybe her instincts were correct, after all, and she was on the right track: he was vulnerable, sensitive. She couldn't lose him now. Instinctively, she turned to the oldest weapon she knew, remembering how it had never failed her.

"You speak English beautifully," she said, flattering him of course, but knowing there was truth in the flattery. "You must have a special talent for languages."

Miro blushed with pleasure. But like so many things, there was pain in the pleasure. The girl's statement also made him think again of Aniel. Poor Aniel. Dead before his time. Good with weapons as Miro had been good with languages. Aniel had been good with his hands as well. His hands, too, were weapons. He struck swiftly and with accuracy. He knew the parts of the body that were most vulnerable to attack. His hands could kill as quickly as a knife or bullet. But Aniel had been a slow student in other respects. Especially language. Miro had excelled at languages. You should have been a scholar, his instructor had once said. In a time of peace, he might have been.

The girl persisted: "Did you go to a special language school?"

"I went to a special school," he said, wondering if she noticed the irony of his words. And then he found himself telling her about this special school that was not really a school at all, not with desks and chairs arranged neatly like the pictures he had seen of American classrooms. The building was sunk into the earth with no windows. The blackboards were sheets of wrinkled paper pinned to the walls. The education received in the school was intense and concentrated. You are here to learn what you must know to survive and what you must know to gain back our homeland, the instructor had said. He was an old man with many scars on his face. He taught the use of weapons and explosives. Combat: with the knife, the gun, the hands. The diagrams of the human body outlined on the blackboard were indelibly stamped on Miro's mind. Even now, Miro could touch certain spots on the body that would cause a victim to grovel with pain. Yet Miro had enjoyed the other lessons more: reading and the languages. The languages were important because everyone was trained for a destination, to carry out revolutionary acts throughout the world . . .

. . . Miro started in surprise. He had been carried away by his words and his memories, and had in fact forgotten the presence of the girl to whom he was addressing those words. Had he revealed too much of himself?

Robert Cormier, *After the First Death*

Considering the Viewpoints

1. Select three quotations each for Kate and Miro, to show the different thoughts and feelings of each within the same narrative.
2. Miro wondered 'did she suspect that she would die before this incident was over?' What is the answer to that question?
3. Kate mentally refers to 'some kind of war'. Select a quotation that you think shows that this war is crucially important to Miro.
4. Why do you think Kate finds Miro 'strange, pathetic' when she also fears him?
5. Miro has a gun but what is 'the oldest weapon' Kate knew, which 'had never failed her'?
6. What was it that Miro enjoyed most in his education which showed that his life might have been different in different circumstances?
7. What do Miro and Kate both think they are achieving in this conversation?

Options

● In pairs take the parts of a hostage and a terrorist, who use the interval of waiting to talk to each other. What would be the aims of each in talking to the other? What might they be trying to find out?

● After five minutes, switch parts and see how well you can maintain your partner's role.

DIFFERENT VIEWPOINTS

This first appeared in the *New Scientist* weekly review of Science and Technology

'The use of animals or objects as central characters can lead to stories which give an unusual view of human behaviour. For example, a fox's version of a hunt; a right hand pocket which resents the over-use it receives from its right handed owner.'
Bob Taylor

Options

● How do you think your family pets would describe everyday life in your household?

● Write one of the following from a pet's viewpoint: feeding time, having a bath, being put out at night. Refer back to your change of reaction at the end of *The Architect* and *Valley of Death*. Try to present a complete – and honest – rounded picture of the whole you.

● Write a script for a radio monologue where the audience will not know, until they reach the end, who it was they were listening to. They should be intrigued to hear a familiar story or situation from an unusual viewpoint, eg

The wolf's version of his meeting with Little Red Riding Hood.
One of the ugly sister's versions of the engagement of Cincerella.
An endangered animal's account of the activities of the environmentalists to save it.
A dog's account of going with its master to dog handling classes.
The littlest bridesmaid's account of the wedding.

A story may be different depending on who is telling it, particularly if they are involved with the subject of the story.

● Read the following case history and then decide which people were the source of the different viewpoints expressed.

A family moved to the south of England into a house which was connected to the house next door. Previously they had lived in a detached house but now they wanted to know about the owner of the house next door, as its kitchen door opened into their new yard and so they had very little privacy.

The house next door was occupied by a group of young people and students, who were the tenants of the house's owner, Mr Barrow. The family were told that Mr Barrow no longer lived in the house because his wife had divorced him and his children had left home. His wife had sued for a divorce on the grounds of cruelty and would sometimes escape to her neighbour's house, bruised and crying.

The house was in a very dilapidated condition and the bathroom was a joke. There was no heating in the bedrooms which were bitterly cold in winter. Mr Barrow did not let his tenants get very far behind with the rent and on one occasion he came round to collect his money because he needed some to buy a birthday present for his daughter.

The family learnt that Mr Barrow had intended to do up the house and spend a lot of time bringing it up to a high standard because he was a joiner by profession. The work that he did was extremely good and he charged very high prices for his services. Usually he 'over-estimated' the quantities of materials needed for a job and would have some left over. He kept all these building materials in a large shed near the house which was full of all sorts of other things, rubbish, junk, and some valuable antiques. At one time he had gone to Australia after letting out the house but came back because, he said, he had 'forgotten to take his tools'.

Considering Sources

● The sources of all this information were the local people the family met before and after they moved in. Try to decide which facts they learnt from which of the following sources:
1. The tenants of the house next door
2. Mr Barrow's work mate
3. Mr Barrow himself
4. The neighbours on the other side of the family's new house.

● Write your own description of a person from different sources, like the one above. List the sources at the end of the description.

● 'Myself as others see me'. Write what is suggested by this title.

● You will probably be aware that you present different aspects of your personality in different situations. What would your teachers think of you if they saw you out of school? What would your parents think of you if they saw you with your friends?

WHAT IS THE TRUTH?

The combination of different viewpoints can often result in a very confusing picture even if they all purport to describe the same event, place or person. Two 'eye-witness' accounts of the same incident can differ considerably.

Guilty or Not Guilty

● Study the following case and try to decide what did actually happen and who is guilty.

● The different testimonies could be dramatised into a court case, with the rest of the class/group as the jury who then have to return a verdict of 'guilty' or 'not guilty'.

THE POLICE STATEMENT: In the early hours of August 25th Richard B. was apprehended in a drunk and disorderly condition not far away from the wreck of a blue coupe car, which had apparently gone off the York Road and into the ditch. The owner of the car, Mr. Johns, had not authorised Richard B. to drive his vehicle which he says he left on the car park at the 'Green Dragon' whilst visiting a friend who lived nearby. The friend has refused to give evidence.

THE DEFENCE: Richard states that on the evening concerned he was celebrating his 'A' level results as they meant that he had won his place at college. He has little recollection of what happened after closing time as he had drunk so much. Witnesses at the 'Green Dragon' will testify that he was in an expansive mood, but that he left alone, on foot, at closing time.

CHARACTER REFERENCE 1 (THE HEADMASTER): Richard has been an unsatisfactory sixth former with a poor attitude to school and the staff. We were grateful to see the end of him in June, and his good 'A' level results are due to his own ability rather than any work he may have put in on his subjects.

CHARACTER REFERENCE 2 (THE GARAGE PROPRIETOR): Rick is a great lad and a wizard with cars. He has been working for me on Saturdays for two years now and has serviced most of our regular clients' vehicles. I shall miss him when he goes away to college.

Options

● Develop each of these characters and improvise their conversation outside the courtroom.

● Introduce another witness, who may make things clearer for the jury.

● Richard discusses his situation with his girlfriend. Where was she that evening?

● Use the case studied for your own 'What is the truth' puzzle. Think of an incident, a theft or an assault, and prepare statements from the witnesses, and character evidence about the accused.

People react very differently to particular places, depending on the associations they have with them.

● Put together a description of a particular place from different viewpoints eg the school as described by:
the caretaker;
the headmaster;
a first year;
a disaffected fifth year.

● Put together a questionnaire about your neighbourhood and its amenities. Take into account its convenience for schools, shops, leisure facilities, public transport, etc.
1. Interview members of your family and some of your neighbours.
2. Write up the results into a description of your area from a range of viewpoints, taking the topic of each question in turn and looking at all the answers on that subject.

● Different views of the same house. Compile a multi-viewpoint picture of your house.
Include: your own description;
how other members of your family see it;
how an estate agent would describe it;
how a possible purchaser's surveyor might describe it (his aim is to reduce the price).
Illustrate with any Estate Agents' description of property, accompanied with a comically ill-assorted drawing of a horribly run-down dilapidated place.

● You will find another example of different viewpoints on the tape. As each character gives his or her opinion of Kelly, how does your view of her develop? *Repromaster 17* may help you, but listen to the tape first.

The following short story, from **The Compass Rose,** *by Ursula Le Guin uses an extremely unusual viewpoint to give the reader a fresh insight into a frequently used horror story device. This is the changing of shape, called a metamorphosis, from one kind of being, usually human, into another. This possibility has provided many nightmare visions.*

Reading is not just a passive experience – we make meanings as we read and different people will find different meanings in the same text. From your own experience of reading a book or story twice, you will know that the second reading is not the same as the first.

● It is important that you note your reactions to this story as you read it. They will probably change and you need to look back on your first impressions when you reach the end.
● The story has been divided into several sections with suggestions for response at the end of each section.
● Write your own ideas in response to each section and then follow the instructions at the end to produce a finished reading journal.

The Wife's Story

He was a good husband, a good father. I don't understand it. I don't believe in it. I don't believe that it happened. I saw it happen but it isn't true. It can't be. He was always gentle. If you'd have seen him playing with the children, anybody who saw him with the children would have known that there wasn't any bad in him, not one mean bone. When I first met him he was still living with his mother, over near Spring Lake, and I used to see them together, the mother and the sons, and think that any young fellow that was that nice with his family must be one worth knowing. Then one time when I was walking in the woods I met him by himself coming back from a hunting trip. He hadn't got any game at all, not so much as a field mouse, but he wasn't cast down about it. He was just larking along enjoying the morning air. That's one of the things I first loved about him. He didn't take things hard, he didn't grouch and whine when things didn't go his way. So we got to talking that day. And I guess things moved right along after that, because pretty soon he was over here pretty near all the time. And my sister said – see, my parents had moved out the year before and gone south, leaving us the place – my sister said, kind of teasing but serious, 'Well! If he's going to be here everyday and half the night, I guess there isn't room for me!' And she moved out – just down the way. We've always been real close, her and me. That's the sort of thing doesn't ever change. I couldn't ever have got through this bad time without my sis.

Well, so he come to live here. And all I can say is, it was the happy year of my life. He was just purely good to me. A hard worker and never lazy, and so big and fine-looking. Everybody looked up to him, you know, young as he was. Lodge Meeting nights, more and more often they had him to lead the singing. He had such a beautiful voice, and he'd lead off strong, and the others following and joining in, high voices and low. It brings the shivers on me now to think of it, hearing it, nights when I'd stayed home from meeting when the children was babies – the singing coming up through the trees there, and the moonlight, summer nights, the full moon shining. I'll never hear anything so beautiful. I'll never know a joy like that again.

1. What kind of person do you imagine is telling this story?
2. Pick out some of the comments which characterise her for you.
3. Where do you think the story is happening? What evidence have you used to decide?
4. Why was the narrator attracted to her husband? Was her judgement of him as a partner correct? Was their partnership successful?
5. How do you interpret the opening few sentences of the story? What do they lead you to expect in the story?
6. Write down what you think might happen next in the story.

READING JOURNAL

So it happened that way maybe three times or four. He'd come back late, and worn out, and pretty near cross for one so sweet-tempered – not wanting to talk about it.

And then the awful thing. I don't find it easy to tell about this. I want to cry when I have to bring it to my mind. Our youngest, the little one, my baby, she turned from her father. Just overnight. He come in and she got scared-looking, stiff, with her eyes wide, and then she began to cry and try to hide behind me. She didn't yet talk plain but she was saying over and over, 'Make it go away! Make it go away!'

The look in his eyes, just for one moment, when he heard that. That's what I don't ever want to remember. That's what I can't forget. The look in his eyes looking at his own child.

I said to the child, 'Shame on you, what's got into you!' – scolding, but keeping her right up close to me at the same time, because I was frightened too. Frightened to shaking.

He looked away then and said something like, 'Guess she just waked up dreaming,' and passed it off that way. Or tried to. And so did I.

He kept way that whole day. Because he knew, I guess. It was just beginning dark of the moon.

It was hot and close inside; and dark, and we'd all been asleep some while, when something woke me up. He wasn't there beside me. I heard a little stir in the passage, when I listened. So I got up, because I could bear it no longer. I went out into the passage, and it was light there, hard sunlight coming in from the door. And I saw him standing just outside, in the tall grass by the entrance. His head was hanging. Presently he sat down, like he felt weary, and looked down at his feet. I held still, inside and watched – I don't know what for.

It was the moon, that's what they say. It's the moon's fault, and the blood. It was in his father's blood. I never knew his father, and now I wonder what become of him. He was from up Whitewater way, and had no kin around here. I always thought he went back there, but now I don't know. There was some talk about him, tales, that come out after what happened to my husband. It's something runs in the blood, they say, and it may never come out, but if it does, it's the change of the moon that does it. Always it happens in the dark of the moon. When everybody's home and asleep. Something comes over the one that's got the curse in his blood, they say, and he gets up because he can't sleep, and goes out into the glaring sun, and goes off all alone – drawn to find those like him.

And it may be so, because my husband would do that. I'd half rouse and say, 'Where you going to?' and he'd say, 'Oh, hunting, be back this evening,' and it wasn't like him, even his voice was different. But I'd be so sleepy, and not wanting to wake the kids, and he was so good and responsible, it was no call of mine to go asking, 'Why?' and 'Where?' and all like that.

1. How does the tone of the story change? What new subject is introduced?

2. What are the reactions of the baby to her father? What are your reactions to hearing this part of the story?

3. Suggest some possibilities which 'then the awful thing' might refer to.

4. What do you expect is going to happen now?

And I saw what he saw. I saw the changing. In his feet, it was, first. They got long, each foot got longer, stretching out, the toes stretching out and the foot getting long, and fleshy, and white. And no hair on them.

The hair began to come away all over his body. It was like his hair fried away in the sunlight and was gone. He was white all over, then, like a worm's skin. And he turned his face. It was changing while I looked. It got flatter and flatter, the mouth flat and wide, and the teeth grinning flat and dull, and the nose just a knob of flesh with nostril holes, and the ears gone, and the eyes gone blue – blue, with white rims around the blue – staring at me out of that flat, soft, white face.

He stood up then on two legs.

I saw him, I had to see him, my own dear love, turned into the hateful one.

I couldn't move, but as I crouched there in the passage staring out into the day I was trembling and shaking with a growl that burst out into a crazy, awful howling. A grief howl and a terror howl and a calling howl. And the others heard it, even sleeping, and woke up.

It stared and peered, that thing my husband had turned into, and shoved its face up to the entrance of our house. I was still bound by mortal fear, but behind me the children had waked up, and the baby was whimpering. The mother anger come into me then, and I snarled and crept forward.

1. Such transformations often occur in horror films – which is more frightening, watching it happen on film or reading a description like this? What are your reasons for your answer?

2. Pick out the details you find most horrific in the description of the husband's new shape.

The man thing looked around. It had no gun, like the ones from the man places do. But it picked up a heavy fallen tree branch in its long white foot, and shoved the end of that down into our house, at me. I snapped the end of it in my teeth and started to force my way out, because I knew the man would kill our children if it could. But my sister was already coming. I saw her running at the man with her head low and her mane high and her eyes yellow as the winter sun. It turned on her and raised up that branch to hit her. But I come out of the doorway, mad with the mother anger, and the others all were coming answering my call, the whole pack gathering, there in that blind glare and heat of the sun at noon.

The man looked round at us and yelled out loud, and brandished the branch it held. Then it broke and ran, heading for the cleared fields and ploughlands, down the mountainside. It ran, on two legs, leaping and weaving, and we followed it.

I was last, because love still bound the anger and the fear in me. I was running when I saw them pull it down. My sister's teeth were in its throat. I got there and it was dead. The others were drawing back from the kill, because of the taste of the blood, and the smell. The younger ones were cowering and some crying, and my sister rubbed her mouth against her forelegs over and over to get rid of the taste. I went up close because I thought if the thing was dead the spell, the curse must be done, and my husband would come back – alive, or even dead, if I could only see him, my true love, in his true form, beautiful. But only the dead man lay there white and bloody. We drew back and back from it, and turned and ran, back up into the hills, back to the woods of the shadows and the twilight and the blessed dark.

Ursula K. Le Guin, from *The Compass Rose*

1. Who is it who is telling the story? What has her husband changed into?

2. What happens to the husband in his transformed state?

3. How soon did you realise which viewpoint you were sharing?

4. Pick out the details which now make it very clear what kind of beings the narrator and her sister actually are once you reach the end of the story.

5. Go back over the story a second time and reconsider some of the phrases such as: 'grouch and whine', 'he'd lead off strong and the others following', 'he gets up because he can't sleep and goes out into the glaring sun', 'a growl that burst out into a crazy, awful howling', 'shoved its face up to the entrance of our house'.

6. Which words and phrases seemed very normal and could apply to both species? For example: 'Our youngest, the little one', 'I heard a little stir in the passage when I listened'.

Reading Journal Activities

1. In pairs work to produce a questionnaire about something you have read. The questions should be applicable to any text, and you should be able to answer them at any stage in your reading.
eg Do you find this section interesting? Which are your most/least favourite characters? How do you think the story will develop from here?

2. Try out the questionnaire on yourself after your next piece of reading and see whether they work. Alter/improve them if necessary.

3. Keep writing the answers each time you read and gradually build up a reading journal over a term.

4. Look back on it the following term to see how your tastes have changed/how you have changed.

5. Use the notes you made in response to *The Wife's Story* to form a complete reading journal of a couple of pages.

COMIC HORROR

Another kind of metamorphosis which is familiar in horror stories, is the change which comes over vampires as they revert to their bloodsucking form, even though they may appear fairly normal by day.

In the next extract, **Monsterman***, Nick Olsen takes on the challenge of his school friends to deal with the caretaker, whom they believe is a vampire. Nick does not believe in anything so stupid, and has already overcome a large dog in the sewers, which others believed to be a werewolf.*

Monsterman

The truth was, of course, that there was no way I could prove that Bellows was a vampire, simply because there are no such things as vampires. All I could hope to do was go through some mumbo-jumbo motions that would con the gullible into believing I knew what I was doing, and then pray that Bellows caught a cold or something. I could claim that this cold was the first sign that my anti-vampire remedies were working, and then after a while people would forget that anyone had ever mentioned that Bellows was a vampire in the first place. If it all sounds a bit like desperate measures, frankly I didn't have much choice. It was either that or admit that the were-wolf business had been one big hoax.

As the point of the whole exercise was to impress Jayne, I made sure that she was with me at break-time when I made my way to Bellows' little room next to the boiler house. I had already discovered that Bellows was out doing something caretakery at another school in the

district, so I was pretty sure I wouldn't be discovered. But, just to add an air of excitement to the whole thing, I told Jayne to watch out for Bellows while I laid my trap.

While Jayne pressed herself against the wall of the corridor in the most obvious way possible – the result of watching too many spy thrillers on television – I set to work. In a few minutes, I had the doorway of Bellows' little room festooned with cloves of garlic dropping down like Christmas decorations, and on the inner wall I tacked up a metal crucifix with Blue-Tak. I was just stepping back to admire my handiwork, when Jayne called out, "He's coming!"

Already? I couldn't believe it! What had happened at the other school? How come he had finished so early? Whatever the reason, I was in deep trouble. Frantically, I looked around for somewhere to hide. Luckily for me, Bellows was like every other school caretaker, their little hidey holes always look as if they've got the junk of several thousand years packed into them. I dived into a corner and squashed myself behind a packing case, pulling a piece of sacking over me, just seconds before Bellows walked in. He stopped as he walked in, obviously sensing that something had been going on in his room. After all, the door was open. He turned, and saw the garlic, and then a most amazing thing happened. Bellows started to stagger about, clutching his throat and coughing. I know some people are allergic to garlic – personally, I avoid it like the plague – but Bellows was obviously really allergic to it in a huge way. As I watched him, his eyes started to water and he staggered forward, reaching out blindly for something to support him. His hand touched the crucifix. There must have been a metal splinter sticking out of it, or maybe he'd caught his finger on a sharp bit, because he snatched his hand back from it as if he'd been stung. For a second his eyes cleared and he saw what it was he'd touched. Coincidentally, by touching it, he'd moved the crucifix in such a way that the light coming in from the corridor outside fell on it and reflected onto his face. The result was astonishing! Bellows gave a scream that sent a cold shiver up my spine and made the hairs on the back of my neck stand up. The next second he was gone, rushing off out of his room and away down the corridor, covering his face with his hands.

Still a little overpowered by all this, I crept out from my hiding place under the sacking and made for the door. When Bellows returned I wanted to be as far away from his room as possible.

"Did you see it?" said Jayne excitedly, leaping out at me from her hiding place opposite.

"Did I just!" I said and, grabbing her hand, hustled her away down the corridor as fast as we could move.

"I saw it all!" she said. "Everything! It worked just the way you said it would! Only so much quicker! The garlic, the crucifix, it was brilliant! You are a genius!"
Jim and Duncan Eldridge, *Monsterman*

A well known modern classic written in the early part of this century by Franz Kafka, is called **Metamorphosis***. It tells how an ordinary young man woke up one morning to find he had become an insect. Kafka shows how Gregor is really more concerned about fulfilling his boring duties in his job than in coping with what has happened to him. Notice the problems he has in coming to terms with his new shape. Do you think he really has accepted what he has become?*

Metamorphosis

As Gregor Samsa awoke one morning from uneasy dreams he found himself transformed in his bed into a gigantic insect. He was lying on his hard, as it were armour-plated, back and when he lifted his head a little he could see his dome-like brown belly divided into stiff arched segments on top of which the bed-quilt could hardly keep in position and was about to slide off completely. His numerous legs, which were pitifully thin compared to the rest of his bulk, waved helplessly before his eyes.

What has happened to me? he thought. It was no dream. His room, a regular human bedroom, only rather too small, lay quiet between the four familiar walls. Above the table on which a collection of cloth samples was unpacked and spread out – Samsa was a commercial traveller – hung the picture which he had recently cut out of an illustrated magazine and put into a pretty gilt frame. It showed a lady, with a fur cap on and a fur stole, sitting upright and holding out to the spectator a huge fur muff into which the whole of her forearm vanished.

Gregor's eyes turned next to the window, and the overcast sky – one could hear raindrops beating on the window gutter – made him quite melancholy. What about sleeping a little longer and forgetting all this nonsense, he thought, but it could not be done, for he was accustomed to sleep on his right side and in his present condition he could not turn himself over. However violently he forced himself towards his right side he always rolled on to his back again. He tried it at least a hundred times, shutting his eyes to keep from seeing his struggling legs, and only desisted when he began to feel in his side a faint dull ache he had never experienced before.

His immediate intention was to get up quietly without being disturbed, to put on his clothes and above all eat his breakfast, and only then to consider what else was to be done, since in bed, he was well aware, his meditations would come to no sensible conclusion. He remembered that often enough in bed he had felt small aches and pains, probably caused by awkward postures, which had proved purely imaginary once he got up, and he looked forward eagerly to seeing this morning's delusions gradually fall way. That the change in his voice was nothing but the precursor of a severe chill, a standing ailment of commercial travellers, he had not the least possible doubt.

COMIC HORROR

To get rid of the quilt was quite easy; he had only to inflate himself a little and it fell off by itself. But the next move was difficult, especially because he was so uncommonly broad. He would have needed arms and hands to hoist himself up; instead he had only the numerous little legs which never stopped waving in all directions and which he could not control in the least.

When he tried to bend one of them it was the first to stretch itself straight; and did he succeed at last in making it do what he wanted, all the other legs meanwhile waved the more wildly in a high degree of unpleasant agitation. "But what's the use of lying idle in bed," said Gregor to himself.

He thought that he might get out of bed with the lower part of his body first, but this lower part, which he had not yet seen and of which he could form no clear conception, proved too difficult to move; it shifted so slowly; and when finally, almost wild with annoyance, he gathered his forces together and thrust out recklessly, he had miscalculated the direction and bumped heavily against the lower end of the bed, and the stinging pain he felt informed him that precisely this lower part of his body was at the moment probably the most sensitive.

So he tried to get the top part of himself out first, and cautiously moved his head towards the edge of the bed. That proved easy enough, and despite its breadth and mass the bulk of his body at last slowly followed the movement of his head. Still, when he finally got his head free over the edge of the bed he felt too scared to go on advancing, for after all if he let himself fall in this way it would take a miracle to keep his head from being injured. And at all costs he must not lose consciousness now, precisely now; he would rather stay in bed.

But when after a repetition of the same efforts he lay in his former position again, sighing, and watched his little legs struggling against each other more wildly than ever, if that were possible, and saw no way of bringing any order into this arbitrary confusion, he told himself again that it was impossible to stay in bed and that the most sensible course was to risk everything for the smallest hope of getting away from it.

Franz Kafka, *Metamorphosis*

All Change!

● In pairs imagine that one of you has turned into some other form, animal, bird or insect. In a dialogue, the changed character tries hard to persuade the other that they really are still their true self, whilst the other insists on treating them as the creature they have become.

● Try to persuade your partner that someone you both know is in fact a shape changer, a werewolf or vampire. Choose someone very ordinary so that persuading them of the truth of this will be very difficult!

● Write a comedy scene about a metamorphosis, like the one above, where someone firmly refuses to believe the evidence of their own eyes.
Then write a very serious account of the same metamorphosis which highlights the frightening aspects.

A book by Paul Gallico called *Jennie* describes how a young boy, after a road accident, hallucinates that he has become a cat, but has to learn how to be a cat, from the wise Jennie.
Imagine you or your character, have become another creature, and describe how you learn to live as that creature, with others of the same species.

THE NEWSPAPER VIEWPOINT

A viewpoint we are often given in the media is that of the journalist. He is hoping for a 'good story'; an item of news which will catch the public interest and imagination and sell that particular paper. Often, however, in the interests of a 'good story' the truth might become exaggerated or 'improved upon'. The 'story' has become more important than the 'truth'.

The following extracts come from **The Sea Crossed Fisherman** *by Yashir Kemal, a modern Turkish writer. They form one of the threads of the book, concerning the fate of a strange young man, Zeynel Çelik, who became a victim of the publicity he caused. The story is set at first in a fishing village called Menekşe, which is near Istanbul, on the Black Sea. Do not be put off by the difficulty of the Turkish names as the story is quite clear in these excerpts.*

The Sea Crossed Fisherman

Extract A

Zeynel had been ten or eleven years old when he turned up in Menekşe, all alone, and took shelter with some fellow countrymen of his. That was nine years ago. In his home, somewhere on the distant Black Sea coast – maybe up on the mountains of Rize, neither Zeynel nor his countrymen had ever once mentioned where – Zeynel had in one night witnessed the murder of all his family: his father and mother, his brothers and sisters, his uncles and their wives and children. Even Zeynel's six-year-old brother had not been spared. Zeynel could never forget the sight of him, sitting in his bed against the wall, bathed in blood, both hands clamped to his mouth, his eyes frozen in a wide lifeless stare. Somehow Zeynel himself had escaped without a scratch. Maybe he had been in the barn during the raid. Maybe he was a sleepwalker and had been wandering in the tea or hazelnut gardens. Or perhaps he'd gone out to make water under the plane tree and had clambered up into its branches at the sound of shooting. In the morning some neighbours found him in his bed, huddled in a ball among the gory corpses, all his limbs trembling. For days afterwards he remained coiled up, rigid, his eyes tightly closed, refusing food and drink. Try as they might, the strongest men could not prise his mouth open. When at last his teeth loosened and food was put before him, he gobbled it up like a wild animal, his eyes rolling with fear, ready to fly at any moment. Some distant relatives had taken him in, but he did not stay there more than a month, and even then he vanished during the day and only glided in cat-like at night. He lived in dread of everything. A bird, an ant, the faintest rustle of a leaf startled him into flight. And then one day he turned up in a boat in the port of Trabzon, far from his home, huddling in the bilge water between two ribs of the hold. The sailors plied him with questions, but could not get a single word out of him, and when they tried to put him ashore he clung to a mast and all the crew together

could not tear him away, short of killing him. So they gave up and set a large bowl of soup and a loaf of bread in front of him, but he would not even glance at the steaming mint-scented soup until he was sure the boat had weighed anchor and was way offshore.

"Here," the captain tackled him, "take this spoon and grub up. Look, we're as far from port as can be and I've no intention of going back just for you."

With the instinct of a wild creature Zeynel sensed that no harm would come to him from the captain. He crept up to the soup and gulped it down quietly, still casting fearful glances around like a caged beast. And so it went on until the boat came to Istanbul, the boy cleaving to a mast at every port, uttering desperate howls if anyone so much as made to touch him. In Istanbul he went straight to Menekse, to the home of Laz Refik, a former neighbour from his home village. For six months he never stepped out of the house, and when he did it was only to run back if anyone spoke or even looked at him. Then suddenly at the age of sixteen or seventeen this timid lad turned into a veritable hellion. Wherever there was trouble, a fight, a robbery, Zeynel was sure to be there. In the space of a few years he became the worst troublemaker this side of Bakirköy . . .

First Reactions

1. How can Zeynel's strange behaviour be explained?
2. Do you find his involvement in trouble-making when he grew up a surprising development?

● Take the parts of various people in the village, who are getting used to having Zeynel among them, and gossiping about his appalling background. You could start as follows:

MR A: I hear Laz Refik is looking after that weird kid Zeynel.
MRS B: Well, they do come from the same village, I hear.
MR A: Yes, somewhere in the mountains of Rize.
MRS C: Have you heard what they say about the massacre up there?
MRS B: No! Tell me . . .

Zeynel, having shot an enemy in the coffee house in Menekşe, flees to Istanbul in need of money. Galatasaray, Perşembe Market and Beyoğlu are parts of the city of Istanbul.

Extract B

At Galatasaray he stopped short before a large bank and stood staring as though mesmerised. Passers-by were jostling him, stepping on his feet, pushing him this way and that, but he paid no attention. Rousing himself from his trance he ran to the Underground, bought a token and got on the train. He was soon out in Perşembe Market. There he bought a good-sized nylon bag, then searched through the market until he found a rusty iron ball that

THE NEWSPAPER VIEWPOINT

looked just like a bomb. He shoved it into the bag and quickly turned back towards Beyoğlu. Unseeing, oblivious of all around him, bumping into people, he planted himself again in front of the bank, unable to take his eyes off the cashier's desk. The entire facade of the bank was made of glass. With a superhuman effort he darted across the street and shot into the bank, making straight for the cashier's desk.

"Hands up!" he cried. "Hands up, all of you!" He opened the bag and rolled the iron ball towards the entrance. "This is a bomb," he announced as he drew his gun. "I want you to put all the money you have into this bag. If you leave a single kurush in the cashbox I'll touch off that bomb as I leave. It's powerful enough to blow up the whole of Beyoglu."

Several bank employees lost no time in stuffing thick wads of money into the bag.

"That's all," a young man with long hair said at last. "There's not another kurush left . . ." His face was ashen.

Zeynel was pale as a sheet too, in a worse state then the bank employees. He heaved the bag onto his back and went to the door, his finger on the trigger of his gun. A crowd had been gathering outside. Panic-stricken, he fired. The crowd backed away hastily, scrambling over each other, and Zeynel, still firing, crossed the street and dashed down the Boğazkesen slope. It was raining again and the day had grown dark. Some people were after him, a policeman, two watchmen . . . He turned, aimed his gun at the policeman's belly and shot him down. The others threw themselves to the ground. Swerving into a narrow alley, he darted into a carpenter's workshop where a young boy, who looked to be about sixteen, was working. At the sight of him the boy screamed. Zeynel swooped upon him like an eagle. "Be quiet," he hissed, "or I'll pump you full of lead." The apprentice shut up at once. "Don't make a sound! I've just robbed a bank. I'll give you some money too." On the spur of the moment he picked up a coil of rope that was lying around and bound the boy's hands. "Is there another room here?"

"Yes." the boy said, quite at ease now, as though this were some sort of game. "Look . . ." He pushed open a small door into a recess that was full of sawdust.

"I'm going to lock you up in here. Where's your boss?"
"He's gone home. He won't come back today."
"What's your name?"
"Mutlu."
"Well, Mutlu, you'll have to stay in there for a while."
"All right," the boy said, secretly thrilled at this adventure. "Did you bag a lot of money from that bank?"

"A lot," Zeynel replied. "Now, get in there." He was just closing the door when he drew it open again. "I ought to gag you really. What if you shout when you hear someone come in?"

"I'd be a stinker if I did, Abi," Mutlu declared. "We're men here. A man doesn't give another away, especially a big brother who's robbed a bank!" . . .

It's Sensational

It is obvious that Zeynel's bank robbery was an amateurish, though very successful job and there was no violence in his treatment of the boy in the workshop where he escaped.

However, this is not the version of events which makes sensational news stories.

● Write the most sensational story you can based on this episode from Zeynel's life. Devise the shortest and most lurid headlines possible. Play up the violence. Exaggerate the amount of money taken. Include an interview with the boy in the workshop.

● In groups use the story for a radio (taped) or TV (videoed) news item. You will need the following:
Newscaster
Journalist for this item
Boy in workshop
Bank clerk
People from Menekşe who knew Zeynel as a child
The sea captain in the first extract
Laz Refik who came from the same village where Zeynel's family were massacred.

The newspapers make the most of this elusive 'gangster'.

Extract C

(1) That morning, Menekşe had been astir exceptionally early. Some boys had been dispatched to get the newspapers from Küçükçekmece. Even Ibo Efendi had loosened his pursestrings for once and ordered three newspapers. When they arrived, groups assembled on the beach, in the coffee-house, outside the houses, and the account of the murder was read aloud and commented upon. Though this differed from one paper to another, there was one point on which they were all in accord. Zeynel and his gang had fired at the houses all night long, had even fired at the sea and the fishing boats. One paper related how Zeynel had burst into the Menekşe coffee-house with nine men, grabbed hold of that notorious thug Ihsan, who had a clean eleven murders to his credit, and after torturing him for some time had shot him three times in each eye . . .

. . . Alerted, the police had surrounded the gangsters, but Zeynel, that old-timer, so bold and swift, had managed to break through and escape. The Menekşe folk believed it all. Very likely, they said, when Zeynel broke into the coffee-house his gang was waiting outside, but what a pity they had not seen the police surrounding him on sea and on land, as the paper wrote. Yet how could the paper say the skirmish had gone on for days and nights when that was not true at all?

(2) Then there was the incident of the trussed-up policemen, which had made a great sensation in the press. The police, having received a tip-off, had set an ambush for Zeynel at the point of the Old Seraglio, in front of the statue of Atatürk, but instead they found themselves trapped in a hail of bullets . . .

Then came the bank hold-up in Beyoğlu, followed by the burning of Fisher Selim's house. Here was a windfall for the newspapers! Now they could fill up their columns every day with the epic doings of this dangerous gangster, and Istanbul, its hand on its heart, would be waiting for the morning papers with growing eagerness every day.
(3) One journalist had by pure chance, he wrote, come upon Zeynel only the day before, drinking whisky in an unnamed casino on the Bosphorus and Zeynel had granted him a long interview. Splashed over the front page of the paper were various pictures of Zeynel posing beside the journalist. Here Zeynel was a tall handlebar-moustached brave and the journalist said that he originated from Tunceli. First, at the age of eleven he had joined a large smuggling network, but it took him only a few years to realise he did not like black-marketeering. He defied their chief and killed him. Policemen he hated. Wherever he saw one he had pledged himself to truss him up and next time he would send his gun to the Chief of the Security Department. Zeynel, the article went on, was about thirty, cool and self-possessed and quite modest too. The reason he had shot Ihsan was because the man had murdered Zeynel's brother. As for the bank hold-up, well, the gang needed money. They couldn't be expected to go hungry, could they? And nothing was easier than to rob a bank. Three more he had to rob in order to secure his material independence and then he'd never touch another man's property again. Thieving and plundering were downright sinful when you had enough money to get by anyway . . .

(4) That was it. After this, in a very short while, Zeynel Celik's gang had grown to redoubtable proportions and events gathered speed, a second bank hold-up taking place in Beyoğlu, a third in Sisli, a fourth in Sirkeci . . .

. . . And, soon after, a couple of new corpses, mother-naked this time, were found in the underpass in Aksaray. No one doubted but that all these murders were the work of Zeynel Celik's gang. Every new day brought a fresh murder, another burglary or hold-up in this or that quarter of Istanbul, and also a whole spate of photographs of Zeynel, holding now a machine-gun, now a Mauser rifle, a carbine, a sword . . .

(5) The Istanbul police were being showered with tip-offs. It seemed as though the citizens had nothing else to do. Only yesterday morning, at the very same time, twenty-three Zeynel Celiks had been spotted in Samatya . . .

All over Istanbul police were hunting Zeynel, leaving no stone unturned, organising raids every day, every hour, making up to a dozen arrests daily, killing a few people, but for some mysterious reason Zeynel always eluded them.
(6) Zeynel Çelik was the topic of the day in every coffee-house in Istanbul. In Menekşe people talked of nothing else . . .

A wind of panic was sweeping over Menekşe. Not one of the people here had ever been kind to Zeynel. They had sent him out fishing in freezing weather without paying him anything. They had made him work for nothing, ordering him about like a servant. And now they lived with the constant fear that Zeynel Çelik's gang would come in the night and set fire to their houses, shooting down anyone who attempted to get out . . .

Discussion

● In groups or pairs discuss the following questions about the story.

Section 1.
1. How can you tell that the people in Zeynel's home town are fascinated by his story in the papers?
2. Which two details of the story about the murder of Ihsan do the local people who were present at the time, have no memory about? Why do they have no memory of these events?
3. Find a quotation to show that the local people of Menekşe accepted what they read in the papers as truth, even if it conflicted with the evidence of their own eyes.

Section 2.
4. What suggests that the public who buy the newspapers are responsible for the exaggerations of the truth that they find in them?

Section 3.
5. Do you believe the description of Zeynel's life and opinions given by the journalist who had come upon him 'By pure chance'? What is the information given about Zeynel in this 'interview'?
6. Why do you think the journalist chose those particular 'facts' for his report?

Section 4.
7. "No one doubted but that all these murders were the work of Zeynel Çelik's gang." Do you doubt it? Why?

Section 5.
8. What shows that the people of Istanbul were beginning to enter into the spirit of the newspaper stories?

Section 6.
9. How did the people of Menekşe react to what they continued to read in the papers about Zeynel?
10. Do you think they had anything to fear from Zeynel and 'his gang'?

THE NEWSPAPER VIEWPOINT

In the story of Zeynel you have read how an emotionally disturbed youth turned to crime and the press did not hesitate to embroider and exaggerate the events and make up totally fictitious interviews with the criminal. He was presented as a gangster in a way that the public had come to expect from thrillers and crime stories.

Schoolboy footballer fulfils lifetime dream

Degree success for school failure

Enraged husband carries out revenge attack

Lorry driver in motorway pile up

Surprise retirement of local head teacher

PROTESTERS OPPOSE PLANNING COMMITTEE DECISION

WEDDING BELLS FOR TRAGEDY WIDOW

CARBON COPY MURDER

Adopted child reunited with natural parent

Jeweller convicted of receiving stolen goods

Here is the News

● Devise a newspaper/broadcast story. You will be telling the same story from two different viewpoints.

One will be the news version of the story as dramatic and far fetched as possible.

One will be an account of what actually happened from an eye witness, or someone who knows the people involved.

Here are some ideas for the subject of the story.

1. Select a headline which appeals to your group – some are sensational, others more likely to be found in local news.

2. Decide on an outline of the story – the bare facts of what actually happened.

3. Prepare a news presentation, either for a paper or radio, playing up the drama, tension and human interest in the story. Invent details about the people involved which will appeal to the readers/audience and fulfil their expectations of a good story.

4. Plan and prepare interviews with the characters involved.

5. Check that you have used sensational language and that the news item reads like a thriller story.

6. Prepare a contrasting version of the story, which shows the 'simple facts'.

7. Present the two versions side by side, one as a newspaper page or radio news report and the other as a simply-written or spoken statement.

By now the 'truth' has become very elusive. What people expect of a sensational story affects the reporting of real life incidents until the fiction becomes more real than the truth. This is what happened in the end to the unhappy Zeynel Çelik, who was unable to convince people that he was the person who had robbed the bank, and committed some of the other crimes.

Finally, Zeynel becomes a victim of his own legend – he has lost his own identity to the gang leader of the newspapers.

Extract D

Suddenly he remembered the night before. He had been drinking in Yani's tavern. A hundred lira he'd tipped the waiter and indulged in all sorts of tomfoolery, drawing his gun and shouting: "I'm Zeynel Çelik! Zeynel Çelik, they call me!" And Yani, the wise old tavern-keeper, had taken him by the arm, saying, "Everyone's Zeynel Çelik these days," and had led him off to the railway station to prevent him from making any more trouble.

"I *am* Zeynel!" Zeynel was yelling. "Zeynel Çelik! Is there anyone who dares to look askance at me? It's me who killed Ihsan, me who robbed the bank, trussed up all those cops, me, me, me!"

"All right, son," Yani had said soothingly, removing the gun from his hand and shoving it back into his belt. "You're whoever you say, the greatest thug in Istanbul. You're Zeynel Çelik . . ."

"But I *am* Zeynel Çelik. Don't you believe me?"

"Yes, yes, I believe you."

"Then why don't you turn me over to the police?"

"Because the police will break every bone in your body if they take you for Zeynel Çelik. That's why, my little lion," Yani had said and left him there, sitting on a bench at the station.

Dimly Zeynel recalled getting into a train and out again at Florya, wandering through the woods, tumbling into the mud, being caught in a flood of neon light, yellow, green, white, purple, floundering this way and that, dazzled, frightened, desperate, yet still yelling like a madman: "I, I, I am Zeynel Çelik, you bastards! Why don't you believe me?" Buttonholing whoever he came across. "Why are you laughing at me?"

"Zeynel Çelik's a giant of a man – you could hew three of the like of you out of him!"

"I am Zeynel Çelik, I, I!" He pounded his chest. "It was I killed Ihsan. Everyone in Menekşe saw me."

"Pish! That's a tall one!"

"Those policemen . . . It was I . . ."

"Pish!"

"And the bank too . . . Look, look at this! This is what you call money . . ."

"Pish!"

"But I am, I *am* Zeynel Çelik . . ."

"You, Zeynel Çelik? Ha-ha!"

"Everyone calls himself Zeynel Çelik these days, son, or takes himself for Zeynel Çelik. Why, there must be dozens shouting in every quarter of the town that they are Zeynel Çelik . . ."

"But it *is* me, I swear it!"

"You poor lad! Don't you ever read the newspapers? Zeynel Çelik trussed up fifteen cops, single-handed. He's not an ordinary person. That bank now, single-handed! And Zühre Paşali . . . Single-handed! He's a man who's got the whole of Istanbul in a tremble. You can't be Zeynel Çelik, lad, nor can anyone else we know."

"I *am* Zeynel Çelik, I tell you."

"Oh come off it! Stop pulling my leg."

"Look those photographs, they're not the real Zeynel Çelik . . ."

"Piss off, will you?"

Yashir Kemal, *The Sea Crossed Fisherman*

CHORUS AND COMMENTARY

When we tell stories about other people, particularly those known to us, we often add some kind of comment on what has happened. We may feel we can learn something in general from the experience of others –

''I wouldn't treat a friend like that! He got what was coming to him!''

– we may want to show the person we are telling how the story might be interpreted, or how it it might be relevant to them –

''Have you heard about the job she's been offered? More money but she doesn't have any time to herself. You'll find it the same.''

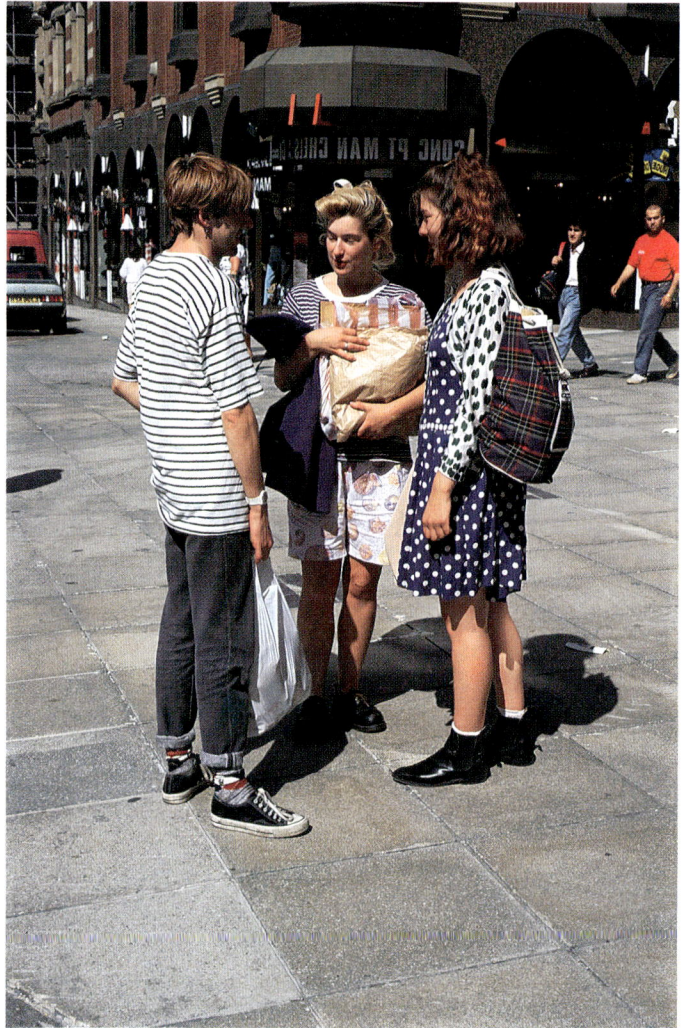

Oral Work – A Two Stage Process

● In small groups work out three or four little stories, anecdotes from everyday life about people you might know. They might have actually happened, or be made up.

1. Write each one down on a separate piece of paper, briefly.
2. Hand in all the anecdotes and redistribute them so that each group receives a different set of stories.
3. Decide on some kind of summing up comment, like those quoted above to put at the end of each anecdote.
4. Display all the work and see how the originators of each anecdote like the comments made on them.

● Using a dramatic form, like a script for a soap opera, devise the story which might have received any of the following comments:
I always knew that love would find a way!
I hate to admit it, but mother did know best!
You lose on the swings, gain on the roundabouts.
I'll never travel with that company after our disastrous holiday!
We all warned him, but he wouldn't take any notice.

● Compare the effects of the following two fragments of a story.

A) Mandy came into registration and asked Jeff, ''Where were you when I rang your house last night?''
''Out,'' replied Jeff.
''And I know where, in case YOU don't want to tell me, and I know who with, you two-timing . . .''

B) The usual registration hubbub was nothing to what broke when Mandy stormed into the room. She made straight for Jeff and asked through clenched teeth, ''Where were you when I rang your house last night?''
Jeff replied coolly, ''Out.''
Mandy erupted volcanically, ''And I know where, in case YOU don't want to tell me, and I know who with, you two-timing . . .''

● Identify the differences between the two. Which has more variety and interest?

● Write a very plain dialogue paragraph like A above giving the barest details of what was said. Exchange with someone else. Rewrite the paragraph you receive, with the extra information added in the descriptive language you use.

Playscript

● Compare the effects of the following two fragments of a play.

A) VIMIT: Can't we have some music now we've eaten?
   PARVATI: OK – I'll get on with my homework while I listen.
   VIMIT: No – I meant you could play your sitar.
   PARVATI: Huh! Whilst you just sit around and laze?
   VIMIT: I'm sure you need the practice.
   PARVATI: Yes and I need my coursework as well.
   VIMIT: Well, do you expect us to sit here in silence?
   PARVATI: What do you think father bought a stereo for?

B) NARRATOR: The family have eaten and now the calm of the evening settles on the house, that quiet time we all look forward to after the stress and rush of the day.
   VIMIT: Can't we have some music now we've eaten?
   PARVATI: OK – I'll get on with my homework while I listen.
   NARRATOR: Now they will settle down and enjoy their favourites from the charts, peacefully together.
   VIMIT: No – I meant you could play your sitar.
   NARRATOR: How will she respond? Does he regard her as there to entertain him? Has she not got exams to do? Would he treat her like this if she were his brother?

● Do the narrator's comments add to the action taking place?
How do they provide another layer of meaning?
Which version gives you a clearer insight into this relationship?

● In pairs:
1. Improvise a scene between two characters – any place, any time.
2. Show the scene to another member of the group/class.
3. Let that person add another speaking part – the narrator/chorus – which provides a commentary, or opens out the action for the audience.
4. Show both scenes, the one without chorus and the one with, to the rest of the class and invite their comments.

Examples of A and B versions of play and prose text can be found on Repromaster 18

Another way of looking at the role of the narrator is to examine folk song. On the tape, Bob Pegg suggests comparing narrative songs with the way a film is structured, and demonstrates how three traditional folk songs use narrative devices.

Inner Voices

A television commercial for an insurance company shows a young man meeting a woman at a party. He asks what she does and she replies that she is in insurance. He replies, 'How interesting!' and as he continues to smile at her you hear his voice over the picture saying 'God, how boring!' He then asks the name of her company and again you hear his voice saying 'Never heard of it' and then he repeats it back to her as if he knows it well.

● In pairs, one person takes the role of somebody waiting for something or someone and the other provides the 'voice over' saying out loud what the character is thinking.

● In groups of four, divide into two pairs. One pair are the shadows of the other. One pair will improvise a conversation, whilst the other pair takes the roles of the inner thoughts of each. For each line of dialogue, the shadow character will speak a line revealing the real unspoken thoughts in the character's mind.

CHORUS AND COMMENTARY

What is truly astonishing about the pair of plays represented in the following two extracts is that they were written 2,500 years apart, yet they both use the same dramatic device.

Oedipus the King

In ancient Athens, in the fifth century BC there was a very important tradition of theatre and the plays that were written then can still be enjoyed today once you understand some of the conventions of Greek drama.

The plays were performed in the open air in large semicircular theatres cut from the ground in concentric tiers of seating, so that the audience looked down on the actors. The actors wore high shoes and masks so they could be seen more clearly.

The action which took place on the stage was very formal with violence only ever being described by a messenger or by the Chorus. The Chorus stood around the edge of the action and commented to the audience on what might be learnt from the behaviour of the characters. They were also occasionally involved in the development of the story itself.

These stories were already well known to the audience from Greek legends and their dramatic enjoyment lay in experiencing a brilliant playwright's interpretation of the psychological implications of the story. Comedy was also very popular, which was often a satire on contemporary politics or personalities.

Thebes, the kingdom over which Oedipus rules, has been suffering from poor harvests and disease. The King sends to the prophetess who is inspired by the god Apollo to find out why this is so and is told that the murderer of the previous king, Laius, has never been identified or punished. When the guilty man is found, and the sin is atoned for, then the kingdom will prosper once more.

The wise priest tells Oedipus that the killer he seeks is none other than himself, but Oedipus refuses to believe this and suspects that the accusation comes from his brother-in-law Creon, whom he thinks may be plotting against him.

At this point in the play the Chorus speaks, first to the audience and then to Creon, who has been sent for.

CHORUS:	Terrible, terrible indeed
	The all-wise seer's tale
	Disturbing, and straining belief.
	I do not know what to say,
	Nor what to look for, now or soon, 5
	My mind flies to and fro.
	I never knew before nor
	Learnt lately of a quarrel
	Between the house of Labdacus
	And Polybus' son to account 10
	For popular rumour that
Oedipus was responsible for the secret	
Murder in the house of Labdacus.	

	Great Zeus and Apollo
	See and know mortal 15
	Ways. But among men,
	That one can prophesy
	More than another is not
	Judged to be true. Wisdom
	Is not fixed in man. 20
	I would not bring blame
	Without clear proof,
	Once, clearly, the winged
	Witch faced him and wisely
This champion met his ordeal. In my mind 25	
He deserves not to suffer ill-repute.	

Enter CREON.

CREON:	Citizens! I have heard King Oedipus
	Has accused me vilely. This I won't bear.
	If at this ill-fated time he believes
	I have harmed him by deed or word, then life 30
	Has lost its meaning for me, slandered thus.
	His words bear hardly on me even more
	If in your sight I am seen as wicked
	And become a traitor to my friends.

CHORUS:	Maybe this accusation was borne of wrath 35
	And not from serious consideration.

CREON:	Then did he say the prophet falsely spoke
	Persuaded by my evil influence?

CHORUS:	So heard I, but I do not know his mind.

CREON:	Was his demeanour straight and eye steadfast 40
	When he laid this accusation at me?

CHORUS:	I know not. What the powerful do I see not.
	But already he appears outside the palace.

At the end of the play it is discovered that Oedipus himself did kill Laius, unaware that that was the identity of the man he met at the crossroads who had rudely refused to get out of his way. To make matters worse Laius was also his own father, and so he had committed the worst sin of all, incest, when he went on to marry Laius' wife, who was in fact his own mother. From being the most powerful and prosperous leader, Oedipus had sunk to being a blind beggar, an outcast.

This is the comment which the Chorus make at the end of the whole tragic story of Oedipus the King.

Inhabitants of Thebes, behold this Oedipus,
Famed for solving the enigma, mightiest
Of men, envied by all who saw his fortune,
How great a flood of misfortune overcame him.

Mortal man must look to his last day:
Call no man happy till he gains the end
Of weary life, and dies, from suffering free.
Sophocles, *Oedipus the King*

1. How do the Chorus feel about the prophet's message? Lines 1–15.
2. How do their feelings relate to what the audience might be feeling? lines 16–23.
3. Why do the Chorus not doubt the words of the prophet?
4. Are they going to make any guesses at the identity of the guilty party? Lines 23–27.
5. How do the Chorus sum up Oedipus' character? Lines 23–26
6. To whom is the Chorus talking now?
7. How has their role changed slightly?
8. How does the Chorus defend Oedipus against the anger of Creon?

Blood Brothers

In this play with music, Willy Russell explores the injustices of the English class system by describing what happened when Mrs Johnstone, the poor cleaning woman, agrees to let her childless employer, Mrs Lyons, bring up one of the Johnstone twins as if it were her own son.

There is a large part in the play for a Narrator, who, just like the ancient Greek Chorus, comments to the audience on what is happening in the play, and occasionally takes a part in the action, talking to the characters.

At this point in the play, Mrs Johnstone has been very happily continuing to work as a cleaner for Mrs Lyons because it means that she can go on seeing her other twin baby boy, whom she has sold to Mrs Lyons in a secret deal known only to the two of them. Mr Lyons believes that his wife's pregnancy took place during his long absence on business. Here Mrs Johnstone is fired by Mrs Lyons and realises that she will not be able to see her other baby boy any more. The Narrator hints that she has no idea what Fate might have in store for her.

The production note for the play says –

The setting for *Blood Brothers* is an open stage, with the different settings and time spans being indicated by lighting changes, with the minimum of properties and furniture. The whole play should flow along easily and smoothly, with no cumbersome scene changes. Two areas are semi-permanent – the Lyons house and the Johnstone house. We see the interior of the Lyons' comfortable home but usually only the exterior front door of the Johnstone house, with the 'interior' scenes taking place outside the door. The area between the two houses acts as communal ground for street scenes, park scenes etc.

and so the Narrator's role is very important in letting the audience know where the next part of the action is taking place. The opening of the play is quoted in **Structure in**

Narrative *page 30 which shows how Willy Russell was aware that his play would still work even if the audience knew from the start what was in store. He knew how the ancient Greeks had used this kind of dramatic irony to give more complexity to the audience's reaction to the play.*
MRS LYONS:
They say . . . they say that if either twins learns that he once was a pair, they shall both immediately die. It means, Mrs Johnstone, that these brothers shall grow up, unaware of the other's existence. They shall be raised apart and never, ever told what was once the truth. You won't tell anyone about this, Mrs Johnstone, because if you do, you will kill them.

MRS LYONS *picks up the money and thrusts it into* MRS JOHNSTONE's *hands.* MRS LYONS *turns and walks away.*

CHORUS AND COMMENTARY

The NARRATOR *enters.*

NARRATOR (*singing*):
Shoes upon the table
An' a spider's been killed.
Someone broke the lookin' glass
A full moon shinin'
An' the salt's been spilled.
You're walkin' on the pavement cracks
Don't know what's gonna come to pass.

Now y'know the devil's got your number,
Y'know he'd gonna find y',
Y'know he's right behind y',
He's starin' through your windows
He's creepin' down the hall.

Ain't no point in clutching
At your rosary
You're always gonna know what was done
Even when you shut your eyes you still see
That you sold a son
And you can't tell anyone.

But y'know the devil's got your number,
Y'know he's gonna find y'.
Y'know he's right behind y'.
He's starin' through your windows
He's creeping down the hall.

Yes, y'know the devil's got your number
He's gonna find y'.

NARRATOR:
There's a full moon shining and a joker in the pack,
The dealers dealt the cards, and he won't take them back,
There's a black cat stalking and a woman who's afraid,
That there's no getting off without the price being paid.

Although the boys are growing up in different circumstances they make friends with each other and share the same girlfriend. It is Micky Johnstone, who had stayed at home with his true mother who marries Linda, but drifts into a life of crime. Edward Lyons, the other twin who has been brought up in a much wealthier household has a successful career and later, Linda goes to him for help, as he is on the town council. The Narrator comments on Linda's plight.

The NARRATOR *enters.*
The NARRATOR *watches* LINDA. *She moves to telephone, but hesitates.*

NARRATOR:
There's a girl inside the woman
Who's waiting to get free
She's washed a million dishes
She's always making tea.

LINDA (*speaking on the 'phone*):
Could I talk to Councillor Lyons, please?

NARRATOR:
There's a girl inside the woman
And the mother she became
And a half remembered song
Comes to her lips again.

LINDA (*on the 'phone*):
Eddie, could I talk to you? Yeh, I remember.

NARRATOR:
The girl would sing the melody
But the woman stands in doubt
And wonders what the price would be
For letting the young girl out.

MRS JOHNSTONE (*singing*):
It's just a light romance,
It's nothing cruel,
They laid no plans . . .
Willy Russell, *Blood Brothers* (1st performed 1983)

Options

● Write a playscript or story using the same basic plot idea; a pair of twins who have grown up in different families and meet again, not knowing how closely they are related.
How did they come to part?
What brings them together again?
How do they feel about each other?
Does the situation develop into co-operation or conflict?
How is it resolved?

● Use any of the line(s) in the Narrator's speeches given in the *Blood Brothers* extract as the idea and the title for a story of your own.

● Improvise a scene of your own which contains one of the following lines:
"There's no getting off without the price being paid."
"There's a girl inside the woman who's waiting to get free."

THEME AND ATMOSPHERE

ATMOSPHERE

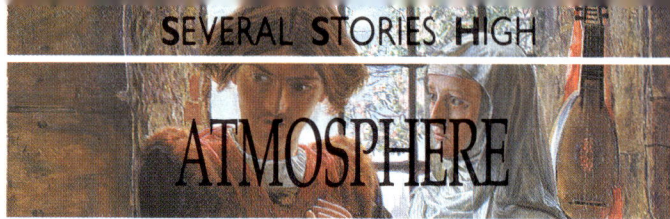

Sometimes the most important part of a narrative is not actually the story, but the atmosphere created by the background, or the characters' thoughts. It may not be what a character does but the state of mind which he or she is in which is of interest to the reader. The writer may choose to back up or emphasise the mood he wants to convey by using an appropriate location. This is especially true in film and television narrative where a director will work with his camera director to produce a particular atmosphere.

You will be familiar with trailers and title sequences which build up the mood or atmosphere of the whole story or situation to come. On radio, suitable music or sound effects will reinforce the atmosphere of the story. Advertisers will also use the technique as they often know they are not trying to sell a product but an image, or a hope or a dream, and they have to persuade the public that buying their product will for example, make the purchaser younger or healthier or improve their life, home, garden or relationships.

Matching Mood to Story

● In pairs or working on your own:

1. Look through magazines to find an advert which aims to create a particular mood in order to sell the product, eg·a fresh country garden with the dew on the flowers, an exotic Eastern temple glittering with rich mosaics.

2. Write a paragraph describing the atmosphere of the picture, choosing words which you feel are the equivalent of the visual effect.

3. Display all the group's pictures and descriptions and see whether you agree with other people's interpretations of the pictures they have chosen.

● In pairs, or a group, try to decide which of the settings in Column A might belong to the stories in Column B.

A	B
An avenue of dripping trees in the rain, with a dejected woman walking a dog along it, umbrella up.	A detective thriller about corrupt gambling.
Quick sequence of shots, a casino, a luxury restaurant, the poolside and back to the casino.	The story of an emigrant family who, although they are prosperous, still regret the move.
A baby's room very prettily decorated where a smart young mother comes in as she hears the baby crying.	An unhappy love triangle story.
An aerial view of the Caribbean dotted with green islands, followed by a picture of inner city streets.	A story focusing on the problems of a successful career woman who decided to include motherhood among all her other commitments.

Mariana in the Moated Grange

This story happens on the fringes of another story and then has been used by later writers and a painter, who were interested not so much in the story as in the atmosphere it seemed to generate.

1. The first appearance of the story

Shakespeare's play **Measure** for **Measure** describes a town where the ruler, a duke, has decided to go into secret retirement for a while. It seems the best way of coping with the state of lawlessness and disorder which have developed in the town. A deputy ruler, Angelo, is placed in charge of the city and he creates harsh new morality laws in an effort to clean it up. Unfortunately a young man, Claudio, is the victim of these laws, as his fiancée is already pregnant.

His sister, Isabella, is told that her brother, Claudio is going to be executed. Isabella at once goes and pleads with the deputy ruler for her brother's life. The deputy ruler finds Isabella very attractive, even though she intends to be a nun so he says he will pardon her brother if she will spend the night with him. Isabella is faced with an impossible decision as she values her chastity as much as her brother's life.

At this stage in the main plot, the real Duke, who had gone into secret retirement, reveals that the deputy was once engaged to be married, to a girl called Mariana, who loves him so much that she would very happily take Isabella's place in the bargain. This girl has been living alone ever since the deputy, who is called Angelo, broke off the engagement because she failed to produce the money for her marriage investment, her dowry.

DUKE: Have you not heard of Mariana, the sister of Frederick the great soldier who miscarried at sea?

ISABELLA: I have heard of the lady, and good words went with her name.

DUKE: She should this Angelo have married; was affianced to her by oath, and the nuptial appointed: between which time of the contract and limit of the solemnity her brother Frederick was wrecked at sea, having in that perished vessel the dowry of his sister. But mark how heavily this befell to the poor gentlewoman: there she lost a noble and renowned brother . . . and with him . . . her marriage dowry; with both, her husband.

ISABELLA: Can this be so? Did Angelo so leave her?

DUKE: Left her in tears and dried not one of them with his comfort.

William Shakespeare, *Measure for Measure*

The solution to the problem? A happy ending?

The Duke then arranges to go to the farmhouse with a moat around it, the moated grange where 'resides this dejected Marina', the exchange is arranged and all turns out well for both women in the end.

2. The story used two hundred and fifty years later

The story of Mariana seems to have been a way in which Shakespeare was able to resolve the impossible situation Isabella was placed in by Angelo's offer, which is the main theme of **Measure for Measure.**

The illustration here shows a painting done in the nineteenth century when Shakespeare's stories were used a great deal.

- Consider the following questions:
1. How does the artist show the intimacy between brother and sister?
2. How does the artist show the conflict between them?
3. Claudio, the brother is unwilling to face the prospect of death and does not know that an offer has been made for his release – how do his attitude and gesture reveal some of this?
4. What do you make of the placing of the figures against the background of the window, and the chains on Claudio's feet?

3. The plight of Mariana

The phrase 'Mariana in the moated grange' awoke the imagination of another person in the nineteenth century, Alfred Tennyson, long before he became Poet Laureate and this is how he imagined she would have felt, abandoned by Angelo, her fiancé, just for money reasons.

Mariana

'Mariana in the moated grange.'
Measure for Measure.

With blackest moss the flower-plots
   Were thickly crusted, one and all:
The rusted nails fell from the knots
   That held the pear to the gable-wall.
The broken sheds look'd sad and strange:
   Unlifted was the clinking latch;
   Weeded and worn the ancient thatch
Upon the lonely moated grange.
     She only said, 'My life is dreary,
       He cometh not,' she said;
     She said, 'I am aweary, aweary,
       I would that I were dead!'

Her tears fell with the dews at even;
   Her tears fell ere the dews were dried;
She could not look on the sweet heaven,
   Either at morn or eventide.
After the flitting of the bats,
   When thickest dark did trance the sky,
   She drew her casement-curtain by,
And glanced athwart the glooming flats.
     She only said, 'The night is dreary,
       He cometh not,' she said;
     She said, 'I am aweary, aweary,
       I would that I were dead!'

Upon the middle of the night,
   Waking she heard the night-fowl crow:
The cock sung out an hour ere light:
   From the dark fen the oxen's low
Came to her: without hope of change,
   In sleep she seem'd to walk forlorn.
   Till cold winds woke the gray-eyed morn
About the lonely moated grange.
     She only said, 'The day is dreary,
       He cometh not,' she said;
     She said, 'I am aweary, aweary,
       I would that I were dead!'

ATMOSPHERE

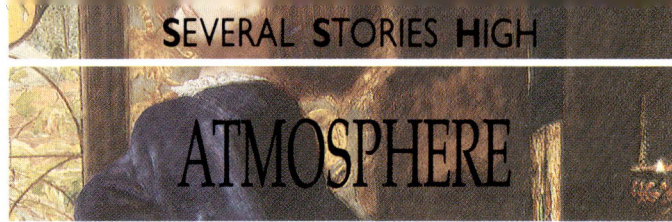

About a stone-cast from the wall
   A sluice with blacken'd waters slept,
And o'er it many, round and small,
   The cluster'd marish-mosses crept.
Hard by a poplar shook alway,
   All silver-green with gnarled bark:
For leagues no other tree did mark
The level waste, the rounding gray.
     She only said, 'My life is dreary,
       He cometh not,' she said;
     She said, 'I am aweary, aweary,
       I would that I were dead!'

And ever when the moon was low,
   And the shrill winds were up and away,
In the white curtain, to and fro,
   She saw the gusty shadow sway.
But when the moon was very low,
   And wild winds bound within their cell,
   The shadow of the poplar fell
Upon her bed, across her brow.
     She only said, 'The night is dreary,
       He cometh not,' she said;
     She said, 'I am aweary, aweary,
       I would that I were dead!'

All day within the dreamy house,
   The doors upon their hinges creak'd;
The blue fly sung in the pane; the mouse
   Behind the mouldering wainscot shriek'd,
Or from the crevice peer'd about.
   Old faces glimmer'd thro' the doors,
   Old footsteps trod the upper floors,
Old voices called her from without.
     She only said, 'My life is dreary,
       He cometh not,' she said;
     She said, 'I am aweary, aweary,
       I would that I were dead!'

The sparrow's chirrup on the roof,
   The slow clock ticking, and the sound
Which to the wooing wind aloof
   The poplar made, did all confound
Her sense; but most she loathed the hour
   When the thick-moted sunbeam lay
   Athwart the chambers, and the day
Was sloping toward his western bower.
     Then, said she, 'I am very dreary,
       He will not come,' she said;
     She wept, 'I am aweary, aweary,
       Oh God, that I were dead!'
Alfred Tennyson

Reading the Poem

1. In the poem the story is only hinted at. How does the refrain to each verse suggest her desperate situation?

2. The house is described in great detail – Shakespeare only tells us that it is a grange, an outbuilding of a monastery, which once had a moat round it. How many factual details can you collect to build up a picture of the place?

3. The mood of the person living there is reflective of the place. What is there about the house which reveals its state of decay?

4. A silence seems to surround Mariana. What actual noises are described and why do you think these were the particular ones chosen?

5. What details can you find that show no one comes there?

6. Note the sounds made by the words of the poem, particularly the rhyming ones. What sounds can you identify and what effect do they have?

● In a group, take the parts of the Duke, Isabella and Mariana. The Duke and Isabella arrive to tell Mariana about the situation which has arisen, and ask if she can help them in this particularly delicate way! Don't forget that Mariana loves Angelo although Isabella hates him for making such an improper offer to her.

4. The story used for another painting

1. Which details in this painting come from the poem?

2. Which details in the painting have been added to enhance the mood?

Options

● Use either of the two paintings shown as the basis for your own story. It does not need to have the same theme/storyline as the Mariana stories you have read.

● Choose a line, a comparison or a sentence from some other piece of writing which has caught your imagination and inspired your own ideas and build up your own story on it. It may be from a pop song lyric, or something you have read at home, or something from school, or a word or sentence heard on radio or television.

● Write some entries from a diary Mariana might have kept whilst she was at the moated grange.

● Improvise your own scene on the theme of an abandoned girlfriend, victim of a broken engagement, who still waits hopefully. Does the story have a happy ending?

● Choose any part of the Claudio/Isabella/Angelo/Mariana story to retell. Set this story of a rejected woman in the twenty-first century – how has the improved status of women altered the situation? Or are you going to imagine that the status of women has taken a backward trend in the future?

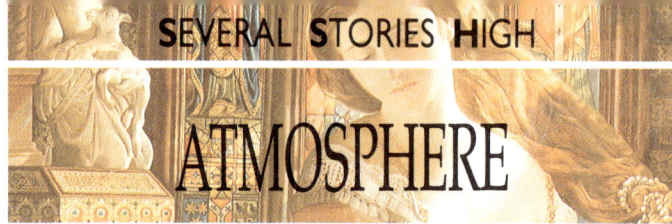

Madeline

XXIII

Out went the taper as she hurried in;
Its little smoke, in pallid moonshine, died:
She clos'd the door, she panted, all akin
To spirits of the air, and visions wide:
No uttered syllable, or, woe betide!
But to her heart, her heart was voluble,
Paining with eloquence her balmy side;
As though a tongueless nightingale should swell
Her throat in vain, and die, heart-stifled, in her dell.

XXIV

A casement high and triple-arch'd there was,
All garlanded with carven imag'ries
Of fruits, and flowers, and bunches of knot-grass,
And diamonded with panes of quaint device,
Innumerable of stains and splendid dyes,
As are the tiger-moth's deep-damask'd wings;
And in the midst, 'mong thousand heraldries,
And twilight saints, and dim emblazonings,
A shielded scutcheon blush'd with blood of queens and kings.

XXV

Full on this casement shone the wintry moon,
And threw warm gules on Madeline's fair breast,
As down she knelt for heaven's grace and boon;
Rose-bloom fell on her hands, together prest,
And on her silver cross soft amethyst,
And on her hair a glory, like a saint:
She seem'd a splendid angel, newly drest,
Save wings, for heaven: – Porphyro grew faint:
She knelt, so pure a thing, so free from mortal taint.

XXVI

Anon his heart revives: her vespers done,
Of all its wreathed pearls her hair she frees;
Unclasps her warmed jewels one by one;
Loosens her fragrant boddice; by degrees
Her rich attire creeps rustling to her knees:
Half-hidden, like a mermaid in sea-weed,
Pensive awhile she dreams awake, and sees,
In fancy, fair St Agnes in her bed,
But dares not look behind, or all the charm is fled.
John Keats, *The Eve of St Agnes*

The story of the poem was invented by Keats whose first inspiration was a visual one. He was shown some fourteenth century frescoes from Pisa, and visited a mediaeval building in Chichester. This gave him a mood and a setting – a cold mediaeval castle where a young girl, Madeline, lives. Her lover, Porphyro, belongs to a rival family, and comes in secret to elope with her, on St Agnes Eve. She intends to carry out a traditional ritual that night, so that she can see her future lover in her dreams. Porphyro hides in the room, just before she comes in, intending to make her dream a reality.

The Poem's Theme

The warmth of the lovers' passion and their urgency to escape contrast strongly with the cold of the night – St Agnes Eve is in January – and the age of the people who help them to elope.

● Follow this pattern for a story whose background supports the theme.

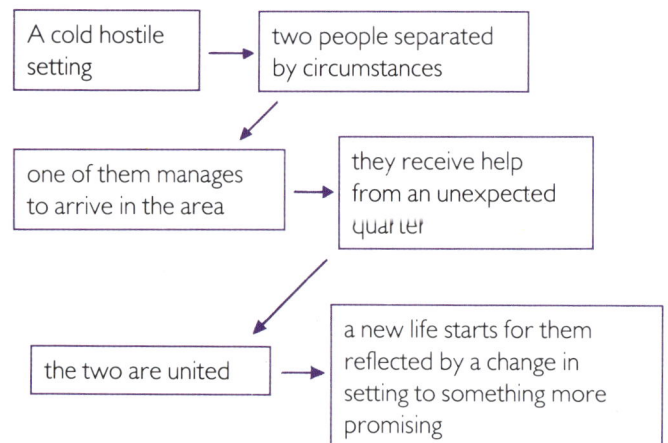

```
A cold hostile    ──▶   two people separated
setting                 by circumstances
                              │
        ◀─────────────────────┘
  │
  ▼
one of them manages  ──▶  they receive help
to arrive in the area      from an unexpected
                           quarter
                              │
        ◀─────────────────────┘
  │
  ▼
the two are united   ──▶  a new life starts for them
                           reflected by a change in
                           setting to something more
                           promising
```

● Again, the poem has inspired a nineteenth century painter, Daniel Maclise. How successful has the painter been in interpreting the poem?

Mood Pictures Quiz

The relationship between words and pictures has been shown to be very close in this section.

● In groups build up a collection of pictures from postcards, magazines, record covers etc which express a particular mood.

Individually, write a few paragraphs to capture the mood of the pictures.

Display several of the pictures with the writing separately to see if other members of the class can identify which matches which.

ATMOSPHERE

Picture Bank

● Share your reactions to the atmosphere of the following pictures with a partner. If there is a particular picture which seems to you exactly to capture a particular mood, describe it, or bring it in.

TIME AND SEASON

So far this section has focused on building up an atmosphere as the most important aspect of the story. Most people have different reactions to the different seasons of the year or times of day. In the following pages several poems and a student's story show different interpretations of autumn and winter.

Seasons

● Compile a list of questions concerning a person's reactions to the different seasons, eg:

Which season do you prefer?

Do you have any particular anniversary in any season?

Do you regard your birthday month in a different way from other months?

1. Obtain responses from several people to your questions.

2. Put together all the responses to the same question and see if a general agreement emerges about the associations we all share for particular seasons.

TIME AND SEASON

In this piece of writing a fourth year pupil responded to the challenge of 'An Autumn Story'. The class were told simply to write any kind of story as long as it had an autumn setting. For many of the pupils, the setting was incidental, though there were quite a few picturesque love stories set amidst falling leaves in the park!

An Autumn Story

The fog had cleared about two hours previously. The night had fallen as pleasantly as a bad attack of dyspepsia. There was no going back now. A rusty leaf stroked the window. He had watched that road for hours; it had seemed like years. He shivered, and reached for the cigarette lighter.

He had a small fire glowing in a few minutes. As little smoke as possible had to be made – no one must know the house was inhabited. Certain things were worrying him – though most of the fog had gone, a misty veil hovered over the part of the road by the old gate. It disconcerted him. Everything had been so well-planned, anything out of the ordinary upset him. His trigger finger was itchy. He was ready to assassinate the ambassador.

The hands of his watch stood stoutly at 6 o'clock. Half an hour to go.

There were no crowds. There was no publicity. The darkness now clutched at the mist that hung, and made it transparent. He had been trained for this one task for months, since April in fact. The Hungarian liberation army had trained him to hit moving objects, almost with his eyes closed.

The ambassador would have come and gone within his range in four seconds. Those four seconds would be the last of his life.

Though at first he thought he was imagining he could make out a figure moving towards him across the fields. There was little light, but this figure seemed to exude its own.

There was only the sound of the whispering wind outside. But suddenly the doors of one of the partitions of the old loft, flung open with such violence the whole house shook. The assassin peered at the doorway. In the doorway was a figure.

The face was that of a man. The man would have been in his mid-forties.

''Good day,'' he said.

''Good day,'' said the figure. ''Have you the correct time, please?''

''Er, ten past six.''

''Thank you.'' The figure had the air of departure. But suddenly he looked at the assassin, knowingly. By this time the latter had recovered to think it most strange that the figure should ask for the time.

''Twenty minutes then,'' said the figure.

He was now in two minds. Should he follow the other man and see if he could stop him before he reached his superiors, or stay where he was? He elected to do the former. He chased wildly the images he thought he saw of the man as he charged down the path. He kicked the gate, which obligingly collapsed in a heap. He pelted down the lane, until he came upon softer ground. He was now running over the fields. He felt his legs get stung by nettles, he tripped, got up, and tripped on the turf. He had to stop the stranger from reporting him. Then up ahead he saw the brown cowled shape. He was standing, almost morosely, by the roadway. But the thing which caught the assassin's attention was a glowing carriage, about a quarter of a mile away. The assassin looked at his watch. Nineteen minutes past six! It had come early!

Without giving another thought to the cowled figure, he charged back to his position at the deserted outhouse.

If the assassin had cared to look carefully between the cowled figure's hands, he would have seen a gleaming, loaded shotgun.

Though he had not thought about it at first, the carriage had seemed ornate and antique. But he brushed that thought aside as he ran at top speed towards the deserted house.

Panting for breath, he careered up the stairs, dived through the opening ravaged by woodworm, and picked his gun up. He was in luck. It was loaded. Twenty one minutes past six. He looked through the sights. He peered almost tentatively through onto the road. He could see leaves. He saw fallen acorns.

He saw the cowled man. What! Yes it was him all right! Then he heard the most surprising sound of all. It was totally unexpected. It was the last sound he would have associated with his task.

It was the sound of an old carriage horn. Taking his gaze away from the figure, he saw a horse-drawn carriage, from inside which there was a ruddy glow. There were faces, peering out silently into the night. Heck! Which one was the ambassador? He was about to fire wildly, when he saw the figure jump out in front of it. 'Now what was happening?' thought the assassin in consternation. In the figure's hand was a gun.

From the second it took that fact to reach his brain, to the second he fired, a peculiar thing happened to the assassin. He did not want the other figure to get his kill, the ambassador. The assassin shot at the carriage.

He then dropped his sniper. He added to the woodworm's efforts by jumping carelessly and increasing the size of the hole in the wall. He tumbled down the stairs. Cut and grazed, he shot out of the front door.

He had three pairs of hands clapped on him. The road was totally deserted apart from a series of police cars. Two minutes later the Hungarian ambassador's car came round the corner.

Report in the Evesham Gazette, 10th November 1821.

An unsuccessful attempt was made on the life of the Duke of Berkshire yesterday. A cowled man, one Septimus Nuttall, ran in front of the Duke and his family's carriages and fired at the said occupants. However, as these shots were fired another shot rang out.

This shot, wherever it came from, hit the said assassin, and didst kill him. The party were much shocked by this incident, and did stop thereby. The shot was said to have come from the house of one Marmaduke Mortimer. The house was deserted when the shot was fired.

None of the said occupants of the coach were injured. The party were delayed by the fog, which had cleared two hours previously.

Gregory Wright

The Background

- Having read the extract consider the following questions:
1. How many details can you find to indicate what time of year it is?
2. Where do references to the fog occur?
3. In what ways has the fog made the assassin's job more difficult?
4. Select three details from the first part of the story which tell you it is taking place in the twentieth century.
5. When do you first realise there is something strange about the other person who seems to be getting in the way of the carefully planned political assassination?
6. What other details seems to suggest things happening not in the present but the past?
7. Whom did the assassin actually shoot?
8. Why was the murder attempt in 1821 unsuccessful?

Options

- Use one of the seasons of the year as the background to a story.
- Describe an event which happens in the present in a place where a similar event has taken place in the past – a lovers' meeting, a death. Show how one event is influenced by the other. You will find a suggested essay plan to help you with this option on *Repromaster 20*

TIME AND SEASON

A charade was the name used to describe an old family game where a person or a group would use costumes and props to present a riddle. The audience had to guess the answer which was a word or phrase represented by the acting.

Charades: September

The squirrel jets along a bough
as if sizzled from a hose.

Autumn's a redhaired girl,
birds at her fingertips.

The squirrel's barking up an oak,
his brown eyes popping acorns.

Autumn's a brazen minx,
shedding lovers fast as leaves.

The squirrel scrats, pounces, nibbles.
Look, he's melted, in beech grey.

Autumn's a martyred queen,
firecoal gems in her crown.

The squirrel's corbel of a face
juts round a pine trunk at me.

Autumn's a crackboned witch,
strips poplars for broomsticks.

The squirrel sits up to pray, white –
is off, a smoketailed comet.

Autumn's a mist hag with
a spade to fill us in.
Geoffrey Holloway

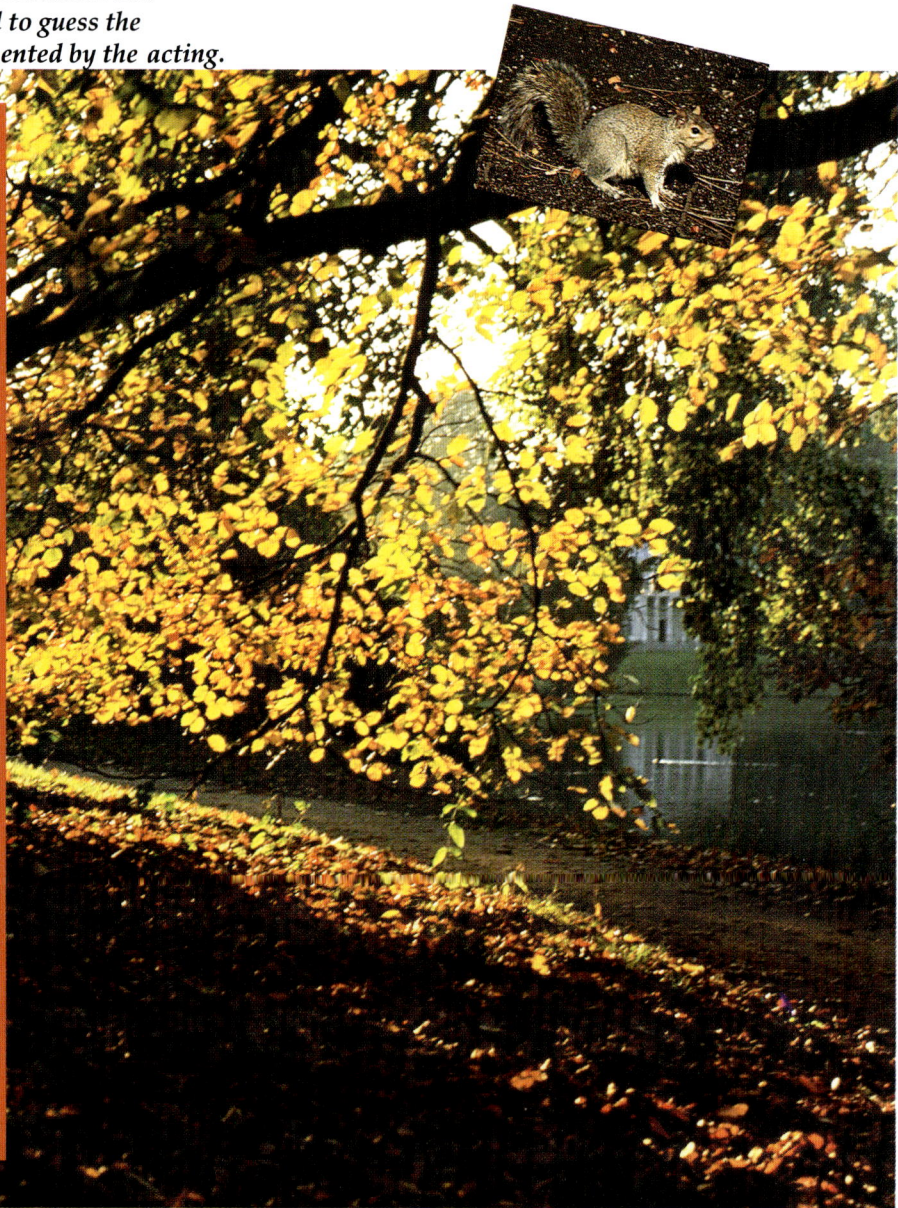

Poetic Comparisons

● In this poem Autumn is represented in a number of different ways. In pairs, one partner researches the verses starting 'Autumn is…' whilst the other studies the verses dealing with the squirrel.

'Autumn is . . .'

1. Work out the five kinds of women that Autumn is compared to.
2. Which of the women have similar characters and which are different?
3. Which of the characters are pleasant and which are unpleasant?
4. Select four details from the poem which seem to you very typical of Autumn.

'The squirrel'

1. How does the writer suggest the squirrel is always active?
2. What comparisons are used to bring the squirrel to life?
3. How many different trees are included in the poem?
4. Select four details from the poem which seem to you very typical of Autumn.

The Thickness of Ice

At first we will meet as friends
(Though secretly I'll be hoping
We'll become much more
And hoping that you're hoping that too).

At first we'll be like skaters
Testing the thickness of ice
(With each meeting
We'll skate nearer the centre of the lake).

Later we will become less anxious to impress,
Less eager than the skater going for gold,
(The triple jumps and spins
Will become an old routine:
We will be content with simple movements).

Later we will not notice the steady thaw,
The creeping cracks will be ignored,
(And one day when the ice gives way
We will scramble to save ourselves
And not each other).

Last of all we'll meet as acquaintances
(Though secretly we will be enemies,
Hurt by missing out on a medal,
Jealous of new partners).

Last of all we'll be like children
Having learnt the thinness of ice,
(Though secretly, perhaps, we may be hoping
To break the ice between us
And maybe meet again as friends).
Liz Loxley

Looking Deeper

1. At first reading the title of this poem suggests that it is about winter and ice. Do you think that is the most important part of the poem?

2. What are the stages in a relationship described here?

3. How can you tell it was not going to be a lasting relationship from their reactions when the ice gives way?

4. Which stages in the relationship are compared to:
'testing the thickness of the ice'
'one day when the ice gives way'
'to break the ice between us'?

● In pairs, take the parts of each one of the couple described in *The Thickness of Ice*. Present a conversation they might have at each different successive stage of the relationship described here.

TIME AND SEASON

● Which of the following two poems is:
1. A description of Autumn as a person?
2. Autumn used as a description of the poet's age?

LXXIII

That time of year thou mayst in me behold
When yellow leaves, or none, or few, do hang
Upon those boughs which shake against the cold,
Bare ruin'd choirs, where late the sweet birds sang.
In me thou see'st the twilight of such day
As after sunset fadeth in the west;
Which by and by black night doth take away,
Death's second self, that seals up all in rest.
In me thou see'st the glowing of such fire,
That on the ashes of his youth doth lie,
As the death-bed whereon it must expire,
Consumed with that which it was nourish'd by.
This thou perceivest, which makes thy love more
   strong,
To love that well which thou must leave ere long.
William Shakespeare

Using Metaphor

● The first twelve lines of this poem are divided into three units of four lines each and each unit contains one comparison. In each case, something is being compared by Shakespeare to the fact that he feels he is well into middle age. Find the three comparisons — two of them have to do with times and seasons.

To Autumn

1

Season of mists and mellow fruitfulness,
　Close bosom-friend of the maturing sun;
Conspiring with him how to load and bless
　With fruit the vines that round the thatch-eves run;
To bend with apples the moss'd cottage-trees,
　And fill all fruit with ripeness to the core;
　　To swell the gourd, and plump the hazel shells
With a sweet kernel; to set budding more,
　And still more, later flowers for the bees,
　Until they think warm days will never cease,
　　For Summer has o'er-brimm'd their clammy cells.

2

Who hath not seen thee oft amid thy store?
　Sometimes whoever seeks abroad may find
Thee sitting careless on a granary floor,
　Thy hair soft-lifted by the winnowing wind;
Or on a half-reap'd furrow sound asleep,
　Drows'd with the fume of poppies, while thy hook
　　Spares the next swath and all its twined flowers:
And sometimes like a gleaner thou dost keep
　Steady thy laden head across a brook;
　Or by a cyder-press, with patient look,
　　Thou watchest the last oozings hours by hours.

3

Where are the songs of Spring? Ay, where are they?
　Think not of them, thou hast thy music too, –
While barred clouds bloom the soft-dying day,
　And touch the stubble-plains with rosy hue;
Then in a wailful choir the small gnats mourn
　Among the river sallows, borne aloft
　　Or sinking as the light wind lives or dies;
And full-grown lambs loud bleat from hilly bourn;
　Hedge-crickets sing; and now with treble soft
The red-breast whistles from a garden-croft;
　And gathering swallows twitter in the skies.

John Keats

Using Personification

● In the first two verses Keats sees Autumn as a person, who 'conspires' or plots with the sun to ripen the fruit and the harvest. Find the four named crops.

● In the second verse the person Autumn is more clearly visualised, as a character carrying out typical country tasks of the season. Find the four autumn jobs described.

● Choose several lines or phrases from either poem which seem to you to describe the season particularly well. Write them out and then explain why you chose them. Compare your choice with your partner's and your reasons with theirs.

Repromaster 21 *explores imagery when related to time and seasons in greater detail, which you may find useful.*

Repromaster 22 *extends all the ideas considered in this section, giving you a chance to look at another poem* **Burnt Sienna** *and explore the ideas behind it.*

PLACE

● Study the following two extracts and see how very different places are used by writers for very different purposes.

Mary Barton

Mary Barton *was written by Mrs Gaskell. Although Mrs Gaskell had been brought up in comfortable surroundings in the South of England, she came to Manchester in the middle of the last century as a vicar's wife, and so was in a very good position to know how the mill workers lived in the poor crowded housing of the city.*

The matter being decided, the party proceeded home, through many half-finished streets, all so like one another that you might have easily been bewildered and lost your way. Not a step, however, did our friends lose; down this entry, cutting off that corner, until they turned out of one of these innumerable streets into a little paved court, having the backs of houses at the end opposite to the opening, and a gutter running through the middle to carry off household slops, washing suds, etc. The women who lived in the court were busy taking in strings of caps, frocks, and various articles of linen, which hung from side to side, dangling so low, that if our friends had been a few minutes sooner, they would have had to stoop very much, or else the half-wet clothes would have flapped in their faces: but although the evening seemed yet early when they were in the open fields – among the pent-up houses, night, with its mists, and its darkness, had already begun to fall.

Many greetings were given and exchanged between the Wilsons and these women, for not long ago they had also dwelt in this court.

Two rude lads, standing at a disorderly looking house-door, exclaimed, as Mary Barton (the daughter) passed, ''Eh, look! Polly Barton's gotten a sweetheart.''

Of course this referred to young Wilson, who stole a look to see how Mary took the idea. He saw her assume the air of a young fury, and to his next speech she answered not a word.

Mrs Barton produced the key of the door from her pocket; and on entering the house-place it seemed as if they were in total darkness, except one bright spot, which might be a cat's eye, or might be, what it was, a red-hot fire, smouldering under a large piece of coal, which John Barton immediately applied himself to break up, and the effect instantly produced was warm and glowing light in every corner of the room. To add to this (although the coarse yellow glare seemed lost in the ruddy glow from the fire), Mrs Barton lighted a dip by sticking it in the fire, and having placed it satisfactorily in a tin candlestick, began to look further about her, on hospitable thoughts intent. The room was tolerably large, and possessed many conveniences. On the right of the door, as you entered, was a longish window, with a broad ledge. On each side of this hung blue-and-white check curtains, which were now drawn, to shut in the friends met to enjoy themselves.

Two geraniums, unpruned and leafy, which stood on the sill, formed a further defence from out-door pryers. In the corner between the window and the fire-side was a cupboard, apparently full of plates and dishes, cups and saucers, and some more nondescript articles, for which one would have fancied their possessors could find no use – such as triangular pieces of glass to save carving knives and forks from dirtying table-cloths. However, it was evident Mrs Barton was proud of her crockery and glass, for she left her cupboard door open, with a glance round of satisfaction and pleasure. On the opposite side to the door and window was the staircase, and two doors; one of which (the nearest to the fire), led into a sort of little back kitchen, where dirty work, such as washing up dishes, might be done, and whose shelves served as larder, and pantry, and store-room, and all. The other door, which was considerably lower, opened into the coal-hole – the slanting closet under the stairs; from which, to the fire-place, there was a gay-coloured piece of oil-cloth laid. The place seemed crammed with furniture (sure sign of good times among the mills). Beneath the window was a dresser with three deep drawers. Opposite the fire-place was a table, which I should call a Pembroke, only that it was made of deal, and I cannot tell how far such a name may be applied to such humble material. On it, resting against the wall, was a bright green japanned tea-tray, having a couple of scarlet lovers embracing in the middle. The fire-light danced merrily on this, and really (setting all taste but that of a child's aside) it gave a richness of colouring to that side of the room. It was in some measure propped up by a crimson tea-caddy, also of japan ware. A round table on one branching leg really for use, stood in the corresponding corner to the cupboard; and if you can picture all this with a washy, but clean stencilled pattern on the walls, you can form some idea of John Barton's home.

The tray was soon hoisted down, and before the merry chatter of cups and saucers began, the women disburdened themselves of their out-of-door things, and sent Mary upstairs with them.

Mrs Gaskell, *Mary Barton*

● What was Mrs Gaskell's intention in choosing to describe John Barton's house in such detail?

● There are plenty of suggestions of a busy social life in the courtyard – the women with their washing and the rude lads at the door of a 'disorderly looking house'. Build up an improvisation of a day in the life of this courtyard, involving as many households as possible, and people of all ages who live there. Which will be the busiest times of day? What occupations will the following have – older women, young boys, men, small children etc?

● In pairs use the idea of the 'hedgehog diagram' shown on page 87 to jot down your responses and note the different ideas at work in the description.

You may find the same information illustrating two different ideas.

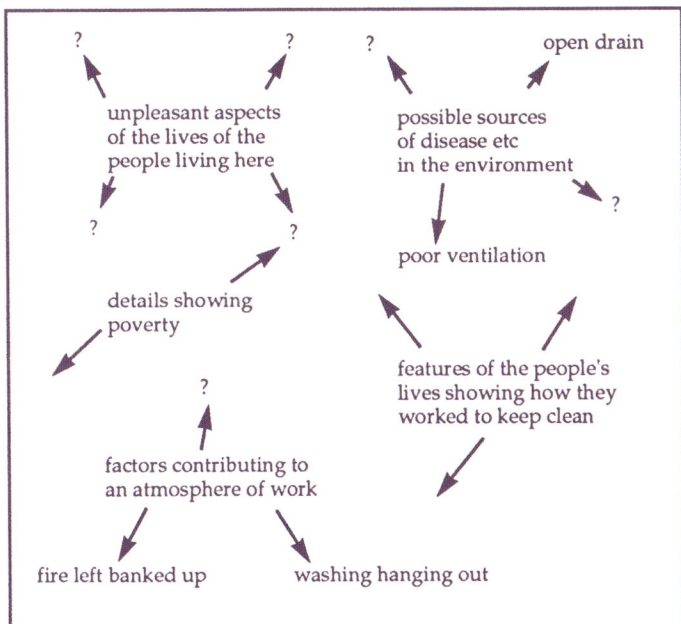

? ? ? open drain

unpleasant aspects of the lives of the people living here

possible sources of disease etc in the environment

? ? ?

details showing poverty

poor ventilation

features of the people's lives showing how they worked to keep clean

?

factors contributing to an atmosphere of work

fire left banked up   washing hanging out

The Aspern Papers

The Aspern Papers were the passionate love letters written by an imaginary famous poet Jeffrey Aspern, to his mistress, the lovely Juliana. The central character in the book is a literary editor who discovers that Juliana, now a very, very old lady, is still alive and lives in Venice with her niece, who is also no longer young. Miss Juliana Bordereau refuses to meet anybody and the editor is desperate to get his hands on the unpublished letters. He takes a gondola ride past their house with another lady he has met, Mrs Prest. He had thought of getting a foothold in the house by taking up lodgings there.

The gondola stopped, the old palace was there, it was a house of the class which in Venice carries even in extreme dilapidation the dignified name. "How charming! It's grey and pink!" my companion exclaimed; and that is the most comprehensive description of it. It was not particularly old, only two or three centuries; and it had an air not so much of decay as of quiet discouragement, as if it had rather missed its career. But its wide front, with a stone balcony from end to end of the *piano nobile* or most important floor, was architectural enough, with the aid of various pilasters and arches; and the stucco with which in the intervals it had long ago been endued was rosy in the April afternoon. It over-looked a clean, melancholy, unfrequented canal, which had a narrow *riva* or convenient footway on either side. "I don't know why there are no brick gables," said Mrs Prest, "but this corner has seemed to me before more Dutch than Italian, more like Amsterdam than like Venice. It's perversely clean, for reasons of its own; and though you can pass on foot scarcely anyone ever thinks of doing so. It has the air of a Protestant Sunday. Perhaps the people are afraid of the Misses Bordereau. I dare say they have the reputation of witches."

I forget what answer I made to this – I was given up to two other reflections. The first of these was that if the old lady lived in such a big, imposing house she could not be in any sort of misery and therefore would not be tempted by a chance to let a couple of rooms. I expressed this idea to Mrs Prest, who gave me a very logical reply. "If she didn't live in a big house how could it be a question of her having rooms to spare? If she were not amply lodged herself you would lack ground to approach her. Besides, a big house here, and especially in this *quartier perdu*, proves nothing at all: it is perfectly compatible with a state of penury. Dilapidated old palazzi, if you will go out of the way for them, are to be had for five shillings a year. And as for the people who live in them – no, until you have explored Venice socially as much as I have you can form no idea of their domestic desolation. They live on nothing, for they have nothing to live on." The other idea that had come into my head was connected with a high blank wall which appeared to confine an expanse of ground on one side of the house. Blank I call it, but it was figured over with the patches that please a painter, repaired breaches, crumblings of plaster, extrusions of brick that had turned pink with time; and a few thin trees, with the poles of certain rickety trellises, were visible over the top. The place was a garden and apparently it belonged to the house. It suddenly occurred to me that if it did belong to the house I had my pretext.

Henry James, *The Aspern Papers*

Following Up the Description

● In pairs work out the answers to these questions:
1. How is the dilapidated 'palace' made to seem like an old person itself?
2. Why do you think the cleanness of the area seems remarkable to these people?
3. What is Mrs Prest's explanation when it is suggested that Miss Bordereau will be a rich person if she lives in such a grand house?
4. What gives the literary editor an idea for a pretext to ask for accommodation?

Options

● Improvise the scene when the literary editor first visits Miss Juliana Bordereau and her niece. Does he have any success with getting lodgings or with getting hold of the love letters? What is her attitude to him considering that he has managed to get in to see her when she tried to prevent this?

● Why do you think the Misses Bordereau were regarded as witches? Devise a scene for some Venetian street urchins who stop outside the palazzo and the gondolier who sometimes takes the niece to church or the market. A stranger passes by and asks them who lives in the Palace.

On the tape you will hear writers talking about the importance of place and atmosphere in creating their stories. Further activities on this section can be found in **Repromaster 23.**

PEOPLE IN PLACE

This unit considers the importance of theme or atmosphere in building up a narrative and all the examples of place descriptions studied so far, from prose texts, have had an important part to play in the story.

Rather than having to think up a plot, you may prefer to describe a place as the proper location for a particular character, as James did in the example.

Mr Bartholomew

In the winding narrow backstreets of Amsterdam is a small alley way with old decaying houses piled on either side of it. Many of the window panes are shattered, like the people who live there, tramps lying on grates, prostitutes and pimps with garish make-up to hide the cracks of age and a cruel life, and old, forgotten people. As you walk up the alley passing signs promising French love or Swedish love but never just love, you pass an old antique shop, looking strangely out of place amongst the filth and whores. For although the building is as decrepit as the rest, more of a shell, with barely four walls and a roof, it exudes innocence, and a time long past of ignorance and naiveté. Looking through the window you see, tainted by the grime, a selection of old broken knives and a watch with the hands missing. Entering, you hear two clocks, striking five and half past three. The bell on the door doesn't ring, the clapper having long since rusted away, like the man sitting down in front of you.

He is short and frail with grey wispy hair, lying lank and lifeless on his scalp, like a dead cat with patches of hair missing. His face is ugly and grey with a long nose and high large nostrils. The skin is cracked and worn, with dust lying in cracks and inflamed sores around his mouth, which is a thin crack surrounded by pale cracked lips. He is wearing a shapeless jacket with frayed elbows and gravy stains speckled down its front. Medals are attached to it, for bravery in a war far away and long forgotten apart from by the maimed and scarred veterans. The shirt he wears is grey and lifeless but once might have been white silk and his trousers are ripped and patched.

You step back, disappointed – he is just another tramp, but as you open the door he awakens with a lung wrenching cough and stares at you with bright intelligent eyes.

"Eh, wot, eurghh? What do you want, young man?"

His voice is clear and stern and as he sees your blank stare he switches to perfect English.

"What do you want?"

"Just looking."

"Hurmph," he coughs in disdain, "you young people are all the same, no respect for your elders, just like my children. They've forgotten me, me who raised them. But in with the new, out with the old, eh?"

Trying to hide your embarrassment at this gruff rebuke you pick up a book and flick it to a page full of poetry.

"What's this?" you timidly enquire.

"Eh? Oh, poetry – Blake or Byron, not sure."
James

This was written by fifth year pupil in an examination. Obviously the end of the examination came just in time as it is not clear how the story might have developed. James had become far more involved in creating a place and a character to go with the place.

Place and Person

- Divide into pairs, each working with another pair.
1. One pair collect details of the place (in the backstreets of Amsterdam).
One pair collect details of the person (Mr Bartholomew).
2. Compare details with each other and see how far the place description has worked to prepare the reader for the person living there.
- In pairs improvise a scene showing how the story of *Mr Bartholomew* might continue.
What was his history?
How had he come to be in the shop?
Why was the storyteller ('you') in the shop?
What happened next?

Amryl Johnson, writer of the next extract, returned to the Caribbean in search of her family's origins and her own identity. Here she describes her first experience of the capital, Port of Spain, in the daylight and the lively characters she saw there.

Port of Spain, Trinidad

I had been enjoying this city by night, taking in the odd calypso tent and show after a late evening on the beach. I would now need to learn to love her by day, also.

The people I met on my way up Independence Square to Frederick Street were out of a magnificent technicolour dream. The people 'liming' on street corners didn't need to work at being individuals. They were. There was a man perched on a bicycle, wearing baseball boots without laces. His orange pants were cut off at the knees where raw edges still frayed hard. The 'Carnival 82' teeshirt had suffered the same fate. Some indiscriminating scissors had removed the sleeves. So he was now quite sleeveless as well as knee to ankleless. A soft, green felt was pulled low over his eyes.

I had no idea they made jeans in that size. He was chatting to a woman with an unbelievably generous bottom held momentarily inactive by the severity of blue denim. Her top half was of the same generous proportions. It had undergone a similar fate. It, also, had been straight-jacketed into submission, tamed and pacified by a controlling influence which held her rigid.

She had squeezed herself into a pink stretch top. I could only hope she would be around and congenial if it started to rain and I was without an umbrella.

The conversation came to meet me while I was yet a little distance from them. Strolling leisurely, I didn't need to eavesdrop.

"But Mavis, I telling you. I walk into we own house and catch she there on the bed with she sweet man."

"Well, boy, you real unlucky, yes. I don't know how you does have so much bad luck with your women and them. Must be somebody do you something."

She lowered her voice as she gave him the next piece of advice. By then I had drawn level so what she had to say reached me anyway.

"Look, Snakie, boy. I heard 'bout this man in Siparia. This friend I have say he good, good. Why you don't go and see if he can't –"

There was a sudden screeching of tyres at my elbow. A second later I could feel the heat from a car wheel as it singed the hairs on my leg.

"Is blind you blind or what? If you take off your damn sunglasses like you some blasted tourist, you go see the cars and them coming up the road. And if you –"

All this was meant for me. Pedestrians, street vendors, limers, all turned to look in the direction of an incensed taxi driver. Everyone but me. I put my nose in the air to look as disdainful as I could while I continued crossing the street. In truth, I was shaking like a leaf. The wheel was like an iron about to be branded into my flesh. The

PEOPLE IN PLACE

memory of it was still searing. And where the devil had he sprung from? He sure as hell wasn't there when I first stepped into the street.

''They should put an L-plate on all you before they let you out. That way we go know –''

The rest of what he had to say was drowned by the klaxoning of horns from the traffic behind him. And where had they suddenly come from? Traffic seemed to appear as if by magic.

There was so much happening on Frederick Street. Commerce, shops, vendors, pedestrians, cars. Frederick Street, as always, busy, teeming with people. Noise ripened in the high temperature to become bolder, louder. People, cars, shops – and Lord Fluke. The refrain from his calypso about the creation reached me.

> 'Naked they come
> Naked they go
> Naked they come
> Naked they go'

The rest of his song was sucked into the vacuum which consumes all energy not moored by gravity, distorting sound. The wind toying with discarded paper made an almost indecipherable rustle.

My sunglasses had a pinkish tint. Perhaps that was the reason why I could no longer tell the difference between reality and what I imagined I saw. But if I took them off I would be blinded by the glare. In that dry, dusty heat, I found myself choking on a desert of mirages. Images coming towards me seemed to seep out of cracks in the pavement. Heat waves transposed shapes, melted movement, absorbed colour. Ghost-like figures wafted

upwards as if seeking light, reaching for substance. Somewhere between the two aspirations they were cut down. Bullet holes like wounds on their cloaks. They bled yellow, purple, orange, red, blue, green. The colours merged, one into the other then fading back to nothing, waned to the level of the gutter to be pulled back beneath the surface. The funnel of sound was now chewing on Lord Fluke's words.

Amryl Johnson, *Sequins for a Ragged Hem*

Discussion

● In groups consider the answers to the following questions:

1. In the opening sentence she describes the people as something 'out of a magnificent technicolour dream'. How does this describe the writing at the end of the extract?

2. Give your own description of the two characters, a man and a woman, in conversation, whom she passed in the street. Did they seem remarkable in this environment? Where do you think such characters would stand out?

3. Why was she nearly run over? What seemed to be the traffic laws in Trinidad?

First Impressions – People and Places

● Try to remember your first impressions when you went somewhere very different from where you usually live. Describe them to your partner or write them down, including as many of the following as possible:

smells;	typical noises and sounds;
unusual food;	curious characters;
different customs;	the sound of another language.

As with Mr Bartholomew, this descriptive passage includes dialogue, and the dialogue contributes to the description. As well as details of sights, sounds and sensations snatches of dialogue help to contribute to the atmosphere in a piece of writing.

Characteristic Language

- Improvise or write a scene which gives a context for the following snatches of dialogue:

1. "I'm not asking 60p a pound for these lovely fresh greens; I'm not asking 50p a pound, no, I'm robbing myself and giving these away at 40p a pound!"

   "I think it's terrible, they only used to be two shillings did beans."
2. "It's a breakthrough! We shall be able to help thousands of sufferers with this drug!"

   "No, we have to be sure the experiment can be repeated with the same results."
3. "And this is the other downstairs room. We prefer to use it because it's at the back."

   "Do you find you get a lot of noise from the road?"

If you are able, it can be interesting to suggest which is a person's country of origin if they do not speak standard English. You will have to observe speech mannerisms closely. Often, commonly used words or phrases can identify a person to others who also know them.

Repromaster 24 *takes these ideas further, giving you the chance to 'Choose a Location'.*

The Importance of Smell

This may seem an unlikely detail to insist on in good descriptive writing but smells are the most evocative means of creating atmosphere. In the next extract from Sequins for a Ragged Hem *Amryl Johnson describes a visit to a very special plantation on the island of Grenada.*

''Garden of Eden all over again. So hazy and unreal. It's like being on another planet.''

Talking to myself. And was there really any wonder?

There were so many dream qualities to the day, I found myself inching forward, one foot in front of the other. When they talked about walking a perfumed path, I always supposed it involved a crowd of people armed with bottles of scent, spraying towards the ground as they went. I was walking a perfumed path. It was not the first time I had found myself in one of the nutmeg-growing regions. Window had taken me on a visit to his village. I was so excited, I picked up the first, then the second. But this was different. Then as now, some of the harvest lay on the ground. Cloves grew there also. Until then I had not realised they were part of a blossom. Indeed, I had never stopped to ask myself how they grew. And if I had, it was unlikely I would have given myself the correct answer. They were the buds of a specific cluster of white flowers. I was walking along a path where nutmegs seemed to grow wild. They lay strewn on the ground, many still inside their lacy red coats of mace. Overhead, the fruit hung like a split peach. The open halves still held their perfume. All around me were laden branches of nutmegs in various stages of development. Some had not as yet ripened sufficiently for the slit which would gradually get wider, revealing the red cloaked kernel, eventually allowing it to fall to the ground. I was walking along a path where nutmegs seemed to grow wild. But of course they did not. Although the area was not cordoned off, the trees were someone's property and the nutmegs were not going to waste. Sooner or later, someone would come to gather them.

Amryl Johnson, *Sequins for a Ragged Hem*

POP VIDEOS

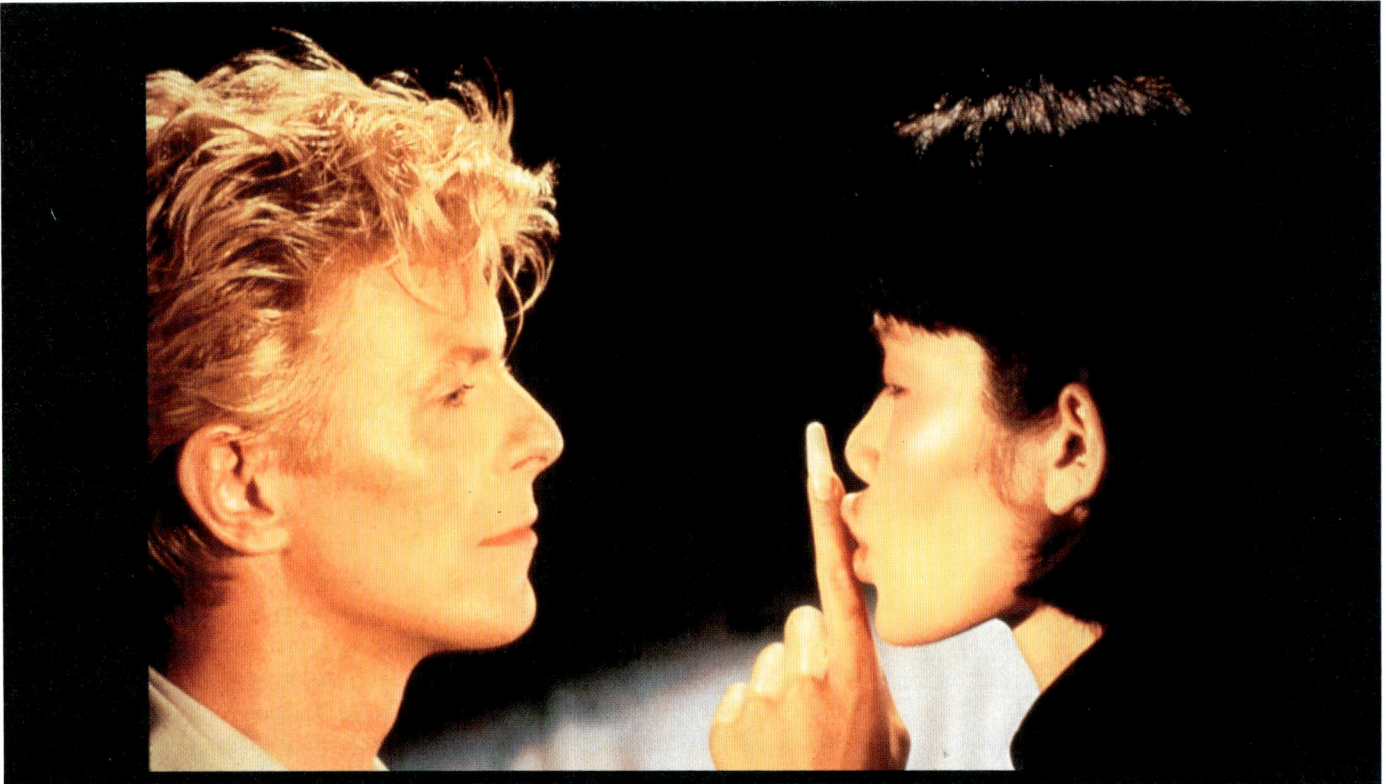

If the idea of a story which is not complete, but which simply creates an atmosphere or suggests a theme, seems strange, you have only to think of the pop videos which many people enjoy watching.

The video maker has worked along with the group to fit a sequence of images which they feel suggest the ideas in the song. Sometimes a complete story is told by the video but more often there is a series of images relating to the theme, and the connections are more like a dream than waking, conscious, logical thinking.

A few years ago, David Bowie was interested in the contrasts between Eastern and Western cultures and made a video for the song 'China Girl' which exploited images of a Chinese girl, as somebody beautiful and exotic, and also as somebody dangerous and threatening. An ordinary western man was seen, going through the streets of a Chinatown where he looked extremely out of place.

Pop Videos – Your Views

● In groups compare ideas on the best and the worst of the current pop videos.

1. Do you agree on which are best and which are worst?
2. Which do you think are the greatest videos of all?
3. Which members of the group prefer a 'story' video and which members of the group prefer a video of a concert, simply showing the group performing? Give reasons for your choice.
4. Which of your current favourite songs would you most like to see a video made for?
5. In your group arrive at an agreed group answer to questions 2 and 3 above.

Thematic Ideas

● What songs do you know which could be described as having any of these themes?

Rivalry (in love, or anything else)
The position of women in society (exploited or dominant)
Fantasy or escape into a dreamworld
The world of the street corner or gangland
The seashore (usually associated with fulfilled love).

● What videos have you found particularly memorable, for their theme or atmosphere? On a single sheet, write the title of the song or the name of the group and then outline what you take to be the theme and add a description of some of the images.

Video Analysis

● You may be surprised to find how much you can increase your understanding and knowledge of a favourite song and video by trying to write it down. To do this you will have to:

1. Videotape the video so that you can pause the image each time you need to write.
2. Prepare a grid (or use *Repromaster 25* which accompanies this section) with three coloumns, for 'Words', 'Image' and 'Camera Angle'.
3. Write out the words to the song, line by line or phrase by phrase in the first column.
4. Watch the video and fill in the other two columns so that you place the screen images beside the words they accompany.

Write Your Own Video

● Choose a favourite musical number which has no video and devise your own to go with it. Set it out in short paragraphs, one for each change of screen image.

These are Lucy's ideas for a video to go with a song by a group whose music she finds full of suggestion. The images recreate the music in another form so it does not matter whether you know the song or not.

Each division in the music corresponds to a division in the arrangement of the sequence of images.

1. The opening music sounds like an echo with the synthesizer. There is complete darkness but as the synthesizer notes come in we see lights in the darkness, like the glowlights carried by very deep sea fish. These lights are in clusters moving slow and hesitantly, or quickly.

2. As the guitar starts, the view rises upwards out of the sea depths slowly into normal waters, and bursts out of the sea with the drum and guitar crescendo, into the night. The view then is very high (long shot) into the sky with stars pinpointing the blackness.

3. As the words begin we have a bird's eye view above the sea, with great white birds soaring below. The sea is blue and wrinkled, way below us. Then the viewpoint plummets back into the sea and down to the coral reefs (close up).

4. With the words 'No-one takes us by the hand and shows us to the land' we see the white towers of a city buried far beneath the waves, in deep dark sea, with fish swimming among them. We can only see tantalising glimpses of the edges of buildings, strange carvings above a doorway, murky through almost black water (fade).

5. In the distance there is a hint of a large patch of darker colour seen only by its movement, about human size, though it has no discernible shape. This moves across the gap between two white edges, and upwards (mix). It is seen only as a movement, and quite slow, to go with the words: 'Something stirs and something tries and starts to rise towards the light'. It should be very vague through the murky sea.

6. We follow this movement up out of the sea into the streets of a normal town where lots of people are pushing past each other.

7. A man bumps into a woman, stops to apologize to her, their eyes meet, they smile. We can see their lips moving as they talk. The woman holds out her hand to the man, as part of the gestures of her hand whilst she is talking. The man takes her hand (close up).

8. The scene flashes back to the underwater images again where the images are becoming clearer, and are definitely two people, a man and a woman close together, hand in hand (to be identified with the couple in the street).

9. A long instrumental section – possibly images flashing backwards through evolution eg mammoth, early mammals, early birds, dinosaurs.

10. As the instruments fade out leaving only misty synthesizer chords, in the background there are strange howling notes on the guitar. All around is deep snow, like the top of a high mountain, with cloud so low the viewpoint is inside the cloud. Within a short distance everything disappears into a blank white nothingness. Beyond the end of the field of vision everything has ceased to exist.

11. Out of the darkness come spiky black reptile birds, some like pterodactyls, and some even stranger, both very close to and almost out of view, and faintly seen through the cloud. The music supplies the cries of the birds.

12. Also through the cloud can be seen huge vague shapes, like brontosaurus type dinosaurs, but only visible as if they were maybe swirls in the mist and it's your eyes fooling you. They are ominous to fit the heaving background music beneath the guitar bird cries.

13. Screen darkens and gradually lightens to reveal the undersea city again. As the music swells the city is seen rising gradually from the very deep to the surface. It breaks through the sea surface accompanied by triumphant chords, with water pouring down the sides of the white towers in the sunlight.

You may find **Repromaster 26,** *which gives a guide to some technical terms of film making, helpful. The storyboard form of presentation is usual for films and video but as you can see above, language is quite adequate for depicting images based on thematic ideas.*

The tape features comments by students about videos and narrative. How far do their views coincide with yours?

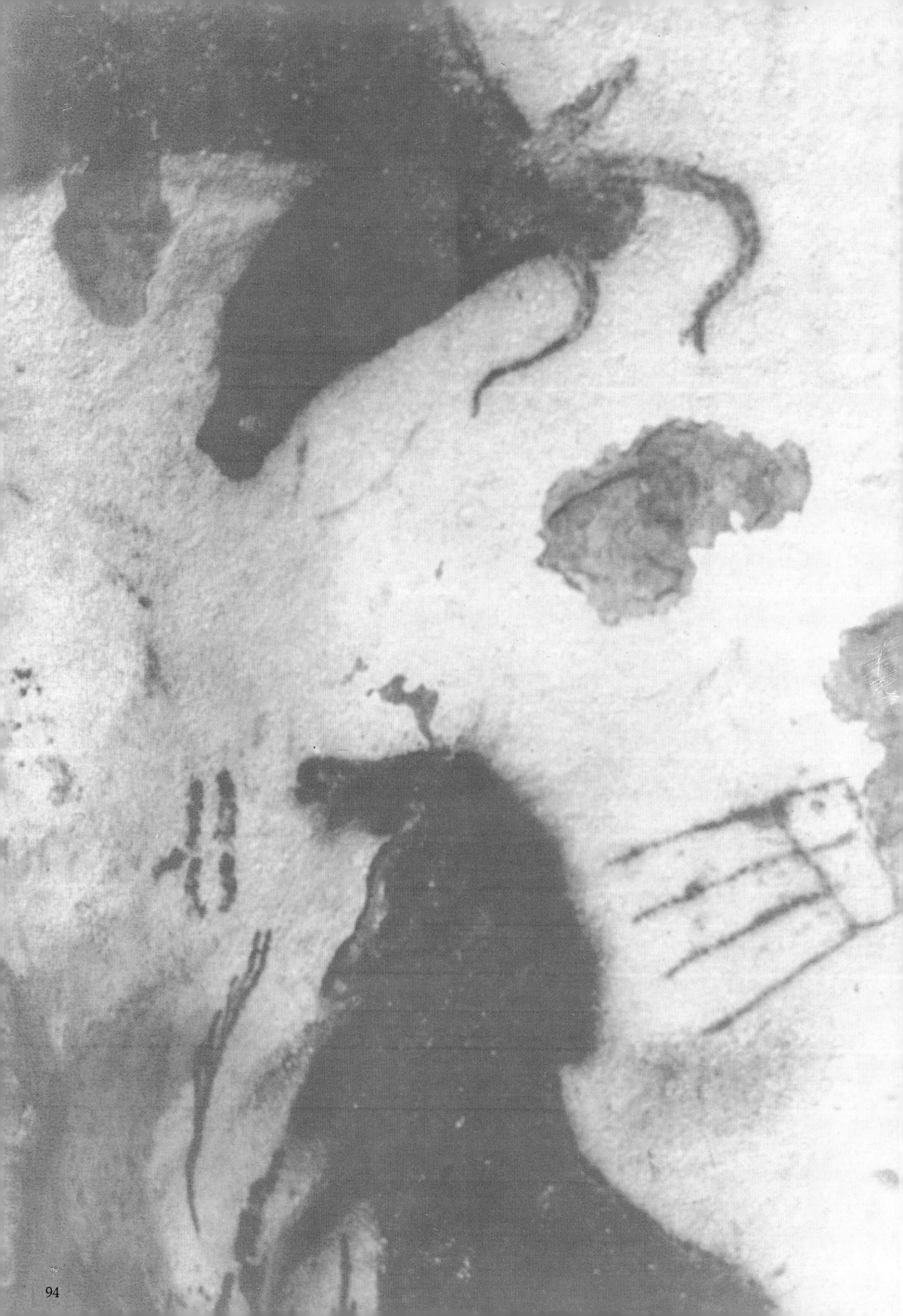

LEGEND AND HEROISM

95

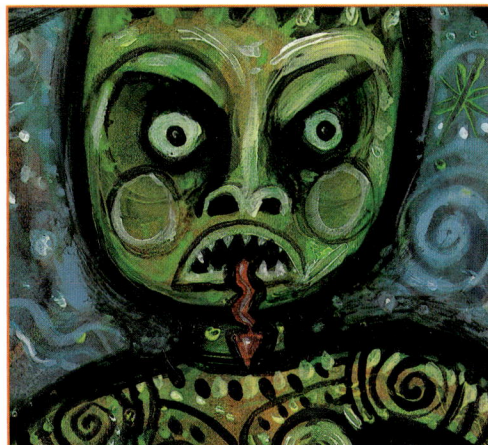

OLDEST STORIES

Stories represent the oldest tradition the world knows. Even though some stories were already written down four thousand years ago, there are other which we can tell were being handed on by word of mouth even earlier than that. 'Reasons for telling stories', which starts on page 10, might help you to work out why story telling is such a basic instinct in humankind. However, there are distinctions between the different kinds of stories told so long ago, and the purpose for which they were told.

● Consider the following three stories based on 'the apple'.

A) In the beginning God created the world as a beautiful garden, and he created man and woman to live there. However, he didn't want them to rival him in his knowledge of what was good and what was bad, so he forbade them to eat the apples of one tree which would make them his equals. In spite of the fact they had everything they needed to make them happy, they broke his command, and ate the apples, and nothing but grief followed for them as they had to leave the lovely garden and work for their living.

B) A princess in ancient Greece was once so proud of her athletic skills that it was declared that any man who could outrun her in a race could have her hand in marriage. One young man, helped by the goddess of Love, took three golden apples and let each of them fall at a crucial point in the race. The princess stopped to pick them up, and lost the race.

C) My dad was going to prune the apple trees in our back garden but he hasn't got round to it, so the ripest apples this year have been very high up. When we picked them, my sister stood on the ladder to hand them down to my mum, and I was up in the branches to hand them down to my sister. I still couldn't reach the really good ones, so we hoped when my friend came to stay we could send him up the tree as he's six foot already. Six foot of quivering cowardice! It was useless, because he weighed much more as well, and didn't dare go out as far as I had on the top branches.

Which Category?

● Study the three definitions below. Which of the 'apple stories' fits which definition?

Legend: A narrative handed down by tradition.

Myth: A purely fictitious narrative usually involving supernatural persons and embodying some popular idea concerning natural or historical phenomena.

Story: A narrative of events, fictitious or not.

● Discuss with your friends which of the following well-known narratives are myths, which are legends and which are stories? (Remember that the distinctions are not always very clear cut.)

1. The origin of Guy Fawkes night
2. The space shuttle disaster
3. The discovery of America
4. The story of Robin Hood
5. The story of Noah's flood
6. The story of Adam and Eve

● Add further examples of your own, particularly of myths, and tell them to the group if they do not know them already.

A Hero Contest

The main characters in myths and legends often seem to be superhuman, even if they are not supernatural.

● In small groups, list all the characters you can think of, real or fictitious, who might be described as 'a hero'.

Compare each list and score one mark for every hero which more than one group has named, and two marks for every hero which only one group has named.

● In the contest above, the distinction between real and imaginary heroes was made, but it should now be possible to divide up the list of heroes still further. The imaginary heroes may be traditional, from legends handed down and often repeated. The real heroes may be modern or historical, and they may belong to one of many different areas of heroism, military, political, sporting etc.

Rearrange your original list under these new headings.

STORYTELLING

The oldest stories, myths and legends, were always told aloud, in the first place, and there are many ways in which telling stories aloud affects the story itself.

Talking About Story

● In small groups discuss the following questions. (The discussion on this topic could be taped.)

1. Have you ever told a familiar story to a little child and found that they complained because it was not the exact version they had heard before?

2. Do you know anyone who is very good at telling stories – they don't have to be children's or folk stories but could be entertaining episodes from their own life or their friends' lives?

3. What is it in the way such people tell their stories which makes everyone want to listen to them?

4. Have you ever been annoyed when someone has told you something they heard elsewhere and they keep stopping and saying, "But it's much funnier the way he does it – what did he say then, I can't just seem to get it right?"

5. Why do you think children are as happy to hear a story well told or read as they are to have more sophisticated entertainment on the television?

6. Why is rapping such a popular form of entertainment? Do you think the rhymes add to the impact of the stories being told?

One way in which stories become altered is through frequent retellings. Each person adds details they like and plays down aspects of the story they think are unimportant.

The ability to tell stories was highly prized in the past, when people were more used to making their own entertainment. In country societies an entertainer, a minstrel who sang and told stories, could always make a living travelling from one place to another and using the same material in a different village or town. Comedians nowadays who used to go round the Music Halls complain that television has meant they are always having to produce new material!

There were several ways by which long stories were committed to memory, such as using a chorus or refrain, so that you could be recalling the next section whilst repeating a part that came so often you didn't even have to think about it.

● See how good the story-telling skills are in your group, by each preparing a short 'story' and then telling it, from memory.
You can choose from any of the following:

1. A children's tale.
2. A joke.
3. Something embarrassing that happened to you.
4. Something stupid that happened to you.
5. An anecdote about something someone in your family did.

The Seal Wife

● Read the following story, or preferably, listen to it being told. It does not deal with a hero but with a local legend, found on the northern coasts of Britain.

On the coasts and islands of the North there is a superstition that among the seals which come inshore and can be seen playing among the waves, there are some who are really women. When no one is watching they come ashore and take off their sealskins and if any man steals the skin then the woman is under his control and she cannot return to the sea until her sealskin is returned to her. There are many stories of wives and mothers who disappeared back to the freedom of the great waves.

Here is the version of this story which Julie Fullarton of the 'Beasties' partnership tells, weaving the spell of the story with her arm movements and gestures. You can follow the telling of the story on the tape.

Once upon a time there lived a young man – a crofter – in a little stone farmhouse overlooking the ocean. He lived all alone except for his cow, a few sheep and some chickens. He owned one field of corn and a little boat, and when he wasn't working his croft or out fishing he would beach-comb. In the evenings, when the sun was setting, he would walk along the water's edge and look to see if the tide had washed up anything that could be of use to him. For instance, trees were very scarce where he lived and sometimes great spars of wood would come into his bay, washed all the way across the sea, perhaps from a shipwreck; and if he was very lucky they would still have great iron nails driven into them. He would pull out the nails, scrape off the rust, and polish them up ready to use again. He would drag the huge planks up the winding path from the bay and use them to start building a barn to keep his corn and lifestock safe during the winter. Once he found a little keg, a barrel, wedged between the rocks at the water's edge. And when he prised the lid up it was full of oranges. The crofter had never seen an orange in his life before, and he didn't know what to do with them.

Now the evening I'm going to tell you about, when this story begins, the young man was very tired. He had finished working his patch of corn and it was too late for the fishing; and there didn't seem to be anything of interest washed up by the sea. So he sat down on the sand and leant his back against a big rock, closed his eyes and listened to the sound of the salt sea travelling into the bay, breaking on the backs of the rocks and smashing onto the shingle, fizzing down among the pebbles.

Then, he thought he heard a strange sound – a bit like a baby crying. He opened his eyes and stared out of the shadow of the rock towards the sound. And there, far out in the dark water of the bay, he could see . . . heads, bobbing up and down. They were seals' heads, and they were calling to each other. As the young man watched, the seals began to swim slowly in towards the shore. He sat very still in the shadow of his rock so they wouldn't notice him. When they came to the water's edge they used their strong flippers to pull themselves over the wet shingle and onto the dry sand. Then they did an amazing thing. They lay down on their sides, rolled over, peeled off their skins and became beautiful girls.

The young man couldn't believe his eyes. The girls ran giggling to the water's edge, joking and squealing and splashing each other, and the crofter noticed that in the middle of the group was one girl who was more beautiful than all the rest put together. "I'm in love!" he thought. "That's the girl for me. I'm going to marry that girl." And then he sighed and hung his head. "She'd never marry a poor crofter. I'm not even good-looking."

Then he noticed a pile of skins that the girls had dropped further along the beach, and he noticed that one of the skins was more beautiful than all the rest put together. It was silver like moonshine and soft as a cloud to touch, and all covered with wee brown dots and squiggles and marks. It was really bonny.

The young man had an idea. "Perhaps if I sneak down the beach and grab that bonny sealskin, the beautiful girl would have to come home with me." And that's just what he did. When the girls had their backs to him, he sneaked out of the shadows down the beach and grabbed the bonny sealskin. The girls saw him. They screamed and dashed around the man, snatching up their skins. They splashed into the waves and became seals again and swam away. All except the beautiful girl who stood wringing her hands with the waves lapping at her ankles. How she begged and pleaded with the crofter to give her back her skin – but he wouldn't. Instead, he turned and climbed back up the winding path to his croft. When he got there he crossed the yard, went into the barn he was building from driftwood, and climbed the ladder. Then he threaded the sealskin in behind the rafters of the barn and covered it over with heather.

When the crofter came out of the barn, there was the seal girl, kneeling in the dirt of the yard amongst the chickens. She was crying her eyes out and she begged him, "Please give my skin back to me, for without it I cannot live in the sea – and I have no home on the land."

The young man replied, "If you marry me, and work hard on my croft, *I* will give you a home." So the poor girl agreed. She had no choice. And things didn't work out so badly for, as I told you, the crofter had fallen head over heels in love with her. And time passed, and the seasons turned, and she worked hard on the croft until, when a year had passed, she had a wee baby boy. She loved the baby very much. She was very busy changing him and feeding him and singing lullabies. The baby made her very happy, and she didn't weep so much for her old life in the sea.

And time passed, and the seasons turned, and she worked hard on the croft; and when another year had passed she had another bonny baby boy. So then she was twice as happy and twice as busy feeding and changing and playing games and singing songs. She thought less and less about her life in the sea. And time passed, and the seasons turned, and she worked hard on the croft until another year went by and . . . guess what? She had *another* bonny baby – a wee girl this time, pretty as a pearl. And then she was so busy looking after them and watching they didn't put things in their mouths or fall off the end of the boat when they went out fishing, that she forgot altogether about her life in the sea.

STORYTELLING

And time passed, and the seasons turned, and the three children grew up bonny and strong till they were old enough to help their mummy and daddy around the croft. Especially at harvest time. The mother and father would go out in the field and cut the corn down, swinging their scythes, while the two boys followed, gathering up the corn into little stacks – stookies we call them – and the youngest child, the wee girl, came behind and bound up the necks of the stookies with twine to hold them together. When the stookies had dried out they were carried to the barn which their daddy had finished building by now, and they were stored away against the winter. It was hard work.

One year, when they had finished getting the harvest in and packing it away in the barn, the father and his three children went into the farmhouse where the mother had cooked up a huge pot of mutton stew. They ate it all and then sat dozing by the fire. Soon the mother clapped her hands and said, ''Right! Off to bed,'' and they all rose up, climbed the stairs, and got ready for bed. Their mother tidied up and, in a wee while, she lit a little candle in a dish and carried it upstairs into the children's bedroom. Then she sat down on the end of the bed and took from the wall her harp, carved from driftwood, and began to pluck a tune, a seal song, the sound of the sea, to lull them to sleep. And when their eyelids had drooped down she gently hung up her harp, blew out the candle, and started to tiptoe from the room. Out of the darkness the eldest boy whispered, ''Mummy, what was that beautiful fur coat Daddy had in the barn tonight?''

''What fur coat, darling? What are you talking about?''

Then the middle child spoke. ''Oh, it was bonny, Mummy. It was silver like moonshine and soft as a cloud to touch, and it was all covered with wee brown dots and squiggles and marks. It was really bonny.''

And the little girl yawned, ''Daddy put it behind the rafters in the barn and covered it over with heather.''

''Listen,'' said their mother, ''and remember what I tell you. I love you very much and I'll never forget you; and you'll never go hungry, you'll always have fish for your tea.'' Then she kissed them each on the forehead and went downstairs. She ran from the house, across the yard, into the barn, up the ladder, and pulled the heather away from the rafters; and there she found her very own sealskin. She threw it around her shoulders and came out into the night and ran down the winding moonlit path to the shore. She was just about to rush into the dark water when she stopped and turned to the land. High on the hillside she could see the fire flicker from the kitchen wndow, and she thought of her three bonny babies fast asleep in bed. But then a great wave came travelling into the bay, and it broke on the backs of the rocks; and it smashed on the shingle at her feet and fizzed away into the pebbles. And it seemed to her as if the ocean was calling her home. She threw herself into the waves, and became a seal and swam away forever.

The next morning, when the children came down, the fire was out and the house felt cold and there was no porridge for breakfast. Their father realised what had happened. They all ran down to the shore and looked out to sea. They could see the heads of the seals bobbing up and down in the dark water of the bay, but no matter how much they called, the seals wouldn't come into the land.

For many years after that the children would go down to the sea and look for their mummy. They never did see her again, but sometimes in the mornings they would find a big fat fish lying across a stone at the water's edge, and they would know that this was their seal mother remembering her promise to them that they would never go hungry, they'd always have fish for their tea.

And years afterwards, when these children were grown up and had crofts and children of their own, they would lie in bed at night in the dark, listening through the open window to the sounds of the sea. And it would remind them of the seal songs their mother used to play for them on her harp of driftwood when they were little – the sound of the sea to lull them to sleep.

The Seal Wife, as told by **Julie Fullarton**

Group Discussion

● Which of the following reactions to the Seal Wife story would you share and which do you disagree with? Discuss each in some detail.

1. I like the opening where you get to know what a remote place it is – anything unusual would be believable there.

2. I don't think it's very convincing – imagine a person who only had oranges once in their whole life.

3. It's good the way she keeps bringing you into the story, like 'the evening I'm going to tell you about'.

4. I think the crofter is really cruel, letting her kneel there in the hen yard and making her work for him.

5. But it's very true to life the way women forget their past sorrows when they have a baby to concentrate on.

6. The odd Scottish details and words are a bit difficult to follow – 'stookies' and 'bonny'.

7. When you hear a story told you get more of the effect of words that sound like the sea, like 'smashed' and 'fizzed'.

8. It's heart-rending when she wants to stay with her children but has to go back to the sea now that she has her sealskin.

Different Versions of the Story

● Read the two poems below which are based on the seal-person theme; one is a traditional ballad, the other is also by Julie Fullarton.
● What differences can you spot between the two poems and between the poems and the story?

The Great Silkie of Sule Skerrie

In Norway there sits a maid:
'By-loo, my baby,' she begins,
'Little know I my child's father
Or if land or sea he's living in.'

Then there arose at her bed feet,
And a grumly guest I'm sure it was he,
Saying 'Here am I, thy child's father,
Although that I am not comely.

'I am a man upon the land,
I am a silkie in the sea,
And when I am in my own country,
My dwelling is in Sule Skerrie.'

Then he hath taken a purse of gold,
He hath put it upon her knee,
Saying 'Give to me my little wee son,
And take thee up the nurse's fee.

'And it shall come to pass on a summer day,
When the sun shines hot on every stone,
That I shall take my little wee son,
And I'll teach him for to swim in the foam

'And you will marry a gunner good
And a proud good gunner I'm sure he'll be.
And he'll go out on a May morning
And he'll kill both my wee son and me.'

And lo, she did marry a gunner good,
And a proud gunner I'm sure it was he;
And the very first shot that e'er he did shoot
He killed the son and the great silkie.

In Norway there sits a maid:
'By-loo, my baby,' she begins,
'Little know I my child's father
Or if land or sea he's living in.'
Traditional

The Song of the Man Who Loved a Seal Woman

When Spring tides are rolling the ocean comes leaping
And breaks on the backs of the rocks in the bay
The salt spray surrounds me and fills up my head
With the tang of her hair in the tang of the sea

Restless in Summer I rise before daybreak
And go to the shoreline to wait for the dawn
I pick up a pebble and there in my hand
Is the cool of her skin in the cool of the stone

Searching for driftwood in sunless October
I look past the sound to the islands beyond
The sea birds are calling, but all I can hear
Is the cry of her voice in the cry of the wind

Another day's rain marks another year's turning
The clouds in the sky are as black as a thorn
Water and wind have conspired to taunt, with
The swell of her limbs in the swell of a dune

And when Spring tides are rolling . . .
Julie Fullarton

● Consider the following aspects of story telling when looking for differences:

Identity of the speaker: Man or woman?
Viewpoint on the action: In what way are they personally involved?
The plot itself: How does the version of the story differ?
The resolution: Who is most hurt by the end of the episode?
Does the situation resolve itself in a satisfactory way?
Your preference: For prose or poetry? A man's viewpoint or a woman's? A sad or a happy ending?

STORYTELLING

Earlier in this section on page 98, there was a challenge to tell any kind of story you knew in an interesting way. Focusing on the material of legends, here are three more traditional stories associated with the sea, which could be retold with different emphases or viewpoints.

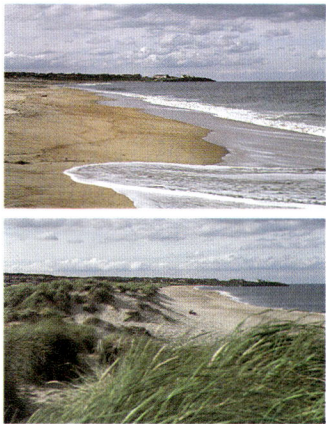

Pomegranate of the Sea

A great King once bought a lovely slave from a merchant. She was so beautiful that he treated her gently but she would never speak to him in reply, though she responded to his loving approach with warm glances. In the end, though he could get no spoken response from her, he arranged for a marriage contract to be drawn up.

After a year of marriage to his joy she spoke and told him that his devotion had outlasted the vow she had taken when she left her people beneath the sea in anger. She was a princess in the land beneath the sea and had quarrelled with her brother, the new King of the Sea.

The King's happiness was fulfilled when a son was born and his wife, Jallanar, which means Pomegranate of the Sea, summoned up her people, who appeared, tall and stately, through the foaming waves. The King of the Land was terrified when the King of the Sea took the baby in his arms and disappeared beneath the water. Shortly, though, they reappeared and Jallanar's brother explained that now the baby would always be safe in the protection of the people of the sea.
From the Arabic

Arion and the Dolphin

Arion was one of the greatest singers the world had known and had made a great fortune performing in Italy. He took ship from Tarentum, a ship manned by Corinthian sailors, to return home to Greece. Once at sea the sailors threatened to kill him for his money, so as a last request he asked to play and sing on the front deck of the ship.

A dolphin following the ship was enchanted by the music and when Arion threw himself into the water to escape death at the hands of the sailors the dolphin took him on his back and brought him safely to shore.

Arion went to Corinth to complain to the ruler of his treatment. When the sailors arrived they were asked by the ruler about Arion and they replied that they had left him safe and well in Italy. At that, Arion appeared from behind a curtain to accuse them and reclaim his wealth.
From the Greek

Urashima and the Turtle

A group of children were teasing a sea turtle, but one, Urashima, defended it and so the turtle befriended him and took him on a magical journey to the kingdom under the sea.

Although he was well entertained by the sea goddess and her creatures, he longed after three years to go back to his village. He was given a closed box to take with him, with instructions not to open it. On returning he was horrified to find everything changed, and longing for consolation in the memories of his happy time under the sea, he opened the box. Instantly he aged three hundred years, the time passed beneath the sea which he had thought to be a mere three years.

From the Japanese

Developing the Outlines

1. Focus on a particular character from any of the sea stories given – tell the story from their viewpoint eg the brother of Jallaner, one of the wicked sailors, the turtle.

2. Provide descriptive detail to help the listener visualise more clearly, eg the inside of the King's palace, how the sea looked to Arion as he faced death, the changes in Urashima's village.

3. Include some conversation eg the merchant's sales talk the King about the slave, the sailors plotting to take Arion's money, Urashima chiding the other children.

OR

1. Start at an interesting point in the story and fill in the earlier details with a flashback eg the moment that Jallanar speaks, Arion's last request, Urashima deciding to return.

2. Tell the story in the first person eg the 'I' of the narrative could be Jallanar herself, or one of the wicked sailors.

These versions could be written or spoken.

Ways of Telling a Story Aloud

As you have seen, Julie Fullarton has a complete text of the story she tells from memory so it can be useful to write the story out first.

A page of notes which are 'prompts' to each stage in the story, each change of action or character, could be prepared and put in front of you as you speak.

If a whole story seems too much, work in a group and divide it up into smaller units, with a different person telling each part. This will need rehearsing, but each person will only have a short section to memorise.

A story can be about anything.

You will find a further example of storytelling on Repromaster 28 *and the accompanying* tape, *when Sam McAughtry relates his tale of* A Belfast Boyhood and Hard Times.

LEGENDS AND MYTHS

Perseus and the Gorgon's Head (Not to Mention the Shower of Gold, the Captive Princess, the Son's Revenge and Many, Many More!!)

You will find below the basic version of the Perseus legend. Don't worry too much about the names, but as you read through the story see which parts of it could fit the basic elements of folk tale mentioned in the title above.

1. Perseus was doomed to be hated through no fault of his own. His mother was Danae and there had been a prophecy from the priestesses at Delphi that Danae's son would kill her father, the son's grandfather. Danae's father was called Acrisius, and when he learnt the prophecy he decided that his daughter should remain childless, so he had her locked up in an underground cellar where no man could touch her.

2. He had reckoned without the gods and their supernatural powers – and most powerful of all, Zeus, the King of the gods, who entered the room in the mystical form of a shower of golden rain and became the father of Danae's child, the boy Perseus.

3. Acrisius was not to be defeated and so he put his daughter and her baby boy into a leaky wooden chest and cast it out to sea. The protection of the gods still followed mother and son, and they were washed safely ashore on the island of Seriphos, whose ruler was Polydectes. Danae was still very young and attractive, and after a while Polydectes fell in love with her, but he found Perseus, now a strong youth, rather an embarrassment. To get rid of Perseus he devised a very elaborate plan. He gave out that he was going to marry, but named Hippodameia as his future wife, and indicated that all those invited to the wedding would have to bring very special gifts. Poor Danae felt they would be shamed in public as they could not afford a suitable wedding gift. Perseus in a fit of extravagance, promised to bring him the head of the Gorgon, the famous death dealing ogress. Polydectes thought he had seen the last of Perseus and would soon be able to lay hands on the lovely mother.

4. Perseus wondered long what had made him take this on, as the Gorgons were fearsome monsters in female form, called Stheno, Euryale and Medusa who lived at the ends of the earth. They were so dreadful that anyone who looked at them was instantly turned to stone. Only Medusa was mortal and could be killed. In addition, no one really knew where they were to be found exactly. While he regretted his folly, the wise goddess Athene appeared to him and inspired him to think of where he could find help. She gave him winged sandals and a highly polished mirror shield.

5. Following Athene's advice Perseus went first to visit three other strange females, the Grey Ladies who lived in the desert who would be able to tell him where to find the Gorgons. They weren't about to tell anyone anything but they did have a weak spot – they had only one eye and one tooth between them and they passed each round. So

Perseus snatched away the eye as it passed from one grey sister to another and easily made them tell him what he wanted to know. Then, he travelled to the Gorgons' desolate area. Using the shield as a mirror rather than looking at Medusa and being turned to stone himself, he cut off the horrible head with curling venomous snakes instead of hair and hastened away using the winged sandals to speed his flight.

6. He had another adventure on his way home, passing by Ethiopia. The queen, Cassiopeia, had boasted she was more beautiful than the lovely Nereids, sea nymphs, and so an appalling sea monster had been sent to devour the people by Poseidon, the god of the Sea. In desperation the King Cepheus, Cassiopeia's husband, found advice from the oracle that his daughter would have to be sacrificed before the monster would stop harrying his country. So as Perseus came by, there was the beautiful Andromeda, chained to a rock by the sea, waiting to be eaten. When the monster came, Perseus simply showed it the Gorgon's head and it became another particularly interesting rock to join the others along the sea coast.

7. When Perseus arrived home with Andromeda, he found his mother, poor Danae, about to become the unwilling bride of Polydectes. As he walked through the hall he was roundly jeered at by the drunken wedding guests, Polydectes' men, for coming so late and so ineffectually. Their jeers froze on their lips as he unveiled the Gorgon's head and held it high for all to see. Later, in gratitude to Athena, he gave the gruesome head to her and she was often portrayed with it in the centre of her shield.

8. Prophecies were always fulfilled, whatever mortals did to avert them and in the end Perseus did kill his grandfather Acrisius, but by accident. Acrisius was among the crowd when Perseus was involved in athletic games and the discus thrown by him accidentally struck and killed the old man.

Basic Elements in the Legend

● Once you have read through the story of Perseus, decide which of the numbered paragraphs might be described by the newspaper-style headings given below. Write out the heading and then put the right paragraph number beside it.

A prophecy comes true

Cruel father locks up daughter

A woman can't resist a knight in shining armour

Proud son tries to keep up family honour

Mother escapes with baby son

Fortune helps those who help themselves

Locked doors don't bar the gods

Approach your problems sideways – they'll not seem so bad

Characters in the Story

The following list has been compiled to help the reader who may find the variety of characters in the Perseus story bewildering. It gives a guide to the part each person plays in the legend.

However, the names have not been placed beside the descriptions.

1. Perseus' grandfather. He had learnt from an oracle that he would be killed by the son of his daughter Danae so he had his daughter shut up in a tower, and later, put to sea with her son, in an attempt to avert this outcome.
2. Daughter of Cepheus and Cassiopeia, King and Queen of Ethiopia. She was chained to a rock as a sacrifice to the sea monster which harassed the kingdom, but rescued by Perseus.
3. Goddess of wisdom, protector of Perseus.
4. Mother of Andromeda, queen of Ethiopia.
5. Father of Andromeda, king of Ethiopia.
6. Mother of Perseus later wooed by Polydectes, King of Seriphos, where she escaped with her son.
7. One of the Gorgons.
8. Three female creatures living at the extreme end of the earth, with snakes for hair and faces which turned people to stone.
9. Three old women with only one eye between them who, in some versions, provided Perseus with the helmet of invisibility.
10. The pretended bride of Polydectes, who really wanted to marry Danae, the mother of Perseus.
11. The only one of the gorgons who was mortal.
12. The son of Danae and Zeus, who killed the gorgon Medusa, freed Andromeda and later killed his grandfather Acrisius, fulfilling the oracle.
13. King of Seriphos, where Danae fled with her baby, who later wanted to marry her.
14. God of the Sea who sent the monster to harass the people of Ethiopia in punishment for their queen's boast that she was more beautiful than the Ocean nymphs.
15. One of the Gorgons.
16. King of the gods who found his way into Danae's tower in the form of a shower of gold, and became the father of Perseus.

● Choose the right name from the list below to fit each description.

Athene	Danae	Cepheus
Zeus	Medusa	Perseus
Hippodameia	Polydectes	
Cassiopeia	Stheno	
Andromeda	Gorgons	
Acrisius	Grey ladies	
Poseidon	Euryale	

You will see pictures of these scenes on pages 110–112.

Research Into Legends

● In groups pool all the legends you already know. See which legends are familiar to everyone in the group and which are known by only one or two people. Try to remember stories you might have been told or read lower down the school or at Junior school.

● Alternatively:
1. Find some collections of legends, preferably from a culture that you do not know, from the library, and choose one which appeals to you.
2. Each member of the group then writes out the legend they find most appealing.
3. Then pick out the names of all the characters involved and arrange them in alphabetical order.
4. Write an explanation of who they are all related to and what part they play in the story/episode.
5. Show the list of characters to another member of the group and invite them to reconstruct the story.
6. Compare the reconstruction with your original version.

LEGENDS AND MYTHS

● Use the list of characters which follows, to reconstruct and write your own version of a legend – one which comes from India.

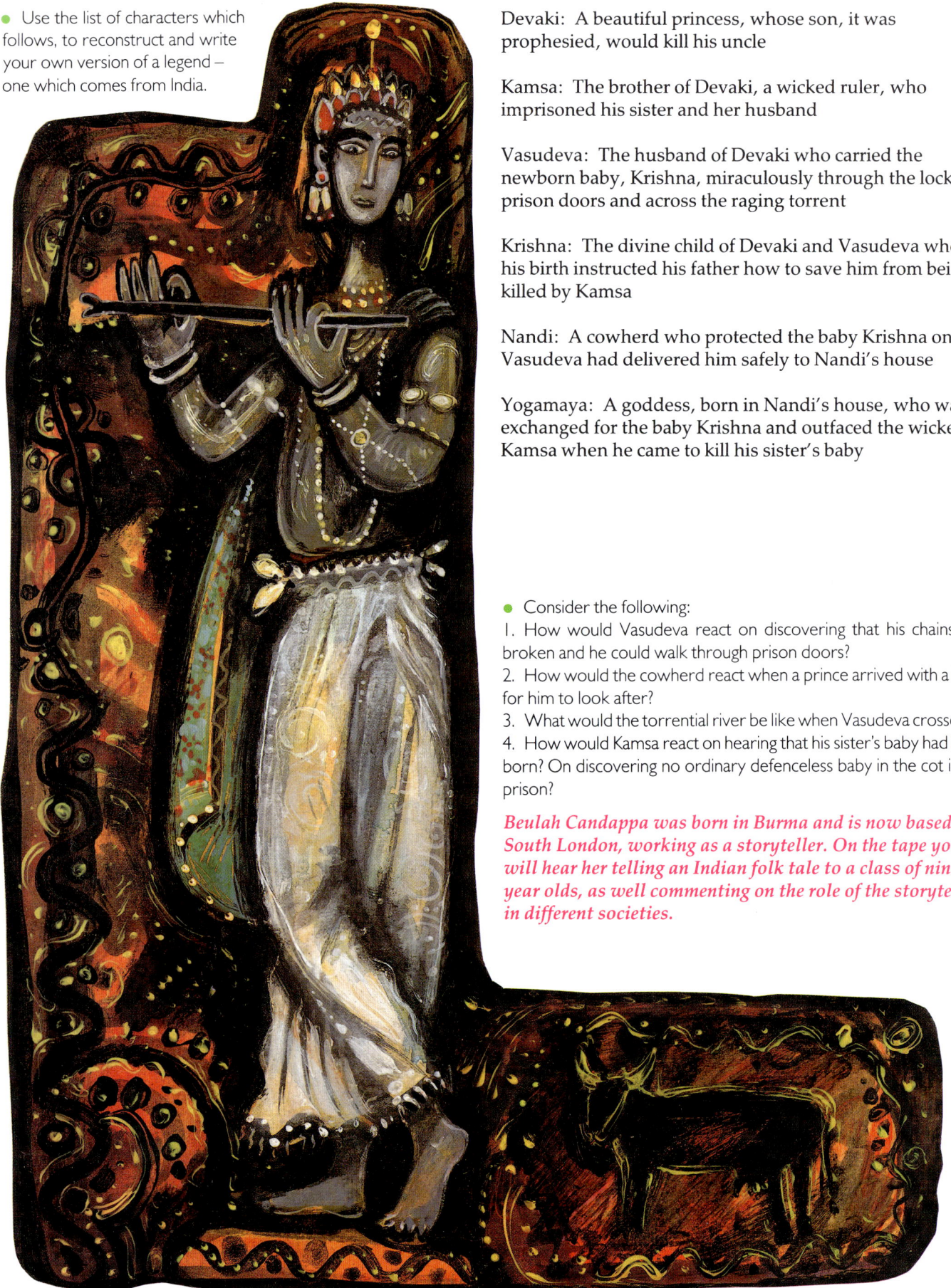

Devaki: A beautiful princess, whose son, it was prophesied, would kill his uncle

Kamsa: The brother of Devaki, a wicked ruler, who imprisoned his sister and her husband

Vasudeva: The husband of Devaki who carried the newborn baby, Krishna, miraculously through the locked prison doors and across the raging torrent

Krishna: The divine child of Devaki and Vasudeva who at his birth instructed his father how to save him from being killed by Kamsa

Nandi: A cowherd who protected the baby Krishna once Vasudeva had delivered him safely to Nandi's house

Yogamaya: A goddess, born in Nandi's house, who was exchanged for the baby Krishna and outfaced the wicked Kamsa when he came to kill his sister's baby

● Consider the following:
1. How would Vasudeva react on discovering that his chains had broken and he could walk through prison doors?
2. How would the cowherd react when a prince arrived with a baby for him to look after?
3. What would the torrential river be like when Vasudeva crossed it?
4. How would Kamsa react on hearing that his sister's baby had been born? On discovering no ordinary defenceless baby in the cot in the prison?

Beulah Candappa was born in Burma and is now based in South London, working as a storyteller. On the tape you will hear her telling an Indian folk tale to a class of nine year olds, as well commenting on the role of the storyteller in different societies.

Creating a Legend

So far in this section many themes have been suggested which are included in actual legends from different cultures (eg the list of headlines for the Perseus legend).

● Try this do-it-yourself kit, working in a pair or a group, to make a legend. You do not need to use all the components, but will have to think of good ways of nailing/splicing/glueing them together convincingly!

A captive princess
A courageous hero
Gods or goddesses who help mortals
Magic aids to invisibility, distance travelling etc.
Wicked relative
A distant location or goal
A substitution of one person for another

A powerful enemy
A difficult task or challenge
Someone in disguise, possibly a god or goddess
Special weapons
A terrible punishment
A prohibition
Monsters or dragons or giants
Mountains, caverns or the underworld

Another approach is to use a recent episode of a serial or soap opera you know and turn that into a legend. Ordinary men and women should become heroes and princesses and ordinary locations should be transformed into something more 'legendary'.

Creating a Myth

You may remember that a myth is a 'purely fictitious narrative usually involving supernatural persons and embodying some popular idea concerning natural or historical phenomena'.

You have seen how myths attempt to explain why something is as it is. This may be because unsophisticated people do not have the scientific explanation, or it may be that something happened or was created so long ago that the true explanation for its existence is no longer known. Science fiction writers like to imagine a future world which does not understand the ruins of our present civilisation.

The next two activities involve myth making which take a standpoint in time and look back, firstly from our present era to the past and secondly from a future age (from their viewpoint) to the past which is our present.

The third story, looks forward to the present from the past.

There already exist many local myths which 'explained' something special about the place to the primitive people who lived there. The strange hill called the Wrekin was said to have been a spadeful of earth dumped there by a giant who had intended to bury the town of Shrewsbury but missed his way. Other giants are said to have hurled rocks, and two prominent crags were described as 'Robin Hood's Stride'.

Options

● Select some local landmark, or even simply a strange name and invent a myth to explain it.

● The people who lived in the Dark Ages thought the ruins of Roman buildings had been constructed by giants. What aspects of our civilisation, if they survived, might puzzle a future race? Try to think of a myth to explain something like one of the following:

a fridge freezer
a supermarket trolley
a drivein car wash

children's playground equipment
an underground train system
a sports' centre

Try telling your myth to someone else in the group and see if they can guess what is being accounted for/described from a future viewpoint.

LEGENDS AND MYTHS

In this story you are sharing the experiences of two tenth century knights, who are waiting to try and kill a dragon which has already destroyed many others. It is said to rush across a particularly spooky stretch of moorland, where time stands still . . .

The Dragon

The night blew in the short grass on the moor; there was no other motion. It had been years since a single bird had flown by in the great blind shell of sky. Long ago a few small stones had simulated life when they crumbled and fell into dust. Now only the night moved in the souls of the two men bent by their lonely fire in the wilderness; darkness pumped quietly in their veins and ticked silently in their temples and their wrists.

Firelight fled up and down their wild faces and welled in their eyes in orange tatters. They listened to each other's faint, cool breathing and the lizard blink of their eyelids. At last, one man poked the fire with his sword.

"Don't, idiot; you'll give us away!"

"No matter," said the second man. "The dragon can smell us miles off, anyway. God's breath, it's cold. I wish I was back at the castle."

"It's death, not sleep, we're after . . ."

"Why? Why? The dragon never sets foot in the town!"

"Quiet, fool! He eats men travelling alone from our town to the next!"

"Let them be eaten and let us get home!"

"Wait now; listen!"

The two men froze.

They waited a long time, but there was only the shake of their horses' nervous skin-like black velvet tambourines jingling the silver stirrup buckles, softly, softly.

"Ah." The second man sighed. "What a land of nightmares. Everything happens here. Someone blows out the sun; it's night. And then, and *then*, oh, God, listen! This dragon, they say his eyes are fire. His breath a white gas; you can see him burn across the dark lands. He runs with sulphur and thunder and kindles the grass. Sheep panic and die insane. Women deliver forth monsters. The dragon's fury is such that tower walls shake back to dust. His victims, at sunrise, are strewn hither and thither on the hills. How many knights, I ask, have gone for this monster and failed, even as we shall fail?"

"Enough of that!"

"More than enough! Out here in this desolation I cannot tell what year this is!"

"Nine hundred years since the Nativity."

"No, no," whispered the second man, eyes shut. "On this moor is no Time, is only Forever. I feel if I ran back on the road the town would be gone, the people yet unborn, things changed, the castles unquarried from the rocks, the timbers still uncut from the forests; don't ask how I know, the moor knows, and tells me. And here we sit alone in the land of the fire dragon, God save us!"

"Be you afraid, then gird on your armour!"

"What use? The dragon runs from nowhere; we cannot guess its home. It vanishes in fog, we know not where it goes. Aye, on with our armour, we'll die well-dressed."

Half into his silver corselet, the second man stopped again and turned his head.

Across the dim country, full of night and nothingness from the heart of the moor itself, the wind sprang full of dust from the clocks that used dust for telling time. There were black suns burning in the heart of this new wind and a million burnt leaves shaken from some autumn tree beyond the horizon. This wind melted landscapes, lengthened bones like white wax, made the blood roil and thicken to a muddy deposit in the brain. The wind was a thousand souls dying and all time confused and in transit. It was a fog inside of a mist inside of a darkness, and this place was no man's place and there was no year or hour at all, but only these men in a faceless emptiness of sudden frost, storm, and white thunder which moved behind the great falling pane of green glass that was the lightning. A squall of rain drenched the turf, all faded away until there was unbreathing hush and the two men waiting alone with their warmth in a cool season.

"There," whispered the first man. "Oh, *there* . . ."

Miles off, rushing with a great chant and a roar – the dragon.

In silence, the men buckled on their armour and mounted their horses. The midnight wilderness was split by a monstrous gushing as the dragon roared nearer, nearer; its flashing yellow glare spurted above a hill and then, fold on fold of dark body, distantly seen, therefore indistinct, flowed over that hill and plunged vanishing into a valley.

"Quick!"

They spurred their horses forward to a small hollow.

"This is where it passes!"

They seized their lances with mailed fists, and blinded their horses by flipping the visors down over their eyes

"Lord!"

"Yes, let us use His name."

On the instant, the dragon rounded a hill. Its monstrous amber eye fed on them, fired their armour in red glints and glitters. With a terrible wailing cry and a grinding rush it flung itself forward.

"Mercy, God!"

The lance struck under the unlidded yellow eye, buckled, tossed the man through the air. The dragon hit, spilled him over, down, ground him under. Passing, the black brunt of its shoulder smashed the remaining horse and rider a hundred feet against the side of a boulder, wailing, wailing, the dragon shrieking, the fire all about, around, under it, a pink, yellow, orange sun-fire with great soft plumes of blinding smoke.

"Did you see it?" cried a voice. "Just like I told you!"

"The same! The same! A knight in armour, by the Lord Harry! We *hit* him!"

"You goin' to stop?"

"Did once; found nothing. Don't like to stop on this moor. I get the willies. Got a *feel*, it has."

"But we hit *something*!"

"Gave him plenty of whistle; chap wouldn't budge."

A steaming blast cut the mist aside.

"We'll make Stokely on time. More coal, eh, Fred?"

Another whistle shook dew from the empty sky. The night train, in fire and fury, shot through a gully, up a rise, and vanished over cold earth, towards the north, leaving black smoke and steam to dissolve in the numbed air minutes after it had passed and gone for ever.

Ray Bradbury, *The Dragon*

Discussion

1. Who are the two people talking in the first part of the story?
2. What happens to them?
3. Who are the people talking at the end of the story?
4. Where are they and what are they doing?
5. Now that you have read the story, can you explain what the dragon actually was?

● Using the headings below explore how the writer builds up the contrasts between past and present by adding to the list already started for you.

Old fashioned words and phrases: Modern words and phrases:

'Women deliver forth monsters' 'chap wouldn't budge'
'his silver corselet'

The paragraph beginning 'across the dim country' is intended to blur the reader's sense of time, so that the present can break through into the past in a moment when time stands still.

Using the Same Technique

● Try writing your own science fiction story where in a time warp, people from the past visit our present and try to explain it in their own terms, by building a myth.

You might use any of these myths:

giants;

angels;

monsters;

cities/countries sinking beneath the sea.

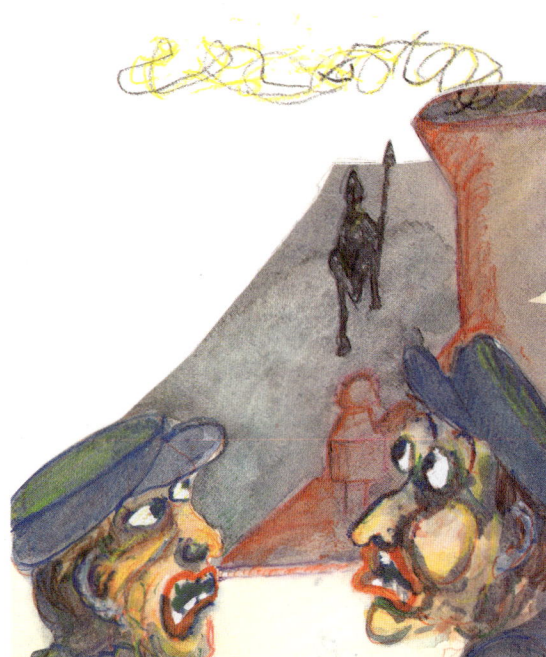

PICTURE STORY

In this section you are asked to think about stories encapsulated in pictures.

● Study the pictures and read the commentary, and then use the questions to stimulate your own discussion on the pictures.

The illustrations on this page come from a series of life-sized colour drawings by a Victorian artist called Edward Burne-Jones.

By studying the three illustrated here you should begin to see how a single image can illustrate more than a single instant in a story. A snapshot shows a suspended moment in time but a carefully thought out and constructed painting should offer much more for detailed 'reading'.

Before he attempts his impossible mission Perseus visits three Grey Ladies (female spirits) who provide him with the winged sandals which will make the journey to the Gorgon's lair possible, the helmet of invisibility so that he can approach Medusa unseen, and a magical bag in which to put the Gorgon's head.

(If these seem childish and 'fairy tale' to you, just think of the episode at the beginning of each of the old James Bond stories where Bond is equipped with amazing devices – exploding pens, specially armed cars, suitcases etc – to help him in his mission!)

The patch of ground on which the nymphs are standing is reflective in just the same way as the mirrored shield of Perseus will reflect the Gorgon's head so that he does not have to look directly into her eyes and be turned to stone as a result.

If you look at the last of these pictures you will see that a mirror is being used again, for Perseus to show the head to his bride, without turning her to stone. Here the mirror is water too, this time in a bowl of a fountain or well. You will discover that images like this can be used to link together a piece of writing just as well as in a visual context.

In the second picture Perseus kills the monster which is going to devour Andromeda. Instead of a large solid kind of whale or hippo, the artist has created a kind of nightmare monster of interlinking coils which would squeeze the life out of its victim. In some versions of the story the monster is turned to stone when Perseus takes the Gorgon's head out of his bag and holds it up. Here he is trying to slice it in half with his sword. Why do you think the conflict has been presented in this way?

PICTURE STORY

The third illustration from the series shows the married couple, their hands entwined (a symbol of marriage) above an octagonal well basin, which could suggest the eternal circle of a ring. The emphasis on geometry and formal completion helps to create the atmosphere of calm and order. Even the possible threat of the Gorgon's head is defused when it is almost lost amid the leaves of a fruitful tree. The leaves and the water are both quite still – why?

The three pictures all convey a different mood, appropriate to the point of the story which the viewer has reached. Another parallel between writing and pictures can be seen, as we would easily become tired of a long story if it were in the same mood all the time. Moments of great drama or excitement become more effective by the contrast of a quieter episode in-between. The nymphs seem calm themselves although Perseus is more anxious as his task is still to be fulfilled. The surging lines of the background hills in the first picture seem to suggest the onward movement, out of this picture and into the next episode which will inevitably take place.

Reading Pictures

1. How do you react differently to Andromeda in the third picture from the second? Why is this?
2. What effect do you think is achieved when we see the wings on the sandals appear to be growing out of Perseus' ankles in the second picture?
3. Describe the shape of the rocks in the second picture. What difficulties do they seem to suggest for Perseus?
4. Look at the marble in the third picture. How is it different from the rocks in the second?
5. What do you think the artist is suggesting about the different relationship of a man and the natural world in each?
6. What would you say the different textures of Perseus' armour, the girl's flesh and the monster's body suggest about the role of each?

The artist chose particular points in the action of the story to illustrate. In the same way a poem might target a significant point in the development of a relationship or a story and explore the emotions of the people involved at that particular instant.

Visual Presentations

● Basing your choice on any legend or story choose two or three moments you might illustrate.
For each one explain:
which characters would be illustrated;
where they would be standing in relation to each other;
what the background would be;
what mood the colouring or shapes of the picture might suggest;
any other important details which would refer to other parts of the story.

Stories From Your Own Life

● Choose one or two photographs of yourself or friends which suggest a longer story. For each one write a few paragraphs describing:
where you were;
who was with you;
what the mood was;
what had happened just before;
what had happened just afterwards;
what you were saying to each other.

● When you consider it, it may not be necessary to include the actual pictures at all, if you described them adequately in words, but simply to link the passages based on them as another kind of personal narrative. Any of these titles would do –
"Moments from the Life of . . ."
"Pictures from an Album"
"Photographs in Words"
"Three Episodes in the Story of . . ."

● Bring in some of your own photos and be prepared to talk about them in an interesting way. The most interesting thing about every individual is their own life story.

DON'T include irrelevant detail;
leave explanations half complete;
miss out names of places or people;
forget to explain facts your listeners wouldn't know about your family and friends;
hint at jokes without explaining them;
use phrases like 'there was this . . .'

DO explain clearly the occasion on which the photo was taken;
give names and details for all the people shown;
explain why this was a special occasion you wanted to treasure;
explain what happened before or after this picture.

Can you explain these two contradictory facts?
1. When someone produces a packet of photos, everyone else will cluster round to see them.
2. Listening to someone describing what is on their photos can be incredibly boring:
"And that's my uncle at the side of the chalet . . ."
"I didn't manage to get all of the dog on . . ."
"Well it does look as though it's leaning sideways but . . ."

HEROES

On the tape you will hear students talking about heroes. How far do you agree with their comments?

Assembling Ideas in Note Form

● Draw up a list of 'heroes'. If you are stuck, think of anyone of whom the phrase 'my hero' might be used.

Arrange the list into two columns headed 'Real' and 'Fiction'.

See if the heroes fall into different categories in each list, eg:

Real:	Fictional:
Sporting heroes	Science fiction heroes
Media personalities	Legendary characters
Famous people	Folk heroes

Compare your list with your friends and see how many names occur more than once on different lists.

Write a brief list of 'qualities' which describes every one of the people on your list in general terms.

Repromaster 29 allows you to consider the role of the 'hero' in more detail, providing role-play activites, ideas for 'A Hero Poster' and 'Media Heroes'.

At the outset of this section a list was compiled of people who might qualify for the title of 'Hero'. It included real and fictitious people, from the past and the present. Since then the focus has been on ancient and legendary heroes, but the idea is still alive. We still admire and revere certain people for something special which seems to set them apart from ordinary people. If you still have the list you made from the beginning of this unit, you will only need to start at 5 below.

Your Own Hero Tale

A Royal person has announced a new award for bravery and humanity to be given to any adult or child whose friends propose them. The proposal has to describe what the person did that seemed so outstanding.

1. Working in groups, invent a character and an incident in which that character behaved with courage or self-sacrifice which you think would qualify them to receive a special award for heroism from a Royal person.

2. Write out the account of the incident with the explanation of the person's qualities displayed. You need several copies of what you have written, one for each working group in the class.

Here is an example which a fourth year class proposed:

I propose that this award goes to the bravest and most heroic dog I have seen.

The dog was walking with his owner by a river when it heard and saw a young girl at the edge of the river playing. She slipped and fell onto the ice. The ice began to crack around her. She could not move as she was unconscious. The owner of the dog ran for help, leaving the dog behind. Passers by saw the dog run down to the girl and try to drag her up to the bank, risking its own life. One of them ran down and pulled the girl to safety, but the ice would not hold any longer, and the dog went under and died. We can not recover the dog until spring. The owner should collect the reward for the dog.

3. Circulate the copies around all the groups in the class so that you can read about the person proposed by each group.

4. Decide which person you would give the award to (each group is excluded from awarding their own candidate with the heroism medal – it works out quite fairly!)

5. Write the name of each person cited on the board and then collect the votes from each group to see who gets the award.

Heroes and the Media

You now have some ideas for your own modern hero story and if you look at newspapers you should see how it could be presented in an interesting way.

● Make the reader build up the story of the person's courage or self-sacrifice from several separate newspaper/magazine articles.

1. A front page spread when the incident first hits the news – if it involves something really dramatic like hostages, hijacking, drugs etc.

2. A second day report from the hospital where victims are recovering (if appropriate).

3. Eyewitness accounts from victims or survivors, given in interview.

4. Background information collected later about the 'hero's' family and friends, their childhood or personal or professional life.

5. A later feature on the awards ceremony.

Do the media always get it right? Perhaps the person about whom all the fuss was made wasn't the right person after all? Maybe someone was beavering away in the background and quietly sloped away once the camera crews arrived.

Another important issue is the way the media treat heroes. It is sometimes remarked that television on-the-spot interviewers can be amazingly insensitive to the feelings of someone who has just emerged from a crisis and may be in pain, or from a contest and may wish to unwind after the effort needed to win. You should be able to provoke many questions from the next pair of improvisations.

The Big Interview

● Present a radio or TV interview at the scene of a crisis or a contest where someone has been outstandingly 'heroic'.
Create a particularly insensitive interviewer who is bound to cause audience resentment and greater sympathy for the person interviewed.

The Inside Story

● Set up an improvisation where local people meet for a gossip in the area where the hero has come from, or the crisis occurred. Through the conversation we gradually learn that the stories on the television weren't anything like the truth and the credit should really go to . . . (The strange tale of Zeynel Celik, told on pages 61–65, tells a similar story.)

The Current Affairs Discussion

● You will probably need to write a script for this serious discussion where prominent people consider the idea of heroism and the damage which publicity, particularly ill-directed publicity, can do. You could tape this as a radio programme or present it live as a 'television' discussion.

All the heroes you have thought of so far in this section have been admirable people; you might have been proud to have done what they did.

However, there remains the hero, in the sense of the main character, who fits the description of 'the person you love to hate'. Many soap operas contain characters who have become popular although they are very unprincipled wicked people. An eighteenth century nobleman, Don Juan, has become a byword for a man whose aim is to have as many women as possible. There are several plays in which he is the main character, and he is the 'superman' of Bernard Shaw's **Man and Superman** *as he claims to do more for women than any conventional husband could do. He can free them from the tyranny of marriage in which they lose their property and identity and become domestic slaves.*

The Anti-Hero

● Brainstorm in your group to produce a list of characters, in real life or fiction, who are men or women we love to hate. Then answer these questions for each character to see if you can build up a picture of the anti-hero.
1. What is so hateful about them?
2. What part do they play in the story to which they belong?
3. Are they universally hated or is there someone who loves them?
4. Do they go against some particular value in their own society?
5. Is there a section of society where they would be welcomed?
6. What differences do you think there are between an anti-hero and a villain?

● Use the blueprint you have produced to write an episode or a whole story which centres on a person you love to hate. Try to show what their motives are, or why they might be hated. You may find it helpful to use one of the following settings:
company rivalry in the modern business world;
a military setting in some past war;
a science fiction scenario;
the world of technological or university research;
a show business setting.

IN THE FAMILY

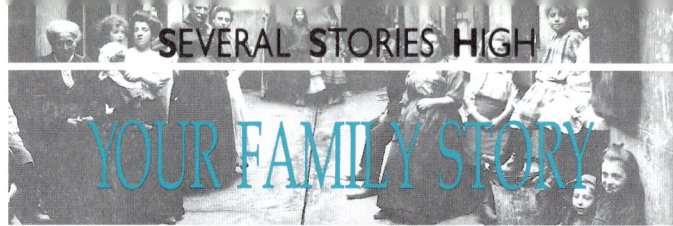

Stories which are very short can pack a great deal of punch, but there are times when we feel we can enjoy a really long story.

● Begin to think of the problems you would tackle in writing a really long story – which of the following will be the most difficult to solve?
1. Thinking of enough ideas to keep the plot going.
2. Keeping track of all the characters involved.
3. Giving individual identities to all the characters.
4. Preventing the background and setting from becoming boring.
5. Deciding which parts to write in detail and which parts to compress.

Many of these problems can be solved if you choose to write about several generations of one family, particularly if the family has lived through an interesting period of history or different members of the family have come from different countries. A very popular format in television is the 'mini series' which frequently follows the fortunes of several generations and may well have been based on a very long best-selling paperback novel.
1) It is easier to follow a long story if some of the characters become very familiar or if there are family likenesses or relationships to connect several characters into a group.
2) It is easier to follow a long time sequence if it can be related to some of the major events in world history which you are already familiar with.

Research

All families have a history which presents us with interesting possibilities. On the tape you can hear students talking about their own family memories and histories. The tape finishes with Julie Fullarton discussing her Scots/Irish ancestry and the opportunities for building stories by using your own background.

● Try asking at home to see if your own real family could provide you with some interesting material for parts of a long family story. See if you can find answers to any of these questions –
1. Do your parents come from the area in which they now live?
2. Have any of your grandparents come from a different part of the country/the world?
3. What trades or professions have been followed by people in your family?
4. Were these followed from choice/by tradition/from necessity?
5. Are there any outstanding or remarkable people who have become something of a tradition in your family?
6. In what ways is your life different from that of your parents/grandparents/great grandparents?
7. Are there any particular places or institutions associated with your family?
8. Are there any family traditions/possessions/heirlooms which are unusual?
9. With the help of your parents/grandparents could you draw up a family tree? (See more on the importance of the family tree on page 134.)

● Use this material to write a whole story or an episode. The example on the opposite page was written by a fourth year.

Richard gives an account of his grandfather's life.

"My Grandfather, Maurice Ziff"

My grandfather's name was Maurice Ziff. Apart from his family and friends, painting and creating art were the most important things in his life. It was no release to him. It wasn't a way of expressing his feelings, either. For the best part of his life, from about twenty-five to seventy-four he painted and drew. He was an artist, one of the most underrated ever.

When he left school he was fourteen and the First World War was still on. When the war was over, he went into his father's trade, which was at the time upholstery. This he did not enjoy, but was extremely good at, and at this time, around 1920, they exported fine furniture and dining room suites all over the country and Europe. My grandfather used to tell me that in those days he would come home and draw or paint, often looking through comics and boys magazines. He always told me though that art was never a release. He always enjoyed it but he said everything had to be done with 'hoghtspu' – yiddish for a good heart.

About 1925 my grandfather sent off some artwork to an all-boys magazine-comic, because at this time his father did not need him in the shop. After a lengthy interview, my grandfather was accepted as a comic illustrator for 'Rocket'. At first he enjoyed this, but as illustrators always have to work to schedules and deadlines, it was forced on him. The editors could obviously see he had talent, but as he was young, they planned to keep him there a while. At this time my grandfather was about twenty-one and was beginning to get fed up of his job in the illustrating business. It wasn't that the work was too much for him, it was that he much preferred to create paintings in his own time, not drawings to someone else's schedule. Also, when drawing for the comics, the writers of the stories, westerns I think they were, always got all the credit. My grandfather was paid a small wage and did most of the work for this popular comic.

In 1931 he left the company producing the comic to help his father again. Soon his father retired, and having only one sister, quite a small family for those days, he was left in charge of the business. My grandmother always said that this was a waste of time. He should, she said, have become a professional artist and sold the business, against his father's wishes. He had the business all through the War, in which he served in the Home Guard and injured his left wrist in the blitz.

By about 1950 slowly the upholstery business died away. My grandfather said that there was just no demand left for it and in 1950 he sold the business. This was when he started seriously to paint. He built up a magnificent portfolio and moved to London. He had been living in Reading. In 1964 my grandparents moved into a flat in Hendon where they lived for the rest of their lives. My grandfather was continually trying to get certain galleries in London to hold an exhibition for him and one of his artist friends. For about thirty years until he died, he was constantly phoning around and organising shows for himself and others.

Sadly his wish never came true. The only people who recognised his true talent, were his immediate family and friends. He was a man who was never downhearted. All the time he made jokes and he also made others happy. Before he died he travelled the world and probably the last thing I heard him say before he went into hospital was that he was satisfied with his life – he couldn't complain. On the third of February 1983 my grandfather died. He died because he was too old to have a kidney machine – younger people needed them more. His love of art is what I will always remember him for, along with his love for family and friends.

The reason I wrote this was that he was the person I knew who was most dedicated to a certain subject. I could have written about the other topic, but I didn't. This is for him – my grandad who loved life and art – art to him was his life.

Richard

● When using material from your own family for narrative you will need to decide:

1. Which format to use (personal reminiscences, third person narrative or playscripts).

2. Whether to write a complete story or just one episode. It may be an idea to summarise the whole story and pinpoint the particular life or episode you will write about.

3. Who are you writing for? Will this piece be mostly treasured in your own family, or do you need to explain to a wider audience some of your own background? Things which are very familiar to you and your family may be strange and unusual to an outsider.

Follow this pattern of choices:

1. Material for a story

Ask in the family about an interesting relative or special memorable event	or	think what you can remember/already know about a special relative

2. Arrangement of material

select one episode to concentrate on	or	write a series of episodes	or	write an overall memory of the person

3. Format of story

straight narrative with description and conversation	or	you telling about the event/person	or	a play/ filmscript

FAMILY LANGUAGE

In the next extract, Paule Marshall, a black American writer, tells how important her personal experiences were, not only for the material of her writing, but especially for the language by which her mother and her mother's friends expressed themselves.

Some years ago, when I was teaching a graduate seminar in fiction at Columbia University, a well known male novelist visited my class to speak on his development as a writer. In discussing his formative years, he didn't realise it but he seriously endangered his life by remarking that women writers are luckier than those of his sex because they usually spend so much time as children around their mothers and their mothers' friends in the kitchen.

What did he say that for? The women students immediately forgot about being in awe of him and began readying their attack for the question and answer period later on. Even I bristled. There again was that awful image of women locked away from the world in the kitchen with only each other to talk to, and their daughters locked in with them.

But my guest wasn't really being sexist or trying to be provocative or even spoiling for a fight. What he meant – when he got round to explaining himself more fully – was that, given the way children are (or were) raised in our society, with little girls kept closer to home and their mothers, the woman writer stands a better chance of being exposed, while growing up, to the kind of talk that goes on among women, more often than not in the kitchen; and that this experience gives her an edge over her male counterpart by instilling in her an appreciation for ordinary speech.

It was clear that my guest lecturer attached great importance to this, which is understandable. Common speech and the plain, workaday words that make it up are, after all, the stock in trade of some of the best fiction writers. They are the principal means by which characters in a novel or story reveal themselves and give voice sometimes to profound feelings and complex ideas about themselves and the world. Perhaps the proper measure of a writer's talent is skill in rendering everyday speech – when it is appropriate to the story – as well as the ability to tap, to exploit, the beauty, poetry and wisdom it often contains . . .

. . . He didn't know it, but he was essentially describing my experience as a little girl. I grew up among poets. Now they didn't look like poets – whatever that breed is supposed to look like. Nothing about them suggested that poetry was their calling. They were just a group of ordinary housewives and mothers, my mother included, who dressed in a way (shapeless house-dresses, dowdy felt hats and long, dark, solemn coats) that made it impossible for me to imagine they had ever been young.

Nor did they do what poets were supposed to do – spend their days in an attic room writing verses. They never put pen to paper except to write occasionally to their relatives in Barbados. ''I take my pen in hand hoping these few lines will find you in health as they leave me fair for the time being,'' was the way their letters invariably began. Rather, their day was spent ''scrubbing floor,'' as they described the work they did.

Several mornings a week these unknown bards would put an apron and a pair of old house shoes in a shopping bag and take the train or streetcar from our section of Brooklyn out to Flatbush. There, those who didn't have steady jobs would wait on certain designated corners for the white housewives in the neighbourhood to come along and bargain with them over pay for a day's work cleaning their houses. This was the ritual even in the winter . . .

. . . They had taken the standard English taught them in the primary schools of Barbados and transformed it into an idiom, an instrument that more adequately described them – changing around the syntax and imposing their own rhythm and accent so that the sentences were more pleasing to their ears. They added the few African sounds and words that had survived, such as the derisive suck-teeth sound and the word "yam", meaning to eat. And to make it more vivid, more in keeping with their expressive quality, they brought to bear a raft of metaphors, parables, Biblical quotations, sayings and the like:

"The sea ain' got no back door," they would say, meaning that it wasn't like a house where if there was a fire you could run out the back. Meaning that it was not to be trifled with, and meaning perhaps in a larger sense that man should treat all of nature with caution and respect.

"I has read hell by heart and called every generation blessed!" They sometimes went in for hyperbole.

A woman expecting a baby was never said to be pregnant. They never used that word. Rather, she was "in the way" or, better yet, "tumbling big". "Guess who I butt up on in the market the other day tumbling big again!"

And a woman with a reputation of being too free with her sexual favours was known in their book as a "thoroughfare" – the sense of men like a steady stream of cars moving up and down the road of her life. Or she might be dubbed " a free-bee," which was my favourite of the two. I liked the image it conjured up of a woman scandalous perhaps but independent, who flitted from one flower to another in a garden of male beauties, sampling their nectar, taking her pleasure at will, the roles reversed.

And nothing, no matter how beautiful, was ever described as simply beautiful. It was always "beautiful-ugly": the beautiful-ugly dress, the beautiful-ugly house, beautiful-ugly car. Why the word "ugly", I used to wonder, when the thing they were referring to was so beautiful, and they knew it. Why the antonym, the contradiction, the linking of opposites? It used to puzzle me greatly as a child.

Paule Marshall, *Merle*

Your Reactions to Paule Marshall's Views

● In pairs compare your opinions. For each of the following statements decide:
1. Whether this is an accurate summary of the ideas in the extract.
2. Whether you personally agree with it.

1. The male novelist was deliverately 'stirring' the women students by suggesting they had an advantage over male writers.
2. He implied that women were removed from real life by staying in the home.
3. He thought that everyday language was most important in writing fiction.
4. Paule Marshall's mother and her friends did not look like poets.
5. The young girl was fascinated by the words and phrases used by the Caribbean women to describe everyday events.

A Writer's Notebook

"Perhaps the proper measure of a writer's talent is skill in rendering everyday speech – when it is appropriate to the story – as well as the ability to tap, to exploit, the beauty, poetry and wisdom it often contains."

Often it is the dialogue in student writing which seems unconvincing, more like people talking in a book than in real life.

In using your own personal and family experiences for your writing do not forget the importance of the language people use. You may already be aware of certain uses of words and phrases in your family which are unusual.

● Use a page of your notebook to jot down any interesting snatches of conversation or words or phrases that you hear over the next week. It may help to use a grid format like this:

Date	Speaker	Words spoken

How to Use the Notes

● Compare your notes with others in the class by tidying them up and presenting them all in a display.
● Use any of the snippets as the basis for a short improvisation.
● Write a short conversation which might be overheard in your family. Try to make it as convincing as possible using your notes of what people actually said.
● Write a dramatic scene involving some profound feeling which still uses everyday language,
eg someone reveals that they love someone else;
　　someone discovers they have been betrayed by someone they trusted;
　　someone remembers the death of someone very close to them.

PERSONAL IDENTITY

If you find out about your grandparents you may soon discover quite a variety of influences which are shaping your own personality.

● Do you know:
1. The names of all four of your grandparents?
2. Where they each came from?
3. Whether they moved to another area?
4. What aspects of your own character have been described as being typical of one or the other side of the family?

Comfort Herself

The following extract describes the moment when Comfort, a girl of mixed race discovers a letter from her Ghanaian father in her mother's handbag, after her mother's sudden death in a road accident.

A) . . . a sausage of blue paper, an airmail letter rolled up small.

Comfort's throat felt tight and her hands were shaking as she unfolded it, as if she was doing something wrong. But the only wrong thing was being up in the bedroom during the day and that was only Ivyside Court wrong. The letter was from Mante and addressed to Margaret Kwatey-Jones in the flat at Brixton.

"Kwatey-Jones," Comfort murmured softly. When had Margaret dropped the Kwatey, even at the nursery she had been just Comfort Jones. The letter had been written eight years before and Comfort's eyes skimmed quickly, looking for her own name. "As for Comfort, it would be better if she came out to Ghana where she belongs. My mother and sisters will take care of her for the time being. As you know such family arrangements are common here and Comfort is Ghanaian after all. A child gets her blood from her mother but her spirit comes from her father. I will send her ticket as soon as I can."

"A child gets her blood from her mother but her spirit comes from her father," Comfort murmured to herself. She hardly knew what it meant but a strange excitement fluttered in the pit of her stomach and then spread through her whole body. As if her spirit was singing.

Comfort Jones you have a long way to go.

Comfort Kwatey-Jones.

Now she knew what she had to do. She had to write to Mante but it would be better not to tell anybody, Comfort thought.

After she has been in Ghana she starts to keep a diary so that she can remember her life in England until that time.

B) Comfort sat on the lorry step where Esi could not see her and untied her diary. 'If I don't go back soon I shall never go back,' she wrote biting her biscuit, 'because I have already missed school for yonks and forgotten everything and Grandmother wants me to stay for always because I write better than anybody else in the compound and add figures quicker and help her with the lorry and because I'm her granddaughter, child of Mante, and her eyes and ears and all that stuff and it's ace looking after the stall and shouting out loud and doing what I like and magic trading for myself and bringing something home and not going to school which I never liked all that much and I've got my own grandmother wanting me to stay so much which is the other best thing in the world.'

Comfort looked up then and shouted at a woman passing, "Buy my soap, pretty lady, this soap will make your skin as soft and sweet as frangipani." The book-man let out a high pitched snort of laughter at such cheek but the woman tossed her head and did not stop and Comfort went back to her diary.

'I like it in Wanwangeri with drumming and dancing every day and pink dust flying and feast days too, so nearly every day is a party and when Bolo died, which was because of spirits or ghosts or because Obodai's other wife was jealous of such a beautiful child (nobody here reckons much on germs) and everybody cried because everybody was feeling the same thing all together and everybody cries much more than England and they laugh and joke much more too and the chief in Akwapawa settles all quarrels and everybody has to keep the custom which is lots and lots of rules but everybody here belongs to everybody and everybody lives every day as it comes and every week as it comes and nobody thinks about tomorrow or next year much and that's the difference but my roots are in England.'

Finally she decides to go back to her English grandparents. In the Kentish village where they live Comfort had met a girl whose family had always lived in that place.

C) Comfort stared up at the grey church wall blotched with green and orange lichen, there were nests of swallows under the roof. Did the swallows come back year after year to the same place, a nest of their own, she wondered. The church was part Norman, Normans had come from France, immigrants, Grandad said. Like everything in Penfold it had stood where it was for a long time. Round white clouds like cherubs billowed across the sky and there were bright green paths mown in the feathery grass where people could walk between the graves. The church was on a slight mound and the Romney marshes stretched away like an endless green ocean. It had been under the sea at one time, Grandad said, it was man-made land drained by the Romans with hundreds of dykes criss-crossing it in straight black lines and grey roads raised on banks above the grass.

"You can sit on my great-granny's grave if you like," Lettie said extending her arm to the marble edge in hostess style. "Grass might be damp."

"Thanks," said Comfort. There was a headstone made of speckly imitation marble with *Letitia Stamp* and the date of her birth and death in gold-filled letters and lots of bright green chips like bath salts.

"Saves weeding, saves cutting the grass," Lettie explained flattening the green chips with the palm of her hand to accommodate the jar of moon daisies. "My great-granny went to school in a white pinny, same school," she nodded her head towards the deserted building. "We got this photo, *Letitia* same as me," her eyes turned to Comfort curiously. "Where are your great-grannies then? You got four, everybody has."

"Well, there's one in Harrogate, I think," Comfort said startled by the question and feeling it shameful not to know for certain but nobody had ever talked to her of great-grandmothers. There must be two in Africa.
Geraldine Kaye, *Comfort Herself*

Looking Closer

● Find short quotations from each of the extracts from *Comfort Herself* which show the following facts –

Extract A:

1. Comfort's father thought *his* family gave Comfort her spirit.
2. She felt excited by the possibility of finding the other side of her personality.
3. Her new name expressed both races which went to make up her personality.
4. It would take a long time to live up to both races.

Extract B:

1. Comfort had wanted to win her Ghanaian grandmother's respect.
2. Comfort liked the Ghanaian way of life.
3. She disliked the lack of forward planning.
4. She felt there was a rational explanation for the death of Bolo although the people were superstitious about it.
5. After enjoying life in Ghana she still felt she belonged in England.

Extract C:

1. The Normans had come to England just like Comfort's father, her grandfather said.
2. The countryside round Penfold went back even further than the Normans.
3. Lettie's name was the same as her great-grandmother's.
4. Comfort's family came from England and Africa.

● Explore the themes running through the examples in this section by using one of the following briefs for a scene, a play scene or just a play for voices.

1. A teenager visits the grave of their grandparents/great grand-parents and meets an old person who knew them well. What does the young person want to ask and what do they learn from the older person?

2. A parent comes by chance upon a photo/an heirloom/a relic/a momento of a grandparent or great grandparent. What is the object and what associations/memories does it spark off? What is the reaction of the younger members of the family on hearing these reminiscences?

3. A person who has been out of the country for twenty years returns home to renew contacts with their family. How have things changed and what kind of reception do they get? Has the person's new life been an improvement on their life while they were still at home?

4. The teenage child of an immigrant family finds it hard to reconcile the traditional way of life of their family, who still keep to the customs of the country of their birth, and the greater freedom of British teenagers. What area of conflict causes most problems – clothes/friends/hours/work? How is the conflict resolved?

● Your own life story so far might be as interesting as Comfort's with important journeys to grandparents. Trace the different strands of your family through your own story.

Further examples and activities based on personal writing can be found on Repromaster 31.

DOCUMENT STORY

The legal evidence for the important events in any family's history can usually be found locked up in deeds boxes, in solicitors' offices or family safe places. Every birth, marriage and death is officially documented and most families keep these documents securely. Other documents, which do not have the same legal validity but are often treasured by a family as more valuable, are the letters which people write which reveal so much to later generations about hopes and fears and relationships. Both of these kinds of written documentary evidence can be:

1. A good source of true stories,
2. A good way of making fictional stories seem authentic.

SOUTH YORKSHIRE TIMES: SATURDAY, JULY 5TH, 1969

Bride followed a family tradition

Miss Penelope Rosemary Jennings, 21-years-old daughter of Mr. Arnold H. Jennings, Headmaster of Ecclesfield Comprehensive School, and of Mrs. Jennings of Clarkegrove Road, Sheffield, made her own bridal gown and also a gold satin embroidered waistcoat which the bridegroom wore with a dark suit at their wedding at Queen's College Chapel, Oxford.

The bridegroom, Mr. William Andrew John Marsterson, is the only son of Mr. and Mrs. H. Marsterson, of Black Heath, London.

The bride, who completed her finals at Queen's College a few days before her marriage, is entering Leeds University to take a Diploma in Education, for she intends to become a teacher.

The bridegroom is a graduate of Queen's College, and has entered the library service of the West Riding County Council. In September he will be setting up a new branch library at Baildon.

The bride and bridegroom met as undergraduates at Queen's College. The bride's brother, Christopher, met his wife at the same college and it was also here that the bride's parents met as undergraduates.

The bride, given away by her father, wore an Edwardian style gown of Chinese ivory wild silk consisting of a blouse and a long A-line skirt, which she made to her own design. Down the front of the gown were two frills in shades of cream and coffee embroidered in Victorian design, and her long sleeved blouse had buttoned cuffs and a severe collar on a band.

The gown had a belt at the waistline fastened by an original Edwardian silver buckle which the bridegroom presented to her. Her hair was fastened back and she wore a blue silk chiffon bow. She had no veil. Her shoes were of cream coloured leather.

GOLD WAISTCOAT

The gold satin waistcoat which the bridegroom wore, had an embroidered design of flowers in an 18th century pattern in shades of gold, cream, coffee, rose and moss green.

The bride's mother, who is a senior lecturer and head of the department of history at Totley Hall College of Education, Sheffield, wore a matching silk dress and fitted coat with navy blue accessories, and a matching cloche hat in pale blue Swiss straw with a large stiff blue chiffon bow at the back.

The bridegroom's mother had chosen navy blue satin trimmed Guipure lace dress and jacket with navy blue accessories, a pink carnation corsage, and a large brimmed pink chiffon picture hat.

The Rev. David Jenkins (Chaplain) officiated at a choral ceremony and the couple took Holy Communion.

An undergraduate friend of the bride composed a piece of music for the wedding, and two others wrote epithalamia wedding odes. As the couple left the Chapel, Oxford University Morris dancers danced in the quadrangle.

Among guests at a reception were friends from Greece. The honeymoon was spent in Florence and Rome. The bride travelled in a turquoise suit with an A-line skirt and a jacket in royal blue wool, a flowered voile blouse in blue and green and white trimmed turquoise hat of Shantung.

Studying the Evidence for the Story

● Look at the documents on this page.
Work out how the various events in them are connected.
To do this you will need to be sure a) what kind of document it is,
b) when the event occured.

I Elizabeth Jennings of 10 Pennington Street, Huddersfield hereby revoke all wills and testamentary dispositions heretofore made by me and Declare this to be my last will.

1. PROVIDED that my husband Arnold Harry Jennings shall survive me for the period of 28 days after my death, I DEVISE AND BEQUEATH ALL my estate of whatsoever kind and wheresoever situate to my said husband absolutely and I appoint him the sole executor of this my will.

2. If my husband shall not survive me as aforesaid then the following provisions shall take effect.

1. (a) I APPOINT William Andrew John Marsterson of 38 Lucy Hall Drive, Baildon, Shipley, Yorkshire and Leonor Ann Walter of 10 Collegiate Crescent, Sheffield (hereinafter called "my trustees") to be executors and trustees of this my will.

(b) I APPOINT William A. J. Marsterson and Leonor A. Walter to be executors and trustees of this my will.

2. I DEVISE AND BEQUEATH all my estate of whatsoever kind and wheresoever situate and not hereby otherwise disposed of unto my trustees upon trust to sell call in and convert the same and any part thereof into money or retain the same in its actual state of investment or condition at the date of my death subject to and after payment of my funeral and testamentary expenses, debts, and death duties to stand possessed of the residue of the said property and money and the investments for the time being representing the same IN TRUST for my two children Christopher Redman Jennings and Penelope Rosemary Jennings the wife of W. A. J. Marsterson equally PROVIDED THAT if any child dies in my lifetime leaving a child or children living at my death who attains the age of 21 years or marry then the share of the child so dying shall be held in trust for such child or children as aforesaid and if more than one in equal shares.

3. ANY monies requiring investment hereunder may be laid out in or upon the acquisition or security or any property of whatsoever nature or wheresoever situate to the intent that my trustees shall have the same full and unrestricted powers of investment in all respects as if they were absolutely entitled thereto beneficially.

4. MY TRUSTEES may apply the whole or any part or parts of the capital or income (or of both capital and income) of the contingent or presumptive share of any infant beneficiary hereunder for the maintenance, education, or advancement or benefit generally of such infant beneficiary in the absolute discretion of my trustees.

5. The power of appropriation conferred by the administration of Estates Act 1925 shall be exercisable by the trustees without any of the consents made requisite by that Act.

6. ANY Trustees being a solicitor or accountant or other person engaged in any profession or business or trade shall be entitled to be paid all usual professional or business or trade charges for business transacted, time expended and acts done by him or any employeee or partner of his in connection with my will including acts done by him which a trustee not being in any profession or business or trade could have done personally.

7. I desire that my body be cremated, and my ashes scattered upon Haworth Moor in the County of Yorkshire.

Death certificate — Certified Copy of an Entry Pursuant to the Births and Deaths Registration Act 1953. Death Entry No. 132. Hubert Lacey MARSTERSON.

Creating Family Documentation

When you have studied the various certificates and linked them together you will have reconstructed a very regular pattern of events in a family.

● Make your own documents to tell a story – follow the decisions below.
1. What are the family called?
2. Whose marriage is the central event?
3. How many children?
4. Name of the person marrying in?
5. Where do they live?
6. Do the dates give enough time between events?

Do not write the story in full – tell it through any of these documents:
Birth/death certificate.
Birth/marriage/death announcement.
Newspaper article.
Obituary (newspaper feature on a recently deceased person).

Make the reader do the work!

Episodes from Family Life

● In groups:
1. Decide on the names and relationships within two family groups. Fill out a set of documents for the people in both families, appropriate to their ages. You could include a couple of death certificates for the other people who have already died.
2. Then select one or two important events, a marriage, a birth.
3. Take the roles of the different characters named in the documents and improvise a set of 'episodes' in the life of the two families, they do not have to build up to a complete sequential narrative (the whole story). Instead, give your audience glimpses into moments in the life of the families you have invented.
4. Your scenes could include:
The reaction in each family to the announcement of the engagement of the son of one and the daughter of the other.
Two prospective grandmothers talking shortly before the birth of a grandchild.
The family rallying round a bereaved parent.
A scene in which one child in the family reveals that they consider themselves to be less privileged than another brother/sister.
A member of one family takes refuge with the other after their own family have thrown them out – why were they thrown out?
The discovery of a document – marriage or birth certificate – which reveals that someone does not belong by birth to the family in which they were brought up.

MARSTERSON.—On September 1st. to Penelope (nee Jennings) and William Marsterson — a son (Thomas William).

FAMILY HISTORY THROUGH LETTERS

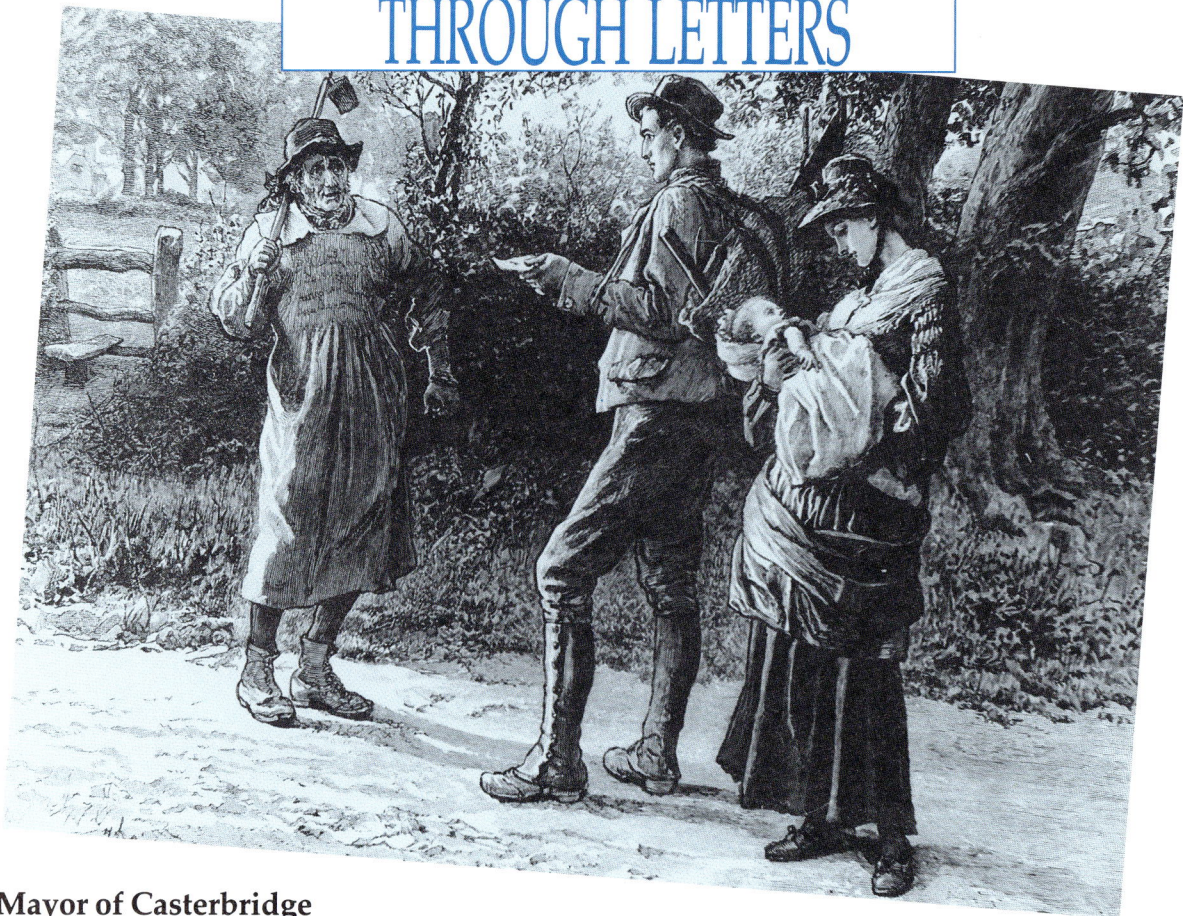

The Mayor of Casterbridge

Earlier in this book, page 34 includes the 'prologue' to this novel, where Michael Henchard in his drunkenness sold his wife and baby daughter to a sailor, an episode he was to regret for the rest of his life. Later he is reunited with his wife Susan and child, after the sailor is lost at sea. Susan does not live long, and when she dies he tells the girl, Elizabeth-Jane, whose memories do not go back to the first years of her life, and who thought the sailor was her father, that she is in fact Elizabeth-Jane Henchard, his daughter. The following extract begins when he leaves her to come to terms with the idea.

Henchard in the meantime had gone upstairs. Papers of a domestic nature he kept in a drawer in his bedroom, and this he unlocked. Before turning them over he leant back and indulged in reposeful thought. Elizabeth was his at last, and she was a girl of such good sense and kind heart that she would be sure to like him. He was the kind of man to whom some human object for pouring out his heart upon – were it emotive or were it choleric – was almost a necessity. The craving of his heart for the re-establishment of this tenderest human tie had been great during his wife's lifetime, and now he had submitted to its mastery without reluctance and without fear. He bent over the drawer again, and proceeded in his search.

Among the other papers had been placed the contents of his wife's little desk, the keys of which had been handed to him at her request. Here was the letter addressed to him with the restriction, *'Not to be opened till Elizabeth-Jane's wedding day.'*

Mrs Henchard, though more patient than her husband, had been no practical hand at anything. In sealing up the sheet, which was folded and tucked in without an envelope, in the old fashioned way, she had overlaid the junction with a large mass of wax without the requisite under-touch of the same. The seal had cracked, and the letter was open. Henchard had no reason to suppose the restriction one of serious weight, and his feeling for his late wife had not been of the nature of deep respect. "Some trifling fancy or other of poor Susan's, I suppose," he said; and without curiosity he allowed his eyes to scan the letter:

"MY DEAR MICHAEL, – For the good of all three of us I have kept one thing a secret from you till now. I hope you will understand why; I think you will; though perhaps you may not forgive me. But, dear Michael, I have done it for the best. I shall be in my grave when you read this, and Elizabeth-Jane will have a home. Don't curse me, Mike – think of how I was situated. I can hardly write it, but here it is. Elizabeth-Jane is not your Elizabeth-Jane – the child who was in my arms when you sold me. No; she died three months after that, and this living one is my other husband's. I christened her by the same name we had given to the first and she filled up the ache I felt at the other's loss. Michael, I am dying, and I might have held my tongue; but I could not. Tell her husband of this or not, as you may judge; and forgive, if you can, a woman you once deeply wronged, as she forgives you.
SUSAN HENCHARD."

Thomas Hardy, *The Mayor of Casterbridge*

Roleplay

- In small groups improvise the scene at breakfast the next day.
1. How do the 'father' and 'daughter' react to each other?
2. Does Henchard tell Elizabeth-Jane the truth?
3. How might his behaviour to her change, even without revealing her true parentage to her?

Henchard's will can be found on **Repromaster 32** *along with more activities.*

Mansfield Park

The final events of this story are told through two letters and a newspaper article. Fanny Price has been brought up with her cousins by her rich relatives at Mansfield Park. She had always wanted to revisit her own true parents and family in Portsmouth, and does so after the marriage of her cousin Maria to Mr Rushworth. While she is away she hears of Maria's adultery with a Mr Henry Crawford but the news reaches her in several garbled versions.

First she has a letter from Mary Crawford, Henry's sister, which she cannot make head or tail of.

'A most scandalous, ill-natured rumour has just reached me, and I write, dear Fanny, to warn you against giving the least credit to it, should it spread into the country. Depend upon it there is some mistake, and that a day or two will clear it up – at any rate, that Henry is blameless, and in spite of a moment's *etourderie* thinks of nobody but you. Say not a word of it – hear nothing, surmise nothing, whisper nothing, till I write again. I am sure it will be all hushed up, and nothing proved but Rushworth's folly. If they are gone, I would lay my life they are only gone to Mansfield Park, and Julia with them. But why would not you let us come for you? I wish you may not repent it.

Yours, &c.'

Fanny stood aghast. As no scandalous, ill-natured rumour had reached her, it was impossible for her to understand much of this strange letter. She could only perceive that it must relate to Wimpole Street and Mr Crawford, and only conjecture that something very imprudent had just occurred in that quarter.

Then her father shows her an article in the newspaper.

"What's the name of your great cousins in town, Fan?"

A moment's recollection enabled her to say, "Rushworth, Sir."

"And don't they live in Wimpole Street?"

"Yes, Sir."

"Then, there's the devil to pay among them, that's all. There, (holding out the paper to her) – much good may such fine relations do you. I don't know what Sir Thomas may think of such matters: he may be too much of the courtier and fine gentleman to like his daughter the less. But by G– if she belonged to me, I'd give her the rope's end as long as I could stand over her. A little flogging for man and woman too, would be the best way of preventing such things."

Fanny read to herself that 'it was with infinite concern the newspaper had to announce to the world, a matrimonial *fracas* in the family of Mr R. of Wimpole Street; the beautiful Mrs R. whose name had not long been enrolled in the lists of hymen, and who had promised to become so brilliant a leader in the fashionable world, having quitted her husband's roof in company with the well known and captivating Mr C. the intimate friend and associate of Mr R. and it was not known, even to the editor of the newspaper, whither they were gone.'

"It is a mistake, Sir," said Fanny instantly; "it must be a mistake – it cannot be true – it must mean some other people."

Finally she receives a much clearer letter from her cousin Edmund asking her to come back as they need her in this crisis.

'Dear Fanny,

'You know our present wretchedness. May God support you under your share. We have been here two days, but there is nothing to be done. They cannot be traced. You may not have heard of the last blow – Julia's elopement; she is gone to Scotland with Yates. She left London a few hours before we entered it. At any other time, this would have been felt dreadfully. Now it seems nothing, yet it is an heavy aggravation. My father is not overpowered. More cannot be hoped. He is still able to think and act; and I write, by his desire, to propose your returning home. He is anxious to get you there for my mother's sake. I shall be at Portsmouth the morning after you receive this, and hope to find you ready to set off for Mansfield. My Father wishes you to invite Susan to go with you, for a few months. Settle it as you like; say what is proper; I am sure you will feel such an instance of his kindness at such a moment! Do justice to his meaning, however I may confuse it. You may imagine something of my present state. There is no end of the evil let loose upon us. You will see me early, by the mail. Yours, &c.'

Jane Austen, *Mansfield Park*

Discussion

1. Why do you think the writer chose to tell this important event in this way?
2. How are you made to share Fanny's confusion about what is going on?
3. How are you made to feel that Fanny is 'out of it all'?
4. What do you think happened next?

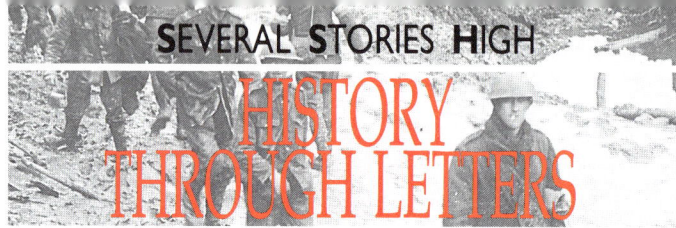

Letters from the Trenches of World War One

Unlike other examples, these are 'real' letters. As you read through them you can begin to tell what kind of person Isaac Rosenberg was.

Winter has found its way into the trenches at last, but I will assure you, and leave to your imagination, the transport of delight with which we welcomed its coming. Winter is not the least of the horrors of war. I am determined that this war, with all its powers for devastation, shall not master my poeting; that is, if I am lucky enough to come through all right. I will not leave a corner of my consciousness covered up, but saturate myself with the strange and extraordinary new conditions of this life, and it will all refine itself into poetry later on.
Isaac Rosenberg, to Lawrence Binyon.

March 1916

The Allowance

I have been in this reg. about two months now and have been kept going all the time. Except that the food is unspeakable, and perhaps luckily, scanty, the rest is pretty tolerable. I have food sent up from home and that keeps me alive, but as for the others, there is talk of mutiny every day. One reg. close by did break out and some men got bayoneted. I don't know when we are going out but the talk is very shortly.
Isaac Rosenberg, to Sydney Schiff.

I never joined the army from patriotic reasons. Nothing can justify war. I suppose we must all fight to get the trouble over. Anyhow before the war I helped at home when I could and I did other things which helped to keep things going. I thought if I'd join there would be the separation allowance for my mother.
Isaac Rosenberg, to Edward Marsh.
The Collected Works of Isaac Rosenberg, ed. Ian Parsons

The Letters

1. How does his first letter contradict the public image of the dedicated soldiers fighting for their country?
2. How would you say he was being 'brave'?
3. Where and why does he use sarcasm in the second letter?
4. How do you think his positive attitude to his experiences is shown?
5. Were you surprised to learn from the third letter that he was a soldier in spite of believing 'nothing can justify war'?
6. How did he think his mother would be helped when he joined the army?

Using Real Material for Narrative

● You may be able to find real letters in published collections or treasured at home on which to base a story or an episode from your own family's story. In your episode be sure to:
1. Explain who the writer is and the recipient.
2. Explain why these people are separated from each other.
3. Explain how long the separation was.
4. Show what happened when they met again, if they did.

Building a Character Through Letters

Isaac Rosenberg was a real person but you could use the same technique for depicting an imaginary character.
● Devise a series of letters through which you build a character. Before creating the letters, decide on the following:

When did your letter writer live?

Where were they when they were writing?

Who were they writing to?

What do their comments on their experiences reveal about them?

What events or experiences do the letters describe?

Did they write differently to different people?

Are you going to include the replies?

A series of letters is an excellent way of telling a story on radio, as different voices can be used for letters from different people.

Story by Letter

● In groups use any of the sets of letters written in response to this section for taping, once you have allocated the different letters to different people to read and written a linking narrative, if necessary.

● Continue any of the extracts used in this section by writing more letters from the characters involved to continue the story.
or
● Decide on the outline of a story (you can use any suggestions from anywhere in the book and tell the story in this way through letters).
1. Allocate the different characters in the story to different members of the group.
2. In different handwriting each write one or two letters from their own character telling their part of the story from their viewpoint.

Eg: A soldier away at war learns that his wife has been out with someone else. His best friend goes home on sick leave and finds the woman and persuades her to return to her mother until the war is over.
The letters:
From the wife's mother to her son:
>   a sad letter at the beginning of the story;
>   an optimistic letter at the end of the story.

From the friend to the soldier:
>   a letter when he arrives home;
>   a letter explaining what has happened.

From the soldier to the wife:
>   a sad letter at the beginning;
>   a forgiving letter at the end.

From the wife to the soldier:
>   a sorry letter explaining how lonely and unhappy she has been.

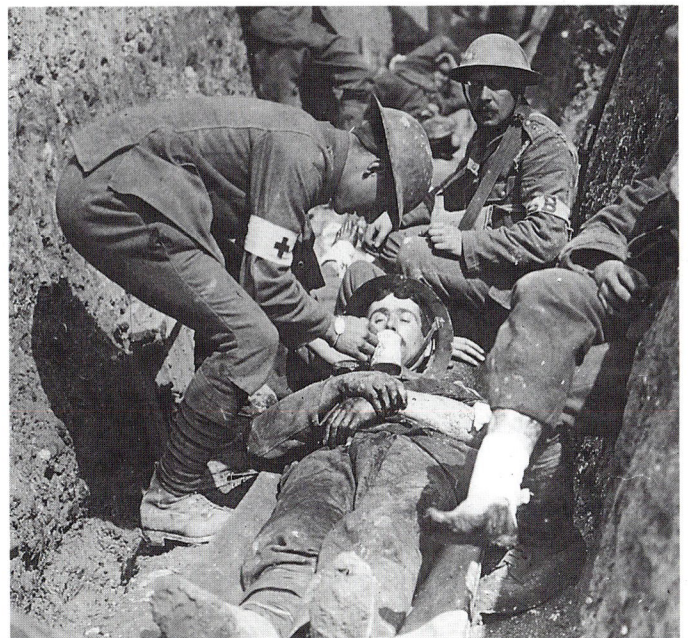

NEWCOMER IN THE FAMILY

You might have your own reasons for wanting to find out about your own family history – but if you are going to make up a family story spanning several generations then it is more interesting if your reader can become involved.

If you tell a true family story, your family will already be interested. You can write about what has made you into what you are today. Other people will be fascinated to know more about someone they know.

A Fictional Family Story

● Decide:

1. Why does your reader want to know about this fictional family?

2. Why do people become so involved in the lives of people who aren't real?

3. What is their involvement with this family you are going to invent?

4. How will your readers find their way around a large new family and sort out its past?

5. Will you choose one person who is told stories from family history?

Lisa St Aubyn De Teran, author of **The Keepers of the House,** *from which the next extracts come, based her story on her own gradual education into the traditions of the family she had married into, hereditary noblemen in South America. She has written the stories, however, for an outside audience, whose viewpoint is that of the new bride.*

Lydia Sinclair has married a Spanish nobleman and gone to live on his family estates in the Andes mountains in South America. Here she comes to know Benito Mendoza who has served the family all his life and is eager to tell her stories from the past –

One night, when Diego had gone early to bed and the house was even stiller than usual, he confided to her: "You are special, Doña, and different, and very like the people that I shall tell you about. You'll survive when I and all in the valley, and the valley itself, are dead and it's through you that we won't be forgotten.

"Do you know, Doña, I have given my whole life to the service of the Beltrán family; and even though they are declining now, I'm proud of it, and of them. The mountains have always upheld the old traditions; and the Beltrán family are like a fortress within the mountains: they are the last survivors. When they fall, I myself and all of us will fall as well. They are the weather-vane of our own failure. I am their oldest retainer and I've outlived most of them and I know more about this valley and its people than anybody else. Someday the Beltráns may be remembered as tyrants or fools, but who will see their splendour and their suffering?" . . .

. . . Benito mulled all these things over in his head, and he brought them out little by little, unravelling them to la Doña. She was one of them, though she did not fully know it yet. The sun chariot would not die, it would rise, thanks to her, in some far-away land. She would find order in the chaos, and action through his words. Almost every evening was spent on the veranda: Benito huddled under his hat, the string fastened tight around his baggy trousers, his machete by his side, and Lydia Sinclair, the new Doña, with her hands round her knees, would sit listening beside him. He told her, "At first, the tales might seem too gloomy, but under the heavy canopy of funeral trappings, you will see that it is just that we have learned to find our strength in death. It lives in our houses. After you, too have felt somebody's death, you will gain the strength to record our lives. Someone's dying will make you strong."

One of the stories tells of how two brothers came to find gold in South America in the eighteenth century and at first thought they had only found two brides, the unmarried daughters of the last Marquis, living in poverty as the house decayed around them.

The Floor of Gold

It was a windy afternoon of late 1785 when the two brothers, Rodrigo and Sancho Beltrán, appeared on the horizon. They had been riding for many months before they came to the Hacienda La Bebella. Far to the south, in their own country, they had plotted and led an uprising that had been betrayed, and both had been banished. Their lives had been spared, in consideration of their eminent and, until then, loyal family, but exile had been inevitable . . .

. . . The brothers were filled with strange feelings as they wound their way to the great house that they had seen in the distance.

They wondered what kind of family would live in such a grand place while surrounded by so much neglect. They wondered, too, what sort of a welcome they would receive – since they planned to ask for shelter . . .

The twin sisters who sat behind the barred window, cloistered in the half-light of their cluttered drawing-room, had stayed that way for over twenty years, since their early childhood. They stared out over the tangled roses and clematis at their vast dowry of lands. Nothing ever moved, except for spiders as they cleaned out their webs, or ants trekking to and from their nests; and yet, that evening something seemed to move out on the skyline. Neither of the sisters could remember anyone ever coming to their house . . .

. . . Now that there were only these two twin girls left, [their father] determined that they should die childless, preferring his name and his lands, his wealth and his superb manners should all be lost rather than break with tradition. He himself had always been prepared to die for his honour and the purity of his blood. The least that his daughters could do was to suffer spinsterhood for their lineage.

The old Marquis knew that the long siege was coming to an end: already the garden walls were caving in; his estates would fall from decay; and people from the village would come and pick over his belongings . . .

NEWCOMER IN THE FAMILY

. . . but he was determined that they should not have his gold. Let them inherit the tangle of weeds that spread for hundreds of thousands of hectares across the hills; let them blister their hands cutting back the undergrowth in search of the scant berries from his coffee plants; but they would not have his easy wealth – not his gold!

So, stealthily, night after night in his house of lethargy, he had raised up the floor tiles of his once splendid hall, and buried a little heap of gold under every tile, until one of the largest fortunes in the country was hidden under the hand-painted ceramics of his floor. His daughters, who were used to hearing strange noises as the house strained and collapsed at night, never suspected the hidden wealth that they walked upon; and they didn't know why their father gloated so, on his deathbed.

Until the Beltrán brothers rode over the hills towards them, the twins spent their time shifting pots and pans to catch the leaks in the roof; being fed by their arthritic servants on gnawed grain, soured wine, and humouring their father through his last years of life. As the old man lay dying, his mind wandered and then returned, time and time again, to extracting promises from his daughters. He made them promise never to leave his estates, and never to marry any of their neighbours or countrymen, no matter what. He made them swear this twofold oath on their bibles and on their rosaries, by all that they held sacred, and by the memory of their dead mother.

The twins watched their father dying, and they relinquished all the hopes that they had ever had of marrying and escaping from the decay of their massive homestead . . .

. . .For the two women, swaddled in their spinsterhood, the arrival of these two men – whose presence and place of origin defied their father's ban – was the solution to all their troubles. The brothers stayed on at the Hacienda La Bebella, lodged in the ramshackle wings of the old house. They brought in labourers from the hills, and livestock from the village, and day by day they brought more life to the dying hacienda. They began to salvage all that they could from the old house, and with the help of local labour they built a new one. Much of the old original material could be seen there: noticeably, the marble columns and stairs, and the stained glass from the chapel. However, they added wooden pillars to the verandas, carved out of whole cedar trunks, and every window led out on to a balcony, so that the old feeling of imprisonment should never be felt in the house, and every room should be open instead of closed; and they called it 'La Casa de Balcon'. Then they carefully transplanted the night-scented jasmine, and its dark leaves and simple starry flowers began to climb up new walls. The last part of the work was to prise up each porcelain tile from the shell of the old house, and re-lay them in their new hall.

They had no idea that the thin layer of tiles concealed a deep bed of gold pieces. Square by square, they unearthed the hidden treasure: never in their lives had they seen such hoards of it, not even in the viceroy's coffers. They were especially careful not to break the tiles that covered their trove, and they attributed to them great symbolic importance, since it was the beauty of the tiles with their animal and insect motifs that had led them to the discovery of the concealed gold. Chest after chest was filled with it, until all the chests were full, and then all the sacks and bags that could be found were filled to bursting and then stitched and tied.

Lisa St Aubyn De Teran, *The Keepers of the House*

Ideas for Discussion – The Floor of Gold

1. Why had the brothers, Rodrigo and Sancho, come to the valley, when so few people came from outside?

2. How are we made to share their feelings as they approached?

3. What is the first picture we get of the two sisters – how are ideas of loneliness and imprisonment suggested?

4. Why had their father, the old Marquis, refused to allow them to marry?

5. What did he fear would happen to his wealth if he did not hide it?

6. Pick out two or three details which show the poverty of the sisters' lives.

7. What did their father make them swear on his deathbed?

8. Find the sentence in paragraph nine which explains that as the brothers, Rodrigo and Sancho, came from a distant country and were noblemen, the sisters could marry them without breaking their promise to their father on his deathbed.

9. In what ways did the brothers begin to put the estates back in order?

10. What caused the treasure to be discovered?

● All the following titles are based on the themes in the *Floor of Gold* but could be used for a new story of your own –

The forgotten house

Two brothers – twin sisters

The hidden valley

Wealth beneath their feet

Renovations reveal riches

A deathbed promise

Creating Atmosphere

● Page 72 goes into detail about the importance of background and atmosphere in a story and *The Floor of Gold* relies on the setting of the ruined hacienda to show up the plight of the sisters who thought they would never marry. Go back through the story and list all the details about plants and animals and insects and all the references to decay or rot.

● Imagine you are the design team for a film to be made of this family saga about the Beltráns in South America. Allocate the following tasks among the group –

1. Use the details in your list to write a brief for the producer explaining what effects you are aiming for in this film.

2. Draw sketches to show interiors and exteriors that will be built as studio sets.

3. Make suggestions (with examples from travel brochure photographs) of suitable locations for the outside filming.

4. List the construction tasks that will be required to build the sets.

5. Decide on suitable background sound effects and write a brief for the composer who will write the film music.

6. Explain what special effects you will require.

7. Combine all the finished work in one large presentation display.

A Sense of Place

A single estate or house is often the central focus for a saga which spans the lives of several generations.

● In groups:

either Choose one of the illustrations to use as your focus

or Draw, describe or find your own picture of a house

then Using the timechart which is available with this unit on *Repromaster 33* to help you, plan the outline of the adventures of several generations who lived in the house you have chosen.

Let each member of the group select one episode to write, in narrative or play form, with each episode using the characters from a different generation

then Present the entire saga, as a drama if you have used play form or with each story episode displayed clockwise with the picture of the house in the centre.

THE FAMILY TREE

Several structures for handling a long family saga have already been suggested. If you want to cover many generations, it is best to work with a group on the writing and tie all the episodes together by the use of a single location. However, you can also focus on specific episodes which are of interest, and miss out areas of family history that are just ordinary.

When planning your writing you can use your own family tree and select outstanding relatives or stories which are well known. If you are inventing a family, you can use a historical fact or event and build a personal experience onto it. You can see the beginnings of the personal stories relating to the family tree below on the opposite page. It is most important that the time scale is credible and realistic. Repromaster 33 has a timechart to go with this unit.

A family tree can provide you with interesting ideas and save you a lot of time in providing links for a very long story. If the family covers several generations, you need:
1. to link up the different generations with historical events;
2. select one or two people whose stories you will tell.

The relationships between the people can be verified by the reader looking back at the family tree.

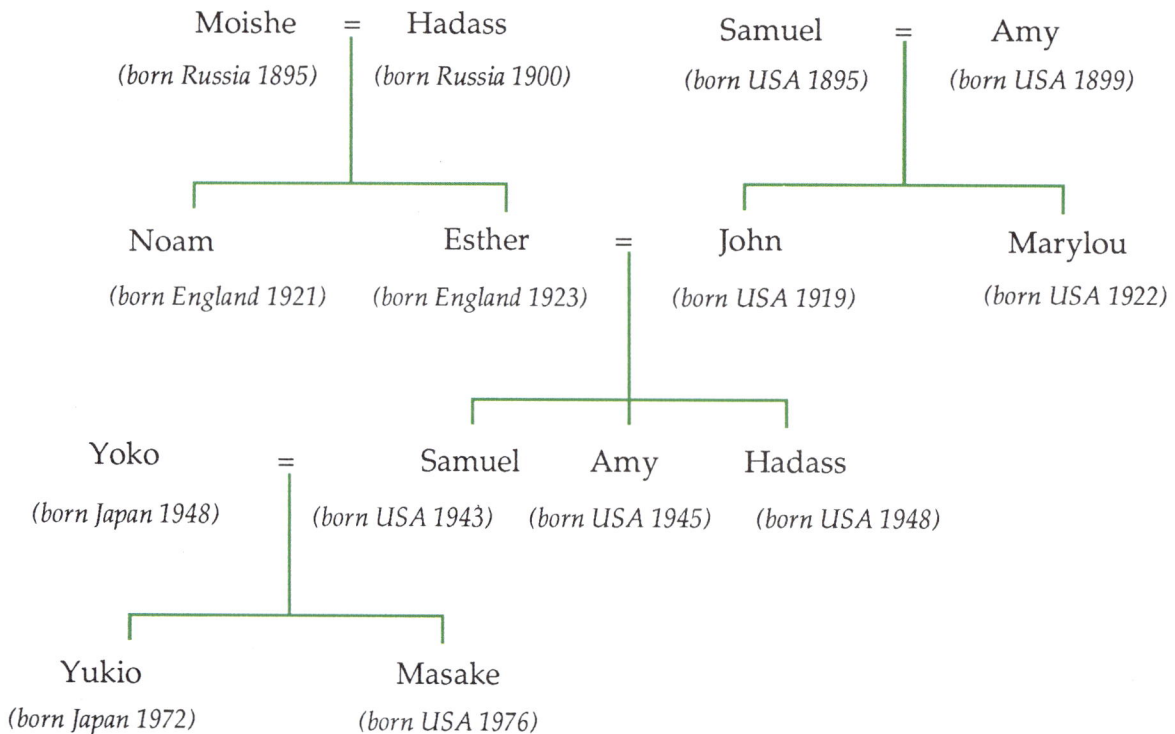

Moishe = Hadass
(born Russia 1895)   (born Russia 1900)

Samuel = Amy
(born USA 1895)   (born USA 1899)

Noam
(born England 1921)

Esther = John
(born England 1923)   (born USA 1919)

Marylou
(born USA 1922)

Yoko =
(born Japan 1948)

Samuel
(born USA 1943)

Amy
(born USA 1945)

Hadass
(born USA 1948)

Yukio
(born Japan 1972)

Masake
(born USA 1976)

Group Discussion

● Study the following family tree and discuss what you can tell about this family from the dates of birth and places of birth of the people mentioned.
● As you look through a family tree you will be able to draw some conclusions if you:
1. Work out how old people were when they died.
2. Work out how old people were when their children were born.
3. See how many brothers and sisters were in each family.
4. Compare whereabouts people were born.

A Fictional Family Tree

Moishe was sorrowful to leave his homeland behind, but Russia was no longer a place for a Jew to live . . .

Hadass (born 1900) had always been an obedient daughter as the Law demanded and after her parents arranged for her to marry Moishe, she then had to go with him to England . . .

Amy (born 1899) was proud of her son in the US marines but horrified when he came home from the war with an immigrant bride . . .

Esther was able to make a new life for herself when as a GI bride, she went back to the States with John, who'd been stationed in England, during the war . . .

Samuel would never have dreamt that being posted by the bank to Tokyo would lead to his falling in love with Japan in such a big way . . .

Yukio envied his younger brother because he was an American citizen, whereas he'd been born before Mum and Dad came back to California.

Studying the Evidence

● In groups, work out the answers to the following:
1. How much younger was Hadass than her husband?
2. Where had they moved to when their children were born?
3. Why should they have left their native country – what happened in Russia in 1917 and how old would they have been then?
4. What nationality was Esther's husband?
5. How do you think they met?
6. Why would Esther have called her daughters Amy and Hadass and her son Samuel?
7. What nationality was Samuel Junior's wife?
8. How do you think they met?
9. Which country did Samuel live in when his first child was born?
10. Which country did Yoko live in when her second child was born?

Options

● Choose one of these characters to write/improvise a story about. An opening line is suggested for the story for some of the people.
● Draw out your own invented family tree which shows how four generations of a family may come from and live in three – or more – different continents.

Background Research

● You will already have realised the importance of accurate historical and contemporary facts for this kind of family saga. You may like to use any of the illustrations of important contemporary events on this page to spark off ideas for your family. Consider:
1. Which part of the world do they live in?
2. Have the family always lived there?
3. Are there any problems/difficulties for them in being where they are?
4. Do they have relatives in another country?
5. Where do they feel they really belong?

Promotional Material

Once you and/or your group have put a great deal of effort into producing a family saga you may enjoy practising some of the promotional ideas used in the media.

A Television Mini-series

● You know the story – design a magazine cover to advertise this forthcoming drama so that there is a large audience for your story.
● Write the trailer that will be shown during the week previous to the mini-series. Stress the most colourful characters and dramatic events of the series.
● Present an interview with some of the stars of the story in which they explain their relationship and the important historical events included in the drama.

A Blockbuster Novel

● Your family saga runs to three volumes – design the posters that advertise it, and a cover for Volume Three.
● Draft the text of the blurb, the writing on the back of the book that gives an enticing idea of what the book is about so that readers will want to buy it.

ACKNOWLEDGEMENTS

Unit 1

Page 9: extract by David Harmer from *Pigs is Pigs* edited by Trevor Millum, published by Unwin Hyman. **Pages 14–19:** extracts from *If on a winter's night a traveller* by Italo Calvino, Copyright © 1979 by Giulio Einaudi editore s.p.a., Torino; English translation Copyright © 1981 by Harcourt Brace Jovanovich Inc; reprinted by permission of Martin Secker & Warburg Limited. **Page 20:** extract from *Les Faux Monnayeurs* by Andre Gide, translated by Dorothy Bussy, Copyright © 1927, 1951 reprinted by permission of Alfred A. Knopf Inc. **Page 21:** extract from *The French Lieutenant's Woman* © John Fowles, first published by Jonathan Cape Ltd. **Page 25:** extract *Odd Man Out* by Martyn Harris, from *Daily Telegraph* November 18th 1988. **Pages 26–27:** photo story *The Bank Manager in the Bri-Nylon Suit* by permission of Midland Bank plc.

Unit 2

Page 32: extract from *Rebecca* © 1938 Daphne du Maurier Browning. Extract from *Staying On* © Paul Scott, reprinted by permission of William Heinemann Limited. Extract from *Blood Brothers* by Willy Russell, published by Methuen, London. **Page 36:** Extract from *Staying On* © Paul Scott, reprinted by permission of William Heinemann Limited. **Page 37:** extracts from *After the First Death* by Robert Cormier, published by Victor Gollancz Ltd. **Page 41:** extract from *The Three Hostages* by John Buchan, by permission of A. P. Watt Ltd on behalf of the Rt. Hon. Lord Tweedsmuir of Elsfield CBE.

Unit 3

Page 48–49: extracts from *Tale Enders* © 1988 Bob Taylor, published by Thomas Nelson & Sons Ltd. **Page 50–51:** extract from *After the First Death* by Robert Cormier, published Victor Gollancz Ltd. **Page 52:** cartoon by David Austin first appeared in *New Scientist*, London, the weekly review of science and technology. **Pages 55–57:** extract from *The Compass Rose* by Ursula K. Le Guin, by permission of A. P. Watt Ltd on behalf of Ursula K. Le Guin. **Page 58:** extract from *Monsterman* by Jim and Duncan Eldridge, published by Methuen Children's Books. **Pages 59–60:** extract from *Metamorphosis* by Franz Kafka, published by Martin Secker & Warburg. **Pages 61–65:** extracts from *The Sea Crossed Fisherman* by Yashar Kemal, published by Collins. **Page 68:** extract from *Oedipus the King* by Sophocles, translated by William Marsterson. **Pages 69–70:** extracts from *Blood Brothers* by Willy Russell, published by Methuen, London.

Unit 4

Page 82: poem *Charades: September* by Geoffrey Holloway from *New Angles 2* published by Oxford University Press, reprinted with his permission. **Page 83:** poem *The Thickness of Ice* by Liz Loxley, reprinted by permission of Faber and Faber Ltd from *Hard Lines: New Poetry and Prose*. **Pages 89–91:** extracts from *Sequins for a Ragged Hem* Copyright © Amryl Johnson, published by Virago Press Ltd 1988.

Unit 5

Pages 98–100: extract from *The Seal Wife*, as told by Julie Fullarton of 'The Beasties'. **Page 101:** poem *The Song of the Man Who Loved a Seal Woman* by Julie Fullarton of 'The Beasties'. **Pages 108–109:** extract from *The Dragon*, reprinted by permission of Don Congdon Associates Inc, Copyright © 1955 Ray Bradbury; renewed 1983 by Ray Bradbury.

Unit 6

Pages 120–121: extract from *Merle*, Copyright © 1983 by Paule Marshall, first published by The Feminist Press, New York 1983, published by Virago Press 1985.
Pages 122–123: extract from *Comfort Herself* Copyright © 1984 Geraldine Kaye, first edition 1986 published by Andre Deutsch Ltd. **Pages 124–125:** the design of the birth, death and marriage certificates are Crown Copyright and are reproduced with the permission of HMSO. **Page 128:** extracts from the *Collected Works of Isaac Rosenberg*, edited by Ian Parsons, published by Chatto & Windus and The Hogarth Press. **Pages 130–132:** extracts from *The Keepers of the House* by Lisa St. Aubyn de Teran, published by Jonathan Cape.

The publishers have made every effort trace all the copyright holders, but if they have inadvertently overlooked any, they will be pleased to make the necessary arrangements at the first opportunity.